Post-Marxism: A Reader

POST-MARXISM: A READER

Edited by
Stuart Sim

Edinburgh University Press

Selection and editorial material © Stuart Sim, 1998

Edinburgh University Press
22 George Square, Edinburgh

Transferred to digital print 2008
Printed and bound by CPI Antony Rowe, Eastbourne

Typeset in Garamond
by Bibliocraft, Dundee,
and printed and bound in Great Britain
at the University Press, Cambridge

A CIP record for this book is available from the
British Library

ISBN 0 7486 1043 X (hardback)
ISBN 0 7486 1044 8 (paperback)

The right of Stuart Sim
to be identified as author of this work
has been asserted in accordance with
the Copyright, Designs and Patents Act 1988.

CONTENTS

ACKNOWLEDGEMENTS

Jackie Jones, Editorial Director of Edinburgh University Press, was a fund of both encouragement and extremely sound advice throughout the various stages of this project. Dr Noel Parker of the Department of Linguistics and International Studies, University of Surrey, gave helpful advice on the selection of material in the field of International Relations. As always, Dr Helene Brandon was a calming influence at the more problematical points of manuscript production.

SOURCES

Grateful acknowledgement is made for permission to reprint copyright material from the following sources (original publication date of translated texts given in parentheses afterwards):

Ernesto Laclau and Chantal Mouffe, *Hegemony and Socialist Strategy: Towards a Radical Democratic Politics*, London: Verso, 1985; David Forgacs, 'Dethroning the Working Class', *Marxism Today*, 29 (5), May 1985 (copyright *Marxism Today* and *New Statesman*); Stanley Aronowitz, 'Theory and Socialist Strategy', *Social Text*, 16 (Winter 1986/7). Copyright 1987, Duke University Press. Reprinted with permission; Norman Geras, 'Post-Marxism?', *New Left Review*, 163, May/June 1987; Ernesto Laclau and Chantal Mouffe, 'Post-Marxism without Apologies', *New Left Review*, 166, November/December 1987; Jean-François Lyotard, *Libidinal Economy*, trans. Iain Hamilton Grant © The Athlone Press, 1993 (translation) (1974), and Indiana University Press; from *Peregrinations: Law, Form, Event*, by J.-F. Lyotard. Copyright © 1988 by Columbia University Press. Reprinted with permission of the publisher; Zygmunt Bauman, *Intimations of Postmodernity*, London: Routledge, 1992; Jean Baudrillard, *The Mirror of Production*, trans. Mark Poster, St Louis, MO: Telos Press, 1975 (1973); Jean Baudrillard, *America*, trans. Chris Turner, London: Verso, 1988 (1986); Edward W. Soja, *Postmodern Geographies: The Reassertion of Space in Critical Social Theory*, London: Verso, 1989; R. B. J. Walker, *Inside/Outside: International Relations as Political Theory*, Cambridge: Cambridge University Press, 1993; Jacques Derrida, *Spectres of Marx: The State of the Debt, the Work of Mourning, and the New International*, trans. Peggy Kamuf, New York: Routledge, 1994 (1993); Heidi Hartmann, 'The Unhappy Marriage of Marxism and Feminism: Towards a More Progressive Union', in L. Sargent, ed., *The Unhappy Marriage of Marxism and Feminism: A Debate on Class and Patriarchy*, London: Pluto Press, 1981 (published in America as *Women and Revolution: A Discussion of the Unhappy Marriage between Marxism and Feminism*. Reprinted with permission from the publisher, South End Press, 116 Saint Botolph Street, Boston, MA 02115, 1981); Rosalind Coward, *Patriarchal Precedents: Sexuality and Social Relations*, London: Routledge and Kegan Paul, 1983; Caroline Ramazanoglu, *Feminism and the Contradictions of Oppression*, London: Routledge, 1989; Sylvia Walby, *Theorizing Patriarchy*, Oxford: Blackwell, 1990.

Editorial Note

Some unacknowledged minor cuts have been made in the text of the anthologised material, where reference has been made to other parts of the original source not included in this volume. References have also been renumbered to fit the edited text.

Introduction

SPECTRES AND NOSTALGIA: *POST*-MARXISM/POST-*MARXISM*

Stuart Sim

Marxism has been such a dominant presence in international cultural and political life for so long that its relatively sudden eclipse in the closing decades of the twentieth century can still come as something of a surprise. The general disenchantment of the French intellectual community against Marxism in the aftermath of the Parisian *événements* in 1968 (when the French Communist Party, the PCF, was felt to have colluded with the State against the workers and students) was followed by a steady erosion of Marxism's political authority, until in the 1980s the Soviet Empire collapsed, and Marxism – in its guise as communism, anyway – ceased to be a significant factor in Western political life. Even the continued existence of Chinese communism provides little sustenance for the Marxist cause, given that, as well as having to cope with considerable levels of dissent internally (Tiananmen Square, for example, and the democracy movement in Hong Kong), that regime has enthusiastically embraced capitalist principles in the economic realm. There is, in short, something of a vacuum where Marxist theory used to be.

One response to that vacuum has been the emergence of a movement known as post-Marxism, which has meant that Marxism has retained a presence in cultural debates in the West, even if, as Jacques Derrida has suggested in his typically idiosyncratic study *Spectres of Marx*, that presence is a somewhat ghostly one. It needs to be pointed out, too, that post-Marxism is by no means a homogeneous movement, and that in fact it covers a range of positions, not all of which are necessarily compatible with each other. Post-Marxists can variously want to reject, revitalise, or renegotiate the terms of their intellectual contract with Marxism. In order to gain an understanding of the nature and significance of post-Marxism as a cultural movement, both in its positive and negative forms, we need to address such divisions, as well as their cultural background.

LACLAU AND MOUFFE

The work of Ernesto Laclau and Chantal Mouffe has played a critical role in the development of post-Marxism, particularly their book *Hegemony and Socialist Strategy:*

Towards a Radical Democratic Politics (1985), which helped to establish post-Marxism as a definite theoretical position in its own right. *Hegemony and Socialist Strategy* also provoked a storm of controversy on the left, to the extent that one commentator, Norman Geras, could damn the book as constituting 'the very advanced stage of an intellectual malady'[1] that it was the duty of the left vigorously to oppose. Laclau and Mouffe did not *invent* post-Marxism, but what they did provide was a theorisation of the scattered pockets of opposition to classical Marxism and communism that had been building up through the 1960s and 1970s (although, as we shall see, it is possible to trace a post-Marxist history well before then). The great virtue of *Hegemony and Socialist Strategy* was that it enabled us to put those scattered pockets of opposition into perspective, such that we could recognise that a new theoretical position had been unfolding gradually over a period.

Laclau and Mouffe's insistence that 'if our intellectual project in this book is *post-*Marxist, it is evidently also post-*Marxist*'[2] suggests a way of positioning ourselves in this field of enquiry. To be *post-*Marxist is to have turned one's back on the principles of Marxism (the case of Jean-François Lyotard or Jean Baudrillard, for example); whereas to be post-*Marxist* is, in the style of Laclau and Mouffe, to attempt to graft recent theoretical developments in poststructuralism, deconstruction, postmodernism, and feminism on to Marxism, such that Marxism can be made relevant to a new cultural climate that is no longer responding to classical Marxist doctrine. Post-Marxism can look like a somewhat unstable coalition of interests. What holds them together is the angle of intervention. One could sum up post-Marxism as a series of hostile and/or revisionary responses to classical Marxism from the poststructuralist/postmodernist/feminist direction, by figures who at one time in their lives would have considered themselves as Marxists, or whose thought processes had been significantly shaped by the classical Marxist tradition.

Post-Marxism is to be differentiated from such phenomena as neo-Marxism, which is a much less critical revision of classical Marxism to take account of changes in global politics and international relations since the Second World War. In fact, the neo-Marxist paradigm in the subject area of international relations has been coming under increasing pressure since the collapse of the Eastern bloc in the late 1980s.[3]

PRECURSORS OF POST-MARXISM

Post-Marxism, as indicated above, did not begin with Laclau and Mouffe, and there are a number of figures whose work significantly prefigures post-Marxism that we should now consider briefly. Some would argue that Marx himself gave the lead to post-Marxism, and that he would have been unlikely to have sanctioned what was later to take place under the authority of his name. In a hostile attack on the Marxist tradition of thought in his book *Libidinal Economy*, Jean-Francois Lyotard has, somewhat unwittingly, given an indication of what it is that makes Marx post-Marxist, when he draws attention to the unsystematic nature of Marx's thought. We then witness, as Lyotard describes it, the perpetual *postponement* of finishing work on *Capital*, a chapter becoming a book, a section a chapter, a paragraph a section, by a process of cancerization of theoretical discourse . . . Is the *non-finito* a characteristic of rational theory? We are able to support this, in these post-relative days; but for Marx (and therefore for Engels the impatient!), it must rather have been a bizarre, worrying fact.[4]

The picture of Marx that is presented here is very far removed from the one fostered by classical Marxism. To that latter tradition, Marx is the arch-exponent of rational argument, a quintessentially systematic thinker whose work constitutes a 'science of society' – with all the sense of order and methodical process that such a phrase conjures up. For Lyotard this is a myth concocted for political reasons, and Marx himself looks much more like a postmodern thinker than the systematiser of popular legend. The villain of the piece is Engels, who supplies, after the event as it were, the ordered structure of thought that Marx is temperamentally unable to.[5] Marxism, in other words, is not *naturally* systematic, nor naturally a 'grand narrative': in Lyotard's picture anyway, it is more like the rhizomes of Deleuze and Guattari, endlessly reconfiguring itself, and never amounting to a final or completed structure.

Georg Lukács is now seen as one of the great apologists for Marxist dialectics, but his early work, too, gestures in a post-Marxist direction; particularly his *History and Class Consciousness*, with its insistence that Marxism is not a body of doctrine as such, but a methodology:

> Let us assume for the sake of argument that recent research had disproved once and for all every one of Marx's individual theses. Even if this were to be proved, every serious 'orthodox' Marxist would still be able to accept all such modern findings without reservation and hence dismiss all of Marx's theses *in toto* – without having to renounce his orthodoxy for a single moment. Orthodox Marxism, therefore, does not imply the uncritical acceptance of the results of Marx's investigations. It is not the 'belief' in this or that thesis, nor the exegesis of a 'sacred' book. On the contrary, orthodoxy refers exclusively to *method*.[6]

The emphasis here is on the dialectic at the expense of any specific notion of Marx's, such as, for example, that the history of the world is the history of class struggle, or that the only way to overcome class struggle is to bring about the dictatorship of the proletariat. Decisive proof, or for that matter disproof, is always difficult to achieve in such cases, but feminists would most certainly contest the notion that the history of the world is only, or even primarily, the history of class struggle. The effective elision of gender relations constitutes one of Marxism's most notorious blind spots.

In retrospect, Lukács's sentiments have a post-Marxist ring to them, especially when he goes on to admit, in however qualified fashion, that the method in question is, in principle at least, susceptible to modification:

> It is the scientific conviction that dialectical materialism is the road to truth and that its methods can be developed, expanded and deepened only along the lines laid down by its founders. It is the conviction, moreover, that all attempts to

surpass or 'improve' it have led and must lead to over-simplification, triviality and eclecticism.[7]

It is more than likely that Lukács would have regarded Laclau and Mouffe-style post-Marxism as guilty of precisely those sins of 'over-simplification, triviality and eclecticism', but that endorsement of development and expansion does seem to invite post-Marxist experimentation.

History and Class Consciousness inspired the work of the Frankfurt School (Theodor Adorno, Max Horkheimer, Herbert Marcuse, and Walter Benjamin, for example), giving rise to what has become known as Western Marxism. Western Marxism is in general characterised by a greater interest in philosophical and aesthetic matters than political and economic (with the latter prevailing in Soviet and Chinese Marxism), and this shift can be seen to have post-Marxist implications. For a start, it calls into question the dominance of the base over the superstructure (more or less an article of faith in classical Marxism), and even reverses this on occasion. Gramsci's work on hegemony is also a critical factor here, since it suggests that the realm of ideas can be an even more important site of ideological contestation than the strictly economic world of the base. Gramsci's influence is widespread throughout the Western Marxist tradition, and the highly flexible, one is even tempted in retrospect to say post-Marxist, policies adopted by the Italian Communist Party of the 1960s and 1970s, when it deliberately sought to cooperate with other political parties in a spirit of compromise, owes much to the intellectual legacy of Gramsci. Rather unfortunately for those who wish to claim the value of the post-Marxist approach, however, this policy was not in itself enough to maintain the Italian Communist Party through the collapse of the Eastern bloc in the 1980s.

Theodor Adorno's 'negative dialectics' represents an even more significant gesture in a post-Marxist direction, to the extent that the concept is now seen to prefigure deconstruction and the work of Derrida. In the way that it resists resolution (for Adorno, contradiction reveals 'the untruth of identity, the fact that the concept does not exhaust the thing conceived'[8]), negative dialectics, or 'non-identity thinking', cuts against the neatness of dialectical materialism, and in so doing opens the door to post-Marxism. As the translator of *Negative Dialectics*, E. B. Ashton, remarks, the book can be regarded as 'an apologia for deviationism, a Marxist thinker's explication of his inability to toe the lines laid down today for proper Marxist thinking'.[9] Adorno goes on to deny that a totalising philosophy of the kind claimed by classical Marxism is even possible; asserting that:

> The thoughts of transcendental apperception or of Being could satisfy philosophers as long as they found those concepts identical with their own thoughts. Once we dismiss such identity in principle, the peace of the concept as an Ultimate will be engulfed in the fall of the identity. Since the basic character of every general concept dissolves in the face of distinct entity, a total philosophy is no longer to be hoped for.[10]

It is hard to see where else one can go *but* into post-Marxism after such a declaration, and it also worth pointing out that both Adorno and Horkheimer could be just as critical of the 'Enlightenment project' as any postmodernist or poststructuralist. For them, as they made clear in their jointly-authored *Dialectic of Enlightenment*, the cult of reason was just as likely to lead to fascism as to universal enlightenment.[11]

Herbert Marcuse's later work (*One-Dimensional Man*, for example[12]) also goes beyond traditional Marxist categories in its attempt to come to terms with a cultural landscape, that of postwar America, that no longer seems to conform to the classical Marxist pattern. Marcuse redefines what is meant by 'working class', for example, and generally hints at the need for a recasting of Marxist theory if it is to remain culturally relevant: a prime case of the development and expansion that Lukács had sanctioned in *History and Class Consciousness*, perhaps, although of a kind that Lukács could not support (Lukács was later to reject that book, in particular the enthusiastic use made of it by student revolutionaries during the *événements*). In Marcuse's view, the middle class is just as much a victim of capitalist exploitation as the working class is, and he is a defender of formal experimentalism in the arts (as Adorno was also), thus laying himself open to the charge of elitism – a sin which makes one highly suspect in the eyes of classical Marxists, concerned as they are with improving the lot of the masses. Although there is no ultimate reason why it should be so (Marx himself said very little on the topic), orthodox Marxism had tended to be very traditional in its aesthetic outlook and generally hostile to artistic experimentalism (modernism proving to be a particularly contentious issue in Marxist aesthetics[13]), and Marcuse's championship of this indicates a need to go beyond the traditional body of Marxist thought, and, indeed, to challenge some of its most hallowed assumptions. Where classical Marxism saw elitism and a threat to the desired proletarianisation of culture, Marcuse, and Adorno too (although the latter's tastes differed significantly from Marcuse), saw a challenge to received wisdom that was closer in spirit to the revolutionary origins of Marxism than any adherence to traditional forms ever could be.

Marcuse's popularity amongst student rebels and activists in the 1960s (Marcuse and Lukács being the favoured theorists of the participants in the *événements*) suggests that he succeeded in his project of developing and expanding Marxism, but only at the cost of damaging the theory's aura of total, unquestionable authority. The moral to be extracted from Marcuse is that Marxism is no longer to be regarded as a body of dogma (as it largely remained in the Soviet tradition), but instead as a flexible method, open to revision and reorientation over the course of time and with exposure to new socio-cultural conditions. Once those possibilities are acknowledged, it could be argued, the days of classical Marxism are numbered.

POST-MARXISM/POST-MARXISM

We can now take a look at what motivates what we have identified as the two main strands of post-Marxist thought, *post*-Marxism and post-*Marxism*, with a view to deciding whether there might be any common ground between them. Is there, perhaps, a residual *nostalgia* for the Marxist world view amongst *post*-Marxists such as Lyotard and Baudrillard that aligns them, in some manner, with Laclau and Mouffe? Or is it the case instead that *post*-Marxism and post-*Marxism* cancel each other out?

Post-Marxism is a relatively simple position to explain, as well as a more coherent one overall than post-*Marxism*. *Post*-Marxists have, in a manner of speaking, lost faith, and while they may feel a sense of anxiety over this (although not always, for some it comes as a welcome release), they can no longer subscribe to the Marxist world view, nor the efficacy of its analytical methods. This realisation can lead to outbursts on the following lines:

> In what language would I have been able to dispute the legitimacy of the Marxist phrase and legitimize my suspicion? In Marxist language? That would have amounted to recognizing that that language was above suspicion, and that the Marxist phrase was legitimate by its very position, even though I might contest or refute it . . . Thus I did not want or was not able to develop by means of a critique, and bring to a 'theoretical' conclusion, something which was at first only a faint and disagreeable insinuation: the suspicion that our radical Marxism was not the universal language.[14]

The passage is taken from Lyotard's essay 'A Memorial of Marxism', and the author's situation recalls that of Victorian intellectuals in that earlier era's crisis of belief, not just in his reluctance to admit the implication of his train of thought, but in his reaction when he finally did so. One could say that for all his hostility to Marxism from 1968 onwards, Lyotard retains something like a Marxist consciousness, rather like those intellectuals of the Victorian age who adhered to Christianity's moral code even when they had ceased to believe in Christianity itself as a religion (perhaps one could refer to them as post-Christian?). In his scathing criticism of 'techno-science' and 'development' (in effect, the multinationals) in his late work *The Inhuman*, for example, one *senses* a nostalgia for the world of Marxist analysis on Lyotard's part (in that world you knew *precisely* what you were supposed to do about the machinations of the multinationals), in spite of the bitterness of his attacks on the Marxist canon from the days of the *événements* onwards.[15]

Baudrillard's rejection of his Marxist past is more in the 'welcome release' mould, but even here in this high-profile desertion from the Marxist cause, a certain air of nostalgia can be detected. This 'sharp-shooting lone ranger of the post-Marxist left', as he is presented to us on the cover of his book *Cool Memories*,[16] can still speak of being, 'not without nostalgia . . . for that good old drama of subject and object',[17] that is such an integral part of both Hegelian and classical Marxist thought. Baudrillard also notes the presence of 'a nostalgia in dialectics, in the work of Benjamin and Adorno, for example', claiming further that '[t]he most subtle dialectics always end in nostalgia'.[18] One would have to say, however, that Baudrillard is fairly single-minded about ridding himself of this nostalgia, and that in a work such as *America*, with its paean to 'desertification' of self and personal identity and contemptuous dismissal of the need for value judgement, we are observing just that process in operation.[19]

Post-*Marxism*, on the other hand, is motivated by a desire to introduce the insights of new theoretical developments such as poststructuralism, postmodernism, and feminism into Marxism. The major problem that confronts the post-*Marxist* is that Marxism is a totalising theory, which cannot really countenance competitors, or indeed, any significant divergence from its doctrines. Marxism claims universal dominion in the world of theory (as well as in the world of political practice) and the notion of pluralism, on which so many of the new theories rest, is, on the face of it, anathema to the classical Marxist world view. Laclau and Mouffe's attempts to resolve this paradox, sincere though they are, and founded in a recognition that cultural change has overtaken the doctrines of classical Marxism, merely point up the scale of the problem. Marxism must drop its pretensions to universal authority, and accept that it has to enter into partnership with an eclectic mix of social protest movements: such as,

> The new feminism, the protest movements of ethnic, national and sexual minorities, the anti-institutional ecology struggles waged by marginalized layers of the population, the anti-nuclear movement, the atypical forms of social struggle in countries on the capitalist periphery.[20]

For the classical Marxist, phenomena such as the above are at best diversions from the main struggle against capitalism, and quite possibly *barriers* to the success of the latter. Marxism has always preferred a united front to a disparate collection of individual struggles over which it cannot exercise control (its authoritarianism coming to the fore at such points). Laclau and Mouffe's prescription for a 'radical democratic politics' founded in the experience of just such a disparate set of conflicts looks like a recipe for disaster to the more traditional Marxist, for whom Marxism minus centralised control is no Marxism at all, but rather 'spontaneism': that theoretical 'perversion' of which Rosa Luxemburg stood accused by the Marxist establishment, and against which Lenin so notably railed.

Ultimately, post-*Marxism* invites a fairly sceptical response, if only on the grounds that the relativism intrinsic to deconstruction and postmodernism is simply incompatible with an absolutist-minded theory such as classical Marxism: a case, perhaps, of trying to square the circle. One is left wondering why post-*Marxism* needs Marxism at all, and what meaningful contribution it can make to a postmodern politics of the kind Laclau and Mouffe are espousing. It is easier to understand what the post- part of the equation does than the Marxism, the latter seemingly dangerously residual, and even dysfunctional in the context of the postmodern and the plural. What remains in post-*Marxism* is not so much Marxism, I would contend, as a series of somewhat empty gestures, whose content is emotional rather than theoretical – although one might still have a great deal of sympathy for the emotion in question. To say that the Marxism serves an almost entirely emotional function in the post-*Marxist* project is, however, just about the most wounding thing one can say of a theory that has set itself up as the ultimate science.

One can say, therefore, that *post*-Marxism and post-*Marxism* do share several key characteristics. There is an element of nostalgia present in both of them, as well as an emotional response to Marxism – and even if this emotional response is essentially negative on the one side and positive on the other, there is a common sense that Marxism *demands* such a response from them, that each side must situate itself in relation to that older body of theory. The other, in this reading crucial, element that *post*-Marxism and post-*Marxism* share is that, in real terms, the post- side dominates.

In each case, I am arguing, it is the postmodernism – that is, the suspicion of grand narratives and universal theories – that drives the theoretical enterprise: not so much a case of cancelling each other out, therefore, as of being two sides of the same coin.

POST-BERLIN WALL

The fall of the Berlin Wall was an extremely symbolic event in terms of the decline of Marxism, and, one could argue, the necessity of a move into post-Marxism. It could also be argued, however, that far from reinforcing the case for a Laclau–Mouffe-style post-*Marxism*, the collapse of the Soviet Empire, so graphically signalled by the fate of the Wall, casts even more doubt on the validity of its Marxist component. Indeed, given the unqualified rejection of Marxism as a political force of any consequence in the West, a real question has to arise as to the continued viability of the theory in the current cultural climate. Nor does it necessarily help to claim, as some commentators do, that communism was some kind of perversion of classical Marxist thought. What Marxists of *any* description have to face up to is the possibility that their theory, by its very nature, *inevitably* promotes authoritarianism and totalitarianism: that Stalin, as a case in point, is a natural consequence of the application of Marxist theory, a phenomenon more likely to happen than not.

Seen from that latter perspective, post-*Marxism* is a doomed attempt to render pluralist an unpluralisable, indeed actively pluralism-resistant, theory: monism and pluralism remain incommensurable, for all the ingenious efforts of theorists such as Laclau and Mouffe. The postmodern side of post-*Marxism* may have no difficulty including paradox within its sphere of operations, but the Marxist side most definitely does. One is tempted to say that Marxism is a universal theory or it is nothing.

FEMINISM

Feminism constitutes yet another nail in the coffin of Marxist theory, which cannot really encompass the radical shift in perspective that feminist theory, in its 'second-wave' form particularly, demands. Much of second-wave feminism would seem to suggest that Marxism lies well beyond revision, in that it is deeply implicated in those very structures of patriarchy that feminism is so concerned to dismantle. At the very least, second-wave feminism is asking for a fundamental renegotiation of its relationship to Marxist theory, and if Marxism survives this process at all (and it does not always do so), then it is almost inevitably only in a post-Marxist form.

At one time feminism and Marxism had seemed natural allies, in that both were committed to projects of emancipation, which appeared to have a large degree of overlap. Marxism provided feminism with a method of analysis which demonstrated how most of the human race had come to be exploited by the forces of capital, which had systematically distorted social relations as its empire had grown. It could be assumed that if economic exploitation was brought to an end, then the exploitative nature of all human relations, including gender relations, would cease. In practice, however, Marxism proved to be highly conservative as regards gender issues, with patriarchal attitudes largely surviving the transition to communism in the Eastern bloc. Western feminists eventually began to challenge what the American critic Heidi Hartmann memorably dubbed 'the unhappy marriage of Marxism and feminism';[21] the subtext being that Marxism tended to view women's liberation as a side issue to the main business of class struggle, which latter phenomenon always had to take priority. Feminists began to point out that emancipation for the working class did not always mean emancipation for women; indeed, the very idea of what emancipation *constituted* came to be bitterly contested.

Patriarchy, in other words, could, and did, exist on both sides of the capitalist/socialist divide, and for that reason alone feminists had to reconsider the value Marxism held for them. It is probably fair to say that the Marxist element of feminist Marxism has been in steady decline for some time now, and that it, too, is in danger of becoming little more than residual.

THE FUTURE OF POST-MARXISM?

Can anything of real substance be retained from Marxism in an intensely pluralist-conscious age such as ours? The *spirit* seems eminently worth retaining, that spirit which rejected economic exploitation of the mass of the populace, and the distorting effect of the capitalist ethos on human relations; but it is a moot point whether this requires theorisation of the kind offered by Laclau and Mouffe – or whether that theorisation can ever attain the level of internal consistency that would render it politically effective. Perhaps it is time to admit that Marxism is beyond revision, either as a method or body of principles (monism and pluralism do not, cannot, mix), and that all that remains is a *nostalgia* for the ideal it appeared to be offering. That nostalgia, with which, as I have said, it is only too easy to sympathise, is embedded to some extent in both *post*-Marxism and post-*Marxism*. A spectre accompanies that nostalgia, however, and of a more sinister kind than we find in Derrida's reading of Marxist history. It is the spectre of all that has been done in the name of Marx and Marxism; the spectre of Stalinism, its purges and show trials, the Chinese 'Cultural Revolution', Tiananmen Square, and Pol Pot, for example. Such a spectre must always remain a check on the nostalgia, reminding us of how easily a totalising theory can become a totalitarian one. Post-Marxism, one might say, sits uneasily on that fault line between 'totalising' and 'totalitarian'.

The nostalgia remains a powerful one all the same, and it seems likely to inform theoretical debate for a while yet, in the sense that nothing so far has come forward to fill the vacuum left by Marxism, and capitalism continues to have a dehumanising edge to it that arouses what must still be called 'socialist' feelings. Zygmunt Bauman, while fully acknowledging the many failings of communism, nevertheless can lament its passing to some extent, in that it leaves us with no viable ideological alternative to a triumphal capitalism, where the individual would appear to be just as much at risk, just as subject to reification and economic exploitation, as ever.[22] Seen from that perspective, post-*Marxism* might still seem a worthwhile project, although that is to damn it with the faintest of praise as the best a socialist can do under all but impossible circumstances. This is post-*Marxism* as romantic gesture, emptied of all real hope. Yet perhaps that is the most one can say: that post-*Marxism* marks not a new beginning, nor a way out of a theoretical cul-de-sac, but the recognition of defeat.

Nevertheless, one suspects that the aftermath of that defeat may be a prolonged one, and that, given the excesses of which global capitalism is still more than capable, post-Marxism, in both its main guises, will be with us for some time to come. It is part of the tragedy of the Marxist tradition (shining ideals, generally dreadful realisation of them) that it can be so hard to muster enthusiasm for this state of affairs.

THE READER

The present volume consists of eighteen pieces, spanning a wide range of disciplines and subject areas across the humanities and social sciences, and is designed to be a source book for the study of both *post*-Marxism and post-*Marxism* from the 1970s onwards. Although, as I have indicated above, post-Marxist tendencies can be traced back more or less to the origins of Marxism itself, it is only really in the last few decades that it takes shape as a specific movement in its own right, thus the decision to restrict the volume's chronological coverage in this way. There is also the point to be made that figures like Adorno and Marcuse, arguably the most significant precursors of post-Marxism, are so well represented in other collections on Marxist theory (and sundry other topics) that it would be somewhat superfluous to include them here yet again.

The reader is divided into three sections; Part I is organised around Laclau and Mouffe, and the reception given to their project to redefine Marxism; Part II considers poststructuralist and postmodernist interventions into the post-Marxist debate; while Part III consists of a selection of feminist interventions. Over the three sections we can see extensive evidence of the revision and rejection of, as well as renegotiation with, Marxist theory, which I have suggested is characteristic of the post-Marxist position in general. The range of disciplines on view, running from politics and philosophy through sociology to human geography and international relations, reveals how deeply embedded post-Marxism is in current intellectual and theoretical debate, as well as the need for a reader of this breadth.

NOTES

1. Norman Geras, 'Post-Marxism?', *New Left Review*, 163 (1987), pp. 40–82 (p. 42).
2. Ernesto Laclau and Chantal Mouffe, *Hegemony and Socialist Strategy: Towards a Radical Democratic Politics*, London: Verso, 1985, p. 5.
3. See, for example, the attack made on this paradigm in R. B. J. Walker, *Inside/Outside: International Relations as Political Theory*, Cambridge: Cambridge University Press, 1993; and Andrew Linklater, *Beyond Realism and Marxism: Critical Theory and International Relations,* Basingstoke: Macmillan, 1990.
4. Jean-François Lyotard, *Libidinal Economy*, trans. by Iain Hamilton Grant, London: Athlone Press, 1993, pp. 96–7.
5. David McLellan, for whom Marx is a restless figure somewhat in the romantic mould, notes similar tendencies; remarking of the work on volumes II and III of *Capital* that, 'Marx amassed a huge amount of material but he now lacked the power of synthesis and the driving force to make something of it. After his death Engels was amazed to find among Marx's papers more than two cubic metres of documents containing nothing but Russian statistics . . . he no longer had the power to create, but at least he could absorb' (*Karl Marx: His Life and Thought*, London: Macmillan, 1973, p. 422).

6. Georg Lukács, *History and Class Consciousness: Studies in Marxist Dialetics*, trans. by Rodney Livingstone, London: Merlin Press, 1971, p. 1.

7. *Ibid.*

8. Theodor W. Adorno, *Negative Dialectics*, trans. by E. B. Ashton, London: Routledge and Kegan Paul, 1973, p. 5.

9. Translator's Note, *Ibid.*, p. xi.

10. *Ibid.*, p. 136.

11. Theodor W. Adorno and Max Horkheimer, *Dialectic of Enlightenment*, trans. by John Cumming, London: Verso, 1979.

12. Herbert Marcuse, *One-Dimensional Man: Studies in the Ideology of Advanced Industrial Society*, Boston: Beacon Press, 1964.

13. For a discussion of the issues involved here, see Stuart Sim, 'Marxism and Aesthetics', in Oswald Hanfling, ed., *Philosophical Aesthetics: An Introduction*, Oxford: Blackwell, 1992, pp. 441–71.

14. Jean-François Lyotard, *Peregrinations: Law, Form, Event*, New York: Columbia University Press, 1988, pp. 52, 54.

15. Jean-François Lyotard, *The Inhuman: Reflections on Time*, trans. by Geoffrey Bennington and Rachel Bowlby, Oxford: Blackwell, 1991; see particularly the chapter, 'Can Thought go on without a Body?'. For more on the complexities of Lyotard's relationship to Marxist thought, see Stuart Sim, *Modern Cultural Theorists: Jean-François Lyotard*, Hemel Hempstead: Prentice Hall, 1996.

16. Jean Baudrillard, *Cool Memories*, trans. by Chris Turner, London and New York: Verso, 1990; the quote itself is taken from the *New York Times*.

17. Jean Baudrillard, 'The Year 2000 Will Not Take Place', trans. by Paul Foss and Paul Patton, in E. A. Grosz, Terry Threadgold, David Kelly, Alan Cholodenko and Edward Colless, eds, *Futur*Fall: Excursions into Post-Modernity*, Sydney: Power Institute of Fine Arts, 1986, pp. 18–28 (p. 23).

18. Jean Baudrillard, *Cool Memories*, p. 4.

19. Jean Baudrillard, *America*, trans. by Chris Turner, London and New York: Verso, 1988.

20. Laclau and Mouffe, *Hegemony and Socialist Strategy*, p. 1.

21. See Heidi Hartmann, 'The Unhappy Marriage of Marxism and Feminism: Towards a More Progressive Union', in L. Sargent, ed., *The Unhappy Marriage of Marxism and Feminism: A Debate on Class and Patriarchy*, London: Pluto Press, 1981, pp. 1–41.

22. See Zygmunt Bauman, *Intimations of Postmodernity*, London: Routledge, 1992; particularly Chapter 8, 'Living without an Alternative'.

I

REDEFINING MARXISM: THE RECEPTION OF LACLAU AND MOUFFE

1

HEGEMONY AND SOCIALIST STRATEGY†

Ernesto Laclau and Chantal Mouffe

The publication of Hegemony and Socialist Strategy: Towards a Radical Democratic Politics *in 1985 represented something of a landmark in the development of post-Marxist thought: arguably the point at which post-Marxism coalesced into a specific theoretical position in its own right, rather than a scattered set of individual responses. Laclau and Mouffe chose to regard the rise of the new social movements, and development of new forms of cultural critique, as an opportunity to revitalise Marxism.* Hegemony and Socialist Strategy *constitutes a rallying cry for the development of a pluralist Marxism, able to enter into dialogue with new theories and world views rather than remaining locked into a narrow and rigid dogmatism. The authors' ultimate goal in the study is the creation of what they call a 'radical democratic politics', where the new protest movements will find full expression. What Laclau and Mouffe are engaged in, therefore, is no less than the redefinition of Marxism as a cultural theory. In particular there is a concern to redefine terms such as 'hegemony', and also the role of the working class within Marxist theory. In the extract below, the introduction to* Hegemony and Socialist Strategy, *Laclau and Mouffe state the case for a reorientation of Marxism to fit changed cultural circumstances, in fairly uncompromising terms. There is a crisis of socialist thought and its central categories, the authors argue, that can no longer be ignored by theorists on the left. They see themselves as challenging the assumptions of classical Marxism, but also striving to retain something of its revolutionary spirit.*

Left-wing thought today stands at a crossroads. The 'evident truths' of the past – the classical forms of analysis and political calculation, the nature of the forces in conflict, the very meaning of the Left's struggles and objectives – have been seriously challenged by an avalanche of historical mutations which have riven the ground on which those truths were constituted. Some of these mutations doubtless correspond to failures and disappointments: from Budapest to Prague and the Polish coup d'etat, from Kabul to the sequels of Communist victory in Vietnam and Cambodia, a

† From E. Laclau and C. Mouffe, *Hegemony and Socialist Strategy: Towards a Radical Democratic Politics*, London: Verso, 1985 (pp. 1–5)

question-mark has fallen more and more heavily over a whole way of conceiving both socialism and the roads that should lead to it. This has recharged critical thinking, at once corrosive and necessary, on the theoretical and political bases on which the intellectual horizon of the Left was traditionally constituted. But there is more to it than this. A whole series of positive new phenomena underlie those mutations which have made so urgent the task of theoretical reconsideration: the rise of the new feminism, the protest movements of ethnic, national and sexual minorities, the anti-institutional ecology struggles waged by marginalised layers of the population, the anti-nuclear movement, the atypical forms of social struggle in countries on the capitalist periphery – all these imply an extension of social conflictuality to a wide range of areas, which creates the potential, but no more than the potential, for an advance towards more free, democratic and egalitarian societies.

This proliferation of struggles presents itself, first of all, as a 'surplus' of the social vis-à-vis the rational and organised structures of society – that is, of the social 'order'. Numerous voices, deriving especially from the liberal-conservative camp, have insistently argued that Western societies face a crisis of governability and a threat of dissolution at the hands of the egalitarian danger. However, the new forms of social conflict have also thrown into crisis theoretical and political frameworks closer to the ones that we shall seek to engage in dialogue in the major part of this book. These correspond to the classical discourses of the Left, and the characteristic modes in which it has conceived the agents of social change, the structuring of political spaces, and the privileged points for the unleashing of historical transformations. What is now in crisis is a whole conception of socialism which rests upon the ontological centrality of the working class, upon the role of Revolution, with a capital 'r', as the founding moment in the transition from one type of society to another, and upon the illusory prospect of a perfectly unitary and homogeneous collective will that will render pointless the moment of politics. The plural and multifarious character of contemporary social struggles has finally dissolved the last foundation for that political imaginary. Peopled with 'universal' subjects and conceptually built around History in the singular, it has postulated 'society' as an intelligible structure that could be intellectually mastered on the basis of certain class positions and reconstituted, as a rational, transparent order, through a founding act of a political character. Today, the Left is witnessing the final act of the dissolution of that Jacobin imaginary.

Thus, the very wealth and plurality of contemporary social struggles has given rise to a theoretical crisis. It is at the middle point of this two-way movement between the theoretical and the political that our own discourse will be located. At every moment, we have tried to prevent an impressionist and sociologistic descriptivism, which lives on ignorance of the conditions of its own discursivity, from filling the theoretical voids generated by the crisis. Our aim has been the exact opposite: to focus on certain discursive categories which, at first sight, appeared to be privileged condensation-points for many aspects of the crisis; and to unravel the possible meaning of a history in the various facets of this multiple refraction. All discursive eclecticism or wavering was excluded from the very start. As is said in an inaugural 'manifesto' of the classical period, when one enters new territory, one must follow the example of 'travellers who, finding themselves lost in a forest, know that they ought not to wander first to one side and then to the other, nor, still less, to stop in one place, but understand that they should continue to walk as straight as they can in one direction, not diverging for any slight reason, even though it was possibly chance alone that first determined them in their choice. By this means if they do not go exactly where they wish, they will at least arrive somewhere at the end, where probably they will be better off than in the middle of a forest.'[1]

The guiding thread of our analysis has been the transformations in the concept of hegemony, considered as a discursive surface and fundamental nodal point of Marxist political theorisation. Our principal conclusion is that behind the concept of 'hegemony' lies hidden something more than a type of political relation *complementary* to the basic categories of Marxist theory. In fact, it introduces a *logic of the social* which is incompatible with those categories. Faced with the rationalism of classical Marxism, which presented history and society as intelligible totalities constituted around conceptually explicable laws, the logic of hegemony presented itself from the outset as a *complementary* and *contingent* operation, required for conjunctural imbalances within an evolutionary paradigm whose essential or 'morphological' validity was not for a moment placed in question. (One of the central tasks of this book will be to determine this specific logic of contingency.) As the areas of the concept's application grew broader, from Lenin to Gramsci, the field of contingent articulations also expanded, and the category of 'historical necessity' – which had been the cornerstone of classical Marxism – withdrew to the horizon of theory. [. . .] [T]he expansion and determination of the social logic implicit in the concept of 'hegemony' – in a direction that goes far beyond Gramsci – will provide us with an *anchorage* from which contemporary social struggles are *thinkable* in their specificity, as well as permitting us to outline a new politics for the Left based upon the project of a radical democracy.

One question remains to be answered: why should we broach this task through a critique and a deconstruction of the various discursive surfaces of classical Marxism? Let us first say that there is not *one* discourse and *one* system of categories through which the 'real' might speak without mediations. In operating deconstructively within Marxist categories, we do not claim to be writing 'universal history', to be inscribing our discourse as a moment of a single, linear process of knowledge. Just as the era of normative epistemologies has come to an end, so too has the era of universal discourses. Political conclusions similar to those set forth in this book could have been approximated from very different discursive formations – for example, from certain forms of Christianity, or from libertarian discourses alien to the socialist tradition – none of which could aspire to be *the* truth of society (or 'the insurpassable philosophy of our time', as Sartre put it). For this very reason, however, Marxism is *one* of the traditions through which it becomes possible to formulate this new conception of politics. For us, the validity of this point of departure is simply based on the fact that it constitutes our own past.

Is it not the case that, in scaling down the pretensions and the area of validity of Marxist theory, we are breaking with something deeply inherent in that theory:

namely, its monist aspiration to capture with its categories the essence or underlying meaning of History? The answer can only be in the affirmative. Only if we renounce any epistemological prerogative based upon the ontologically privileged position of a 'universal class', will it be possible seriously to discuss the present degree of validity of the Marxist categories. At this point we should state quite plainly that we are now situated in a post-Marxist terrain. It is no longer possible to maintain the conception of subjectivity and classes elaborated by Marxism, nor its vision of the historical course of capitalist development, nor, of course, the conception of communism as a transparent society from which antagonisms have disappeared. But if our intellectual project in this book is *post*-Marxist, it is evidently also post-*Marxist*. It has been through the development of certain intuitions and discursive forms constituted within Marxism, and the inhibition or elimination of certain others, that we have constructed a concept of hegemony which, in our view, may be a useful instrument in the struggle for a radical, libertarian and plural democracy. Here the reference to Gramsci, though partially critical, is of capital importance. In the text we have tried to recover some of the variety and richness of Marxist discursivity in the era of the Second International, which tended to be obliterated by that impoverished monolithic image of 'Marxism-Leninism' current in the Stalin and post-Stalin eras and now reproduced, almost intact though with opposite sign, by certain forms of contemporary 'anti-Marxism'. Neither the defenders of a glorious, homogeneous and invulnerable 'historical materialism', nor the professionals of an anti-Marxism à la nouveaux philosophes, realise the extent to which their apologias or diatribes are equally rooted in an ingenuous and primitive conception of a doctrine's role and degree of unity which, in all its essential determinations, is still tributary to the Stalinist imaginary. Our own approach to the Marxist texts has, on the contrary, sought to recover their plurality, to grasp the numerous discursive sequences – to a considerable extent heterogeneous and contradictory – which constitute their inner structure and wealth, and guarantee their survival as a reference point for political analysis. The surpassing of a great intellectual tradition never takes place in the sudden form of a collapse, but in the way that river waters, having originated at a common source, spread in various directions and mingle with currents flowing down from other sources. This is how the discourses that constituted the field of classical Marxism may help to form the thinking of a new left: by bequeathing some of their concepts, transforming or abandoning others, and diluting themselves in that infinite intertextuality of emancipatory discourses in which the plurality of the social takes shape.

NOTE

1.   Descartes, 'Discourse on Method', in *Philosophical Works* Vol. 1, Cambridge 1968, p.96.

2

RADICAL DEMOCRACY: ALTERNATIVE FOR A NEW LEFT†

Ernesto Laclau and Chantal Mouffe

In this second extract from Hegemony and Socialist Strategy *Laclau and Mouffe set out the principles for a 'radical democratic politics'. They argue that the left has no alternative, in the current cultural climate, but to commit itself to pluralism and the construction of links with the various new social movements that have sprung up in the later twentieth century. What is being asked for is nothing less than the recasting of the 'political imaginary' of the left, as it has traditionally been understood. This is a process that will involve discarding certain apparently sacred principles of Marxist and socialist thought; such as the belief that the working class is to be regarded as the 'privileged agent' of social change. We shall not achieve the desired state of radical democracy, Laclau and Mouffe contend, unless we embrace the myriad of struggles against social and political oppression taking place around the world today. Socialism, from this point of view, although a necessary element of radical democracy, is nevertheless only one element amongst many. What is required in the new 'articulation' of interests that radical democracy demands, is cooperation, and, it should be said, good will on the part of the participants. Critics of Laclau and Mouffe's project feel they are weak on how to ensure that this good will is maintained in any loose coalition of interests, such as the one they are prescribing.*

The conservative reaction thus has a clearly hegemonic character. It seeks a profound transformation of the terms of political discourse and the creation of a new 'definition of reality', which under the cover of the defence of 'individual liberty' would legitimise inequalities and restore the hierarchical relations which the struggles of previous decades had destroyed. What is at stake here is in fact the creation of a new historic bloc. Converted into organic ideology, liberal-conservatism would construct a new hegemonic articulation through a system of equivalences which would unify multiple subject positions around an individualist definition of rights and a negative conception of liberty. We are once again faced, then, with the displacement of the frontier of

† From E. Laclau and C. Mouffe, *Hegemony and Socialist Strategy: Towards a Radical Democratic Politics*, London: Verso, 1985 (pp. 176–93).

the social. A series of subject positions which were accepted as *legitimate differences* in the hegemonic formation corresponding to the Welfare State are expelled from the field of social positivity and construed as negativity – the parasites on social security (Mrs Thatcher's 'scroungers'), the inefficiency associated with union privileges, and state subsidies, and so on.

It is clear, therefore, that a left alternative can *only* consist of the construction of a different system of equivalents, which establishes social division on a new basis. In the face of the project for the reconstruction of a hierarchic society, the alternative of the Left should consist of locating itself fully in the field of the democratic revolution and expanding the chains of equivalents between the different struggles against oppression. *The task of the Left therefore cannot be to renounce liberal-democratic ideology, but, on the contrary, to deepen and expand it in the direction of a radical and plural democracy.* We shall explain the dimensions of this task in the following pages, but the very fact that it is possible arises out of the fact that the *meaning* of liberal discourse on individual rights is not definitively fixed; and just as this unfixity permits their articulation with elements of conservative discourse, it also permits different forms of articulation and redefinition which accentuate the democratic moment. That is to say, as with any other social element, the elements making up the liberal discourse never appear as crystallised, and may be the field of hegemonic struggle. It is not in the abandonment of the democratic terrain but, on the contrary, in the extension of the field of democratic struggles to the whole of civil society and the state, that the possibility resides for a hegemonic strategy of the Left. It is nevertheless important to understand the radical extent of the changes which are necessary in the political imaginary of the Left, if it wishes to succeed in founding a political practice fully located in the field of the democratic revolution and conscious of the depth and variety of the hegemonic articulations which the present conjuncture requires. The fundamental obstacle in this task is the one to which we have been drawing attention from the beginning of this book: essentialist apriorism, the conviction that the social is sutured at some point, from which it is possible to fix the meaning of any event independently of any articulatory practice. This has led to a failure to understand the constant displacement of the nodal points structuring a social formation, and to an organisation of discourse in terms of a logic of 'a priori privileged points' which seriously limits the Left's capacity for action and political analysis. This logic of privileged points has operated in a variety of directions. From the point of view of the determining of the fundamental antagonisms, the basic obstacle, as we have seen, has been *classism*: that is to say, the idea that the working class represents the privileged agent in which the fundamental impulse of social change resides – without perceiving that the very orientation of the working class depends upon a political balance of forces and the radicalisation of a plurality of democratic struggles which are decided in good part *outside* the class itself. From the point of view of the *social levels* at which the possibility of implementing changes is concentrated, the fundamental obstacles have been *statism* – the idea that the expansion of the role of the state is the panacea for all problems; and *economism* (particularly in its technocratic version) – the idea that from a successful economic strategy there necessarily follows a continuity of political effects which can be clearly specified.

But if we look for the ultimate core of this essentialist fixity, we shall find it in the fundamental nodal point which has galvanised the political imagination of the Left: the classic concept of 'revolution', cast in the Jacobin mould. Of course, there would be nothing in the concept of 'revolution' to which objection could be made if we understood by it the overdetermination of a set of struggles in a point of political rupture, from which there follow a variety of effects spread across the whole of the fabric of society. If this were all that was involved, there is no doubt that in many cases the violent overthrow of a repressive regime is the condition of every democratic advance. But the classic concept of revolution implied much more than this: it implied the *foundational* character of the revolutionary act, the institution of a point of concentration of power from which society could be 'rationally' reorganised. This is the perspective which is incompatible with the plurality and the opening which a radical democracy requires. Once again radicalising certain of Gramsci's concepts, we find the theoretical instruments which allow us to redimension the revolutionary act itself. The concept of a 'war of position' implies precisely the *process* character of every radical transformation – the revolutionary act is, simply, an internal moment of this process. The multiplication of political spaces and the preventing of the concentration of power in one point are, then, preconditions of every truly democratic transformation of society. The classic conception of socialism supposed that the disappearance of private ownership of the means of production would set up a chain of effects which, over a whole historical epoch, would lead to the extinction of all forms of subordination. Today we know that this is not so. *There are not*, for example, necessary links between anti-sexism and anti-capitalism, and a unity between the two can only be the result of a hegemonic articulation. It follows that it is only possible to construct this articulation on the basis of separate struggles, which only exercise their equivalential and overdetermining effects in *certain* spheres of the social. This requires the autonomisation of the spheres of struggle and the multiplication of political spaces, which is incompatible with the concentration of power and knowledge that classic Jacobinism and its different socialist variants imply. Of course, every project for radical democracy implies a socialist dimension, as it is necessary to put an end to capitalist relations of production, which are at the root of numerous relations of subordination; but socialism is *one* of the components of a project for radical democracy, not vice versa. For this very reason, when one speaks of the socialisation of the means of production as one element in the strategy for a radical and plural democracy, one must insist that this cannot mean only workers' self-management, as what is at stake is true participation by all subjects in decisions about what is to be produced, how it is to be produced, and the forms in which the product is to be distributed. Only in such conditions can there be *social appropriation* of production. To reduce the issue to a problem of workers' self-management is to ignore the fact that the workers' 'interests' can be constructed in such a way that they do not take account of ecological demands or demands of other groups which, without being producers, are affected by decisions taken in the field of production.[1]

From the point of view of a hegemonic politics, then, the crucial limitation of the traditional left perspective is that it attempts to determine *a priori* agents of change, levels of effectiveness in the field of the social, and privileged points and moments of rupture. All these obstacles come together into a common core, which is the refusal to abandon the assumption of a sutured society. Once this is discarded, however, there arises a whole set of new problems which we should now tackle. These may be summarised in three questions which we shall address in turn:

1. How do we determine the *surfaces of emergence* and the *forms of articulation* of the antagonisms which a project for radical democracy should embrace?
2. To what extent is the pluralism proper to a radical democracy compatible with the effects of equivalence which, as we have seen, are characteristic of every hegemonic articulation?
3. To what extent is the logic implicit in the displacements of the democratic imaginary sufficient to define a *hegemonic project*?

On the first point it is evident that, just as the apriorism implicit in a topography of the social has proved untenable, so it is impossible to define *a priori* the surfaces on which antagonisms will be constituted. Thus, although several left politics may be conceived and specified in certain contexts, there is not *one* politics of the Left whose *contents* can be determined in isolation from all contextual reference. It is for this reason that all attempts to proceed to such determination *a priori* have necessarily been unilateral and arbitrary, with no validity in a great number of circumstances. The exploding of the uniqueness of meaning of the political – which is linked to the phenomena of combined and uneven development – dissolves every possibility of fixing the signified in terms of a division between left and right. Say we try to define an ultimate content of the left which underlies all the contexts in which the word has been used: we shall never find one which does not present exceptions. We are exactly in the field of Wittgenstein's language games: the closest we can get is to find 'family resemblances'. Let us examine a few examples. In recent years much has been talked about the need to deepen the line of separation between state and civil society. It is not difficult to realise, however, that this proposal does not furnish the Left with any theory of the surface of emergence of antagonisms which can be generalised beyond a limited number of situations. It would appear to imply that every form of domination is incarnated in the state. But it is clear that civil society is also the seat of numerous relations of oppression, and, in consequence, of antagonisms and democratic struggles. With a greater or lesser clarity in their results, theories such as Althusser's analysis of 'ideological state apparatuses' sought to create a conceptual framework with which to think these phenomena of displacement in the field of domination. In the case of the feminist struggle, the state is an important means for effecting an advance, frequently *against* civil society, in legislation which combats sexism. In numerous underdeveloped countries the expansion of the functions of the central state is a means of establishing a frontier in the struggle against extreme forms of exploitation by landowning oligarchies. Furthermore, the state is not a homogenerous medium, separated from civil society by a ditch, but an uneven set of branches and functions, only relatively integrated by the hegemonic practices which take place within it. Above all, it should not be forgotten that the state can be the seat of numerous democratic antagonisms, to the extent that a set of functions within it – professional or technical, for example – can enter into relations of antagonism with centres of power, within the state itself, which seek to restrict and deform them. None of this means to say, of course, that in certain cases the division between state and civil society *cannot* constitute the fundamental political line of demarcation: this is what happens when the state has been transformed into a bureaucratic excrescence imposed by force upon the rest of society, as in Eastern Europe, or in the Nicaragua of the Somozas, which was a dictatorship sustained by a military apparatus. At any event, it is clearly impossible to identify either the state or civil society *a priori* as *the* surface of emergence of democratic antagonisms. The same can be said when it is a question of determining the positive or negative character, from the point of view of the politics of the Left, of certain organisational forms. Let us consider, for example, the 'party' form. The party as a political institution can, in certain circumstances, be an instance of bureaucratic crystallisation which acts as a brake upon mass movements; but in others it can be the organizer of dispersed and politically virgin masses, and can thus serve as an instrument for the expansion and deepening of democratic struggles. The important point is that inasmuch as the field of 'society in general' has disappeared as a valid framework of political analysis, there has also disappeared the possibility of establishing a *general* theory of politics on the basis of topographic categories – that is to say, of categories which fix in a permanent manner the meaning of certain contents as differences which can be located within a relational complex.

The conclusion to be drawn from this analysis is that it is impossible to specify *a priori* surfaces of emergence of antagonisms, as there is no surface which is not constantly subverted by the overdetermining effects of others, and because there is, in consequence, a constant displacement of the social logics characteristic of certain spheres towards other spheres. This is, among other things, the 'demonstration effect' that we have seen in operation in the case of the democratic revolution. A democratic struggle can autonomise a certain space within which it develops, and produce effects of equivalence with other struggles in a different political space. It is to this plurality of the social that the project for a radical democracy is linked, and the possibility of it emanates directly from the decentred character of the social agents, from the discursive plurality which constitutes them as subjects, and from the displacements which take place within that plurality. The original forms of democratic thought were linked to a *positive* and *unified* conception of human nature, and, to that extent, they tended to constitute a single space within which that nature would have to manifest the effects of its radical liberty and equality: it was thus that there was constituted a public space linked to the idea of citizenship. The public/private distinction constituted the separation between a space in which differences were erased through the universal equivalence of citizens, and a plurality of private spaces in which the full force of those differences was maintained. It is at this point that the overdetermination of effects linked to the democratic revolution begins to displace the line of demarcation between the public and the private and to *politicise* social relations; that is, to multiply the spaces in which the new logics of equivalence dissolve the differential positivity of the social: this is the long process which stretches from the workers' struggles of the nineteenth century to the struggle of women, diverse racial and sexual minorities, and diverse marginal groups, and the new anti-institutional struggles in the present century. Thus what has been exploded is the idea and the reality itself of a unique space of constitution of the political. What we are witnessing is a politicisation far more radical than any we have known in the past, because it tends to dissolve the distinction between the public and the private, not in terms of the encroachment on the private by a unified public space, but in terms of a proliferation of radically new and different political spaces. We are confronted with the emergence of a *plurality of subjects*, whose forms of constitution and diversity it is only possible to think if we relinquish the category of 'subject' as a unified and unifying essence.

Is this plurality of the political not in contradiction, however, with the unification resulting from the equivalential effects which, as we know, are the condition of antagonisms? Or, in other words, is there not an incompatibility between the proliferation of political spaces proper to a radical democracy and the construction of collective identities on the basis of the logic of equivalence? Once again, we are faced here with the apparent dichotomy autonomy/hegemony, to which we have already referred . . . and whose political implications and effects we should now consider. Let us consider the question from two perspectives:

1. from the point of view of the *terrain* on which the dichotomy can present itself as exclusive; and
2. from the point of view of the possibility and the historical conditions of the emergence of that terrain of exclusion.

Let us begin, then, by considering the terrain of the incompatibility between equivalential effects and autonomy. First, the logic of equivalence. We have already indicated that, inasmuch as antagonism arises not only in the dichotomised space which constitutes it but also in the field of a plurality of the social which always overflows that space, it is only by coming out of itself and hegemonizing external elements that the identity of the two poles of the anatagonism is consolidated. The strengthening of specific democratic struggles requires, therefore, the expansion of chains of equivalence which extend to other struggles. The equivalential articulation between anti-racism, anti-sexism and anti-capitalism, for example, requires a hegemonic construction, which, in certain circumstances, may be the condition for the consolidation of each one of these struggles. The logic of equivalence, then, taken to its ultimate consequences, would imply the dissolution of the autonomy of the spaces in which each one of these struggles is constituted; not necessarily because any of them become subordinated to others, but because they have all become, strictly speaking, equivalent symbols of a unique and indivisible struggle. The antagonism would thus have achieved the conditions of total transparency, to the extent that all unevenness had been eliminated, and the differential specificity of the spaces in which each of the democratic struggles was constituted had been dissolved. Second, the logic of autonomy. Each of these struggles retains its differential specificity with respect to the others. The political spaces in which each of them is constituted are different and unable to communicate with each other. But it is easily seen that this *apparently* libertarian logic is only sustained on the basis of a new closure. For if each struggle transforms the moment of its specificity into an absolute principle of identity, the set of these struggles can only be conceived of as an *absolute system of differences*, and this system can only be thought of as a closed totality. That is to say, the transparency of the social has simply been transferred from the uniqueness and intelligibility of a system of equivalences to the uniqueness and intelligibility of a system of differences. But in both cases we are dealing with discourses which seek, through their categories, to dominate the social as a *totality*. In both cases, therefore, the moment of totality ceases to be a *horizon* and becomes a *foundation*. It is only in this rational and homogeneous space that the logic of equivalence and the logic of autonomy are contradictory, because it is only there that social identities are presented as *already* acquired and fixed, and it is only there, therefore, that two *ultimately* contradictory social logics find a terrain in which these *ultimate* effects can develop fully. But as, by definition, this ultimate moment never arrives, the incompatibility between equivalence and autonomy disappears. The status of each changes: it is no longer a case of *foundations* of the social order, but of *social logics*, which intervene to different degrees in the constitution of every social identity, and which partially limit their mutual effects. From this we can deduce a basic precondition for a radically libertarian conception of politics: the refusal to dominate – intellectually or politically – every presumed 'ultimate foundation' of the social. Every conception which seeks to base itself on a knowledge of this foundation finds itself faced, sooner or later, with the Rousseauian paradox according to which men should be obliged to be free.

This change in the status of certain concepts, which transforms into social logics what were previously foundations, allows us to understand the variety of dimensions on which a democratic politics is based. It allows us, first of all, to identify with precision the meaning and the limits of what we may call the 'principle of democratic equivalence'. We are able to specify the meaning because it becomes clear that the mere displacement of the egalitarian imaginary is not sufficient to produce a transformation in the identity of the groups upon which this displacement operates. On the basis of the principle of equality, a corporatively constituted group can demand its rights to equality with other groups, but to the extent that the demands of various groups are different and in many cases incompatible among themselves, this does not lead to any real equivalence between the various democratic demands. In all those cases in which the problematic of possessive individualism is maintained as the matrix of production of the identity of the different groups, this result is inevitable. For there to be a 'democratic equivalence' something else is necessary: the construction of a new 'common sense' which changes the identity of the different groups, in such a way that the demands of each group are articulated equivalentially with those of the others – in Marx's words, 'that the free development of each should be the condition for the free development of all'. That is, equivalence is always hegemonic insofar as it does not simply establish an 'alliance' between given interests, but modifies the very identity of the forces engaging in that alliance. For the defence of the interests of the workers not to be made at the expense of the rights of women, immigrants or consumers, it is necessary to establish an equivalence between these different struggles. It is only on this condition that struggles against power become truly democratic, and that the demanding of rights is not carried out on the basis of an individualistic problematic, but in the context of respect for the rights to equality of other subordinated groups. But if this is the meaning of the principle of democratic equivalence, its limits are also clear. This total equivalence never exists; every equivalence is penetrated by a constitutive precariousness, derived from the unevenness of the social. To this extent, the precariousness of every equivalence demands that it be complemented/limited by the logic of autonomy. It is for this reason that the demand for *equality* is not sufficient, but needs to be balanced by the demand for *liberty*, which leads us to speak of a radical and *plural* democracy. A radical and non-plural democracy would be one which constituted *one* single space of equality on the basis of the unlimited operation of the logic of equivalence, and did not recognise the irreducible moment of the plurality of spaces. This principle of the separation of spaces is the basis of the demand for liberty. It is within it that the principle of pluralism resides and that the project for a plural democracy can link up with the logic of liberalism. It is not liberalism as such which should be called into question, for as an ethical principle which defends the liberty of the individual to fulfil his or her human capacities, it is more valid today than ever. But if this dimension of liberty is constitutive of every democratic and emancipatory project, it should not lead us, in reaction to certain 'holistic' excesses, to return purely and simply to the defence of 'bourgeois' individualism. What is involved is the production of *another* individual, an individual who is no longer constructed out of the matrix of possessive individualism. The idea of 'natural' rights prior to society – and, indeed, the whole of the false dichotomy individual/society – should be abandoned, and replaced by another manner of posing the problem of rights. It is never possible for individual rights to be defined in isolation, but only in the context of social relations which define determinate subject positions. As a consequence, it will always be a question of rights which involve other subjects who participate in the same social relation. It is in this sense that the notion of 'democratic rights' must be understood, as these are rights which can only be exercised collectively, and which suppose the existence of equal rights for others. The spaces constitutive of the different social relations may vary enormously, according to whether the relations involved are those of production, of citizenship, of neighbourhood, of couples, and so on. The forms of democracy should therefore also be plural, inasmuch as they have to be adapted to the social spaces in question – direct democracy cannot be the only organisational form, as it is only applicable to reduced social spaces.

It is necessary, therefore, to broaden the domain of the exercise of democratic rights beyond the limited traditional field of 'citizenship'. As regards the extension of democratic rights from the classic 'political' domain to that of the economy, this is the terrain of the specifically anti-capitalist struggle. Against those champions of economic liberalism who affirm that the economy is the domain of the 'private', the seat of natural rights, and that the criteria of democracy have no reason to be applied within it, socialist theory defends the right of the social agent to equality and to participation as a producer and not only as a citizen. Some advances have been made in this direction by theorists of the pluralist school such as Dahl and Lindblom,[2] who today recognise that to speak of the economy as the domain of the private in the era of multinational corporations is senseless, and that it is therefore necessary to accept certain forms of worker participation in the running of enterprises. Our perspective is certainly very different, as it is the very idea that there can be a natural domain of the 'private' which we wish to question. The distinctions public/private, civil society/political society are only the result of a certain type of hegemonic articulation, and their limits vary in accordance with the existing relations of forces at a given moment. For example, it is clear that neo-conservative discourse today is exerting itself to restrict the domain of the political and to reaffirm the field of the private in the face of the reduction to which this has been submitted in recent decades under the impact of the different democratic struggles.

Let us take up again at this point our argument regarding the mutual and necessary limitations between equivalence and autonomy. The conception of a plurality of political spaces is incompatible with the logic of equivalence only on the assumption of a closed system. But once this assumption is abandoned, it is not possible to derive from the proliferation of spaces and the ultimate indeterminacy of the social the impossibility of a society signifying itself – and thus thinking itself – as a totality, or the incompatibility of this totalising moment with the project for a radical democracy. The construction of a political space with equivalential effects is not only not incompatible with democratic struggle, but is in many cases a requirement for it. The construction of a chain of democratic equivalences in the face of the neo-conservative offensive, for example, is one of the conditions of the struggle of the Left for hegemony in the present circumstances. The incompatibility therefore does not lie in equivalence as a social logic. It arises only from the moment at which this space of equivalences ceases to be considered as *one* political space among others and comes to be seen as the centre, which subordinates and organizes all other spaces. It arises, that is, in the case where there takes place not only the construction of equivalents at a certain level of the social, but also the transformation of this level into a unifying principle, which reduces the others to differential moments internal to itself. We see then, paradoxically, that it is the very logic of openness and of the democratic subversion of differences which creates, in the societies of today, the possibility of a closure far more radical than in the past: to the extent that the resistance of traditional systems of differences is broken, and indeterminacy and ambiguity turn more elements of society into 'floating signifiers', the possibility arises of attempting to institute a centre which radically eliminates the logic of autonomy and reconstitutes around itself the totality of the social body. If in the nineteenth century the limits of every attempt at radical democracy were found in the survival of old forms of subordination across broad areas of social relations, at the present those limits are given by a new possibility which arises in the very terrain of democracy: the logic of totalitarianism.

Claude Lefort has shown how the 'democratic revolution', as a new terrain which supposes a profound mutation at the symbolic level, implies a new form of institution of the social. In earlier societies, organised in accordance with a theological-political logic, power was incorporated in the person of the prince, who was the representative of God – that is to say, of sovereign justice and sovereign reason. Society was thought as a body, the hierarchy of whose members rested upon the principle of unconditional order. According to Lefort, the radical difference which democratic society introduces is that the site of power becomes an empty space; the reference to a transcendent guarantor disappears, and with it the representation of the substantial unity of society. As a consequence a split occurs between the instances of power, knowledge, and the law, and their foundations are no longer assured. The possibility is thus opened up of an unending process of questioning: 'no law which can be fixed, whose dictates are not subject to contest, or whose foundations cannot be called into question; in sum, no representation of a centre of society: unity is no longer able to erase social division. Democracy inaugurates the experience of a society which cannot be apprehended or controlled, in which the people will be proclaimed sovereign, but in which its identity will never be definitively given, but will remain latent.'[3] It is in this context, according to Lefort, that the possibility must be understood of the emergence of totalitarianism, which consists of an attempt to re-establish the unity which democracy has shattered between the loci of power, law and knowledge. Once all references to extra-social powers have been abolished through the democratic revolution, a purely social power can emerge, presenting itself as total and extracting from itself alone the principle of law and the principle of knowledge. With totalitarianism, rather than designating a vacant site, power seeks to make itself material in an organ which assumes itself to be the representative of a *unitary* people. Under the pretext of achieving the unity of the people, the social division made visible by the logic of democracy is thereupon denied. This denial constitutes the centre of the logic of totalitarianism, and it is effected in a double movement: 'the annulment of the signs of the division of the state and society, and of those of the internal division of society. These imply the annulment of the differentiation of instances which govern the constitution of political society. There are no longer ultimate criteria of the law, nor ultimate criteria of knowledge, which are separate from power.[4]

If we examine them in the light of our problematic, it is possible to link these analyses to what we have characterised as the field of hegemonic practices. It is because there are no more assured foundations arising out of a transcendent order, because there is no longer a centre which binds together power, law and knowledge, that it becomes possible and necessary to unify certain political spaces through hegemonic articulations. But these articulations will always be partial and subject to being contested, as there is no longer a supreme guarantor. Every attempt to establish a definitive suture and to deny the radically open character of the social, which the logic of democracy institutes, leads to what Lefort designates as 'totalitarianism'; that is to say, to a logic of construction of the political which consists of establishing a point of departure from which society can be perfectly mastered and known. That this is a *political logic* and not a type of social organisation is proved by the fact that it cannot be ascribed to a particular political orientation: it may be the result of a politics of the 'left', according to which every antagonism may be eliminated and society rendered completely transparent, or the result of an authoritarian fixing of the social order in hierarchies established by the state, as in the case of fascism. But in both cases the state raises itself to the status of the sole possessor of the truth of the social order, whether in the name of the proletariat or of the nation, and seeks to control all the networks of sociability. In the face of the radical indeterminacy which democracy opens up, this involves an attempt to reimpose an absolute centre, and to re-establish the closure which will thus restore unity.

But if there is no doubt that one of the dangers which threatens democracy is the totalitarian attempt to pass beyond the constitutive character of antagonism and deny plurality in order to restore unity, there is also a symmetrically opposite danger of a lack of all reference to this unity. For, even though impossible, this remains a horizon which, given the absence of articulation between social relations, is necessary in order to prevent an implosion of the social and an absence of any common point of reference. This unravelling of the social fabric caused by the destruction of the symbolic framework is another form of the disappearance of the political. In contrast to the danger of totalitarianism, which imposes immutable articulations in an authoritarian manner, the problem here is the absence of those articulations which allow the establishment of meanings common to the different social subjects. Between the logic of complete identity and that of pure difference, the experience of democracy should consist of the recognition of the multiplicity of social logics along with the necessity of their articulation. But this articulation should be constantly re-created and renegotiated, and there is no final point at which a balance will be definitively achieved.

This leads us to our third question, that of the relationship between democratic logic and hegemonic project. It is evident from everything we have said so far that the logic of democracy cannot be sufficient for the formulation of any hegemonic project. This is because the logic of democracy is simply the equivalential displacement of the egalitarian imaginary to ever more extensive social relations, and, as such, it is only a logic of the elimination of relations of subordination and of inequalities. The logic of democracy is not a logic of the positivity of the social, and it is therefore incapable of founding a nodal point of any kind around which the social fabric can be reconstituted. But if the subversive moment of the logic of democracy and the positive moment of the institution of the social are no longer unified by any anthropological foundation which transforms them into the front and reverse sides of a single process, it follows clearly that every possible form of unity between the two is contingent, and is therefore itself the result of a process of articulation. This being the case, no hegemonic project can be based exclusively on a democratic logic, but must also consist of a set of proposals for the positive organisation of the social. If the demands of a subordinated group are presented purely as negative demands subversive of a certain order, without being linked to any viable project for the reconstruction of specific areas of society, their capacity to act hegemonically will be excluded from the outset. This is the difference between what might be called a 'strategy of opposition' and a 'strategy of construction of a new order'. In the case of the first, the element of negation of a certain social or political order predominates, but this element of negativity is not accompanied by any real attempt to establish different nodal points from which a process of different and positive reconstruction of the social fabric could be instituted – and as a result the strategy is condemned to marginality. This is the case with the different versions of 'enclave politics', whether ideological or corporative. In the case of the strategy of construction of a new order, in contrast, the element of social positivity predominates, but this very fact creates an unstable balance and a constant tension with the subversive logic of democracy. A situation of hegemony would be one in which the management of the positivity of the social and the articulation of the diverse democratic demands had achieved a maximum of integration – the opposite situation, in which social negativity brings about the disintegration of every stable system of differences, would correspond to an organic crisis. This allows us to see the sense in which we can speak of the project for a radical democracy as an alternative for the Left. This cannot consist of the affirmation, from positions of marginality, of a set of anti-system demands; on the contrary, it must base itself upon the search for a point of equilibrium between a maximum advance for the democratic revolution in a broad range of spheres, and the capacity for the hegemonic direction and positive reconstruction of these spheres on the part of subordinated groups.

Every hegemonic position is based, therefore, on an unstable equilibrium: construction starts from negativity, but is only consolidated to the extent that it succeeds in constituting the positivity of the social. These two moments are not theoretically articulated: they outline the space of a contradictory tension which constitutes the specificity of the different political conjunctures. (As we have seen, the contradictory character of these two moments does not imply a contradiction in our argument, as, from a logical point of view, the coexistence of two different and contradictory social logics, existing in the form of a mutual limitation of their effects, is perfectly possible.) But if this plurality of social logics is characteristic of a tension, it also requires a plurality of spaces in which they are to be constituted. In the case of the strategy of construction of a new order, the changes which it is possible to introduce in social positivity will depend not only on the more or less democratic character of the forces which pursue that strategy, but also upon a set of structural limits established by other logics – at the level of state apparatuses, the economy, and so on. Here it is important not to fall into the different forms of utopianism which seek to ignore the variety of spaces which constitute those structural limits, or of apoliticism, which reject the traditional field of the political in view of the limited character of the changes which it is possible to implement from within it. But it is also of the greatest importance not to seek to limit the field of the political to the management of social positivity, and to accept only those changes which it is possible to implement at present, rejecting every charge of negativity which goes beyond them. In recent years there has been much talk, for example, of the need for a 'laicisation of politics'. If by this one understands a critique of the essentialism of the traditional Left, which proceeded with absolute categories of the type '*the* Party', '*the* Class', or '*the* Revolution', one would not dissent. But frequently such 'laicisation' has meant something very different: the total expulsion of utopia from the field of the political. Now, without 'utopia', without the possibility of negating an order beyond the point that we are able to threaten it, there is no possibility at all of the constitution of a radical imaginary – whether democratic or of any other type. The presence of this imaginary as a set of symbolic meanings which totalise as negativity a certain social order is absolutely essential for the constitution of all left-wing thought. We have already indicated that the hegemonic forms of politics always suppose an unstable equilibrium between this imaginary and the management of social positivity; but this tension, which is one of the forms in which the impossibility of a transparent society is manifested, should be affirmed and defended. Every radical democratic politics should avoid the two extremes represented by the totalitarian myth of the Ideal City, and the positivist pragmatism of reformists without a project.

This moment of tension, of openness, which gives the social its essentially incomplete and precarious character, is what every project for radical democracy should set out to institutionalise. The institutional diversity and complexity which characterises a democratic society should be conceived of in a very different manner from the diversification of functions proper to a complex bureaucratic system. In the latter it is always exclusively a question of the management of the social as positivity, and every diversification takes place, in consequence, within a rationality which dominates the whole set of spheres and functions. The Hegelian conception of the bureaucracy as a universal class is the perfect theoretical crystallisation of this perspective. It has been transferred to the sociological plane in so far as the diversification of levels within the social – following a functionalist, structuralist or any other similar perspective – is linked to a conception of each of these levels as constituting moments of an intelligible totality which dominates them and gives them their meaning. But in the case of the pluralism proper to a radical democracy, *diversification* has been transformed into a *diversity*, as each of these diverse elements and levels is no longer the expression of a totality which transcends it. The multiplication of spaces and the institutional diversification which accompanies it no longer consist of a rational unfolding of functions, nor do they obey a subterranean logic which constitutes the rational principle of all change, but they express exactly the opposite: through the irreducible character of this diversity and plurality, society constructs the image and the management of its own impossibility. The compromise, the precarious character of every arrangement, the antagonism, are the primary facts, and it is only within this instability that the moment of positivity and its management take place. The advancing of a project for radical democracy means, therefore, forcing the myth of a rational and transparent society to recede progressively to the horizon of the social. This becomes a 'non-place', the symbol of its own impossibility.

But, for this very reason, the possibility of a *unified discourse* of the Left is also erased. If the various subject positions and the diverse antagonisms and points of rupture constitute a *diversity* and not a *diversification*, it is clear that they cannot be led back to a point from which they could all be embraced and explained by a single discourse. Discursive *discontinuity* becomes primary and constitutive. The discourse of radical democracy is no longer the discourse of the universal; the epistemological niche from which 'universal' classes and subjects spoke has been eradicated, and it has been replaced by a polyphony of voices, each of which constructs its own irreducible discursive identity. This point is decisive: there is no radical and plural democracy without renouncing the discourse of the universal and its implicit assumption of a privileged point of access to 'the truth', which can be reached only by a limited number of subjects. In political terms this means that just as there are no surfaces which are privileged *a priori* for the emergence of antagonisms, nor are there discursive regions which the programme of a radical democracy should exclude *a priori* as possible spheres of struggle. Juridical institutions, the educational system, labour relations, the discourses of the resistance of marginal populations construct original and irreducible forms of social protest, and thereby contribute all the discursive complexity and richness on which the programme of a radical democracy should be founded. The classic discourse of socialism was of a very different type: it was a discourse of the universal, which transformed certain social categories into depositories of political and epistemological privileges; it was an *a priori* discourse concerning differential levels of effectiveness within the social – and as such it reduced the field of the discursive surfaces on which it considered that it was possible and legitimate to operate; it was, finally, a discourse concerning the privileged points from which historical changes were set in motion – the Revolution, the General Strike, or 'evolution' as a unifying category of the cumulative and irreversible character of partial advances. Every project for radical democracy necessarily includes, as we have said, the socialist dimension – that is to say, the abolition of capitalist relations of production; but it rejects the idea that from this abolition there necessarily follows the elimination of the other inequalities. In consequence, the de-centring and autonomy of the different discourses and struggles, the multiplication of antagonisms and the construction of a plurality of spaces within which they can affirm themselves and develop, are the conditions *sine qua non* of the possibility that the different components of the classic ideal of socialism – which should, no doubt, be extended and reformulated – can be achieved. And as we have argued abundantly in these pages, this plurality of spaces does not deny, but rather requires, the overdetermination of its effects at certain levels and the consequent hegemonic articulation between them.

Let us come to a conclusion. This book has been constructed around the vicissitudes of the concept of hegemony, of the new logic of the social implicit within it, and of the 'epistemological obstacles' which, from Lenin to Gramsci, prevented a comprehension of its radical political and theoretical potential. It is only when the open, unsutured character of the social is fully accepted, when the essentialism of the totality and of the elements is rejected, that this potential becomes clearly visible and 'hegemony' can come to constitute a fundamental tool for political analysis on the left. These conditions arise originally in the field of what we have termed the 'democratic revolution', but they are only maximised in all their deconstructive effects in the project for a radical democracy, or, in other words, in a form of politics which is founded not upon dogmatic postulation of any 'essence of the social', but, on the contrary, on affirmation of the contingency and ambiguity of every 'essence', and on the constitutive character of social division and antagonism. Affirmation of a 'ground' which lives only by negating its fundamental character; of an 'order' which exists only as a partial limiting of disorder; of a 'meaning' which is constructed only as excess and paradox in the face of meaninglessness – in other words, the field of the political as the space for a game which is never 'zero-sum', because the rules and the players are never fully explicit. This game, which eludes the concept, does at least have a name: hegemony.

NOTES

1. Apart from the fact that our reflexion is located in a very different theoretical problematic, our emphasis on the need to articulate a plurality of forms of democracy corresponding to a multiplicity of subject positions distinguishes our approach from that of the theorists of 'participatory democracy' with whom we nevertheless share many important concerns. On 'participatory democracy', see C. B. Macpherson, *The Life and Times of Liberal Democracy*, Oxford, 1977, chapter 5 and C. Pateman, *Participation and Democratic Theory*, Cambridge, England, 1970.
2. Cf. R. Dahl, *Dilemmas of Pluralist Democracy*, New Haven and London 1982, and C. Lindblom, *Politics and Markets*, New York 1977.
3. C. Lefort, *L'invention démocratique*, Paris 1981, p. 173.
4. Ibid., p. 100.

3

DETHRONING THE WORKING CLASS?†

David Forgacs

Hegemony and Socialist Strategy's demand for a scaled-down, pluralist Marxism created a considerable stir on the left, and very quickly generated a literature of response. David Forgacs's review article in Marxism Today *(1985) constitutes one of the more sympathetic responses to the book, although it is not without some serious misgivings as to the overall validity of the Laclau–Mouffe project. Forgacs's main point is that, no matter how attractive the book's ideas might be, it is hard to see how they can ever be put successfully into practice. Like so many on the left, Forgacs can only regard pluralism as a problematical concept, more likely to dilute than to promote the cause of socialism.*

Since the late 1970s the innovative work of Ernesto Laclau and Chantal Mouffe has been widely drawn on by the Left in order to analyse the radical realignment of social forces that has been taking place.

Hegemony and Socialist Strategy builds on this earlier work. It also intervenes provocatively in two key areas of current debate. First, it has a lot to say about relations between the working class and other social movements. It contends that the working class has no necessary or preordained 'leading role' and argues that an effective strategy for the Left must link together a number of autonomous movements in a relation of mutual equivalence, not of dominance and subordination. Second, it deals with the connections between socialism and democracy. It insists that a 'radical democracy' must be both pluralistic and compatible with individual freedoms. Socialism will be only one of its components, albeit a necessary one.

Laclau and Mouffe mean, then, to carry out a deliberately 'post-Marxist' operation of dislodging the working class from the central place it occupies in Marxist theory. Their intention is not to downgrade the political importance of organised labour but to show that progressive political movements are not necessarily constructed along class lines and indeed that many of them are increasingly taking a non-class form. The

† From D. Forgacs, 'Dethroning the Working Class?', *Marxism Today*, 29 (5), May 1985, p. 43.

term 'hegemony' in this book designates precisely the linking together or 'articulation' of heterogeneous struggles and demands into a bloc. [. . .]

The notion that the working class is a privileged agent of revolutionary transformation depended, in classical Marxism, on the view that the essence of the class is constituted at the economic level by productive work and the sale of labour power. Its 'necessary' political radicalism was then derived or inferred from its economic essence. If it failed to act in a revolutionary way, this was because of 'false consciousness', or a temporary stabilisation of the economy or other 'contingent' factors. Forms of radical political action by groups outside the working class (like the petty bourgeoisie) or along non-class lines (feminism, nationalism) were either dismissed as marginal or explained in subordinate relation to the fundamental class struggle.

The error behind this logic, according to Laclau and Mouffe, lies in the belief that economic relations are more 'real' than political or ideological ones and serve as their foundation (the 'base/superstructure' dualism). They link this belief to the 'essentialist' view that individuals and classes are coherent, unified subjects whose actions and consciousness reflect their underlying essence. Against this the authors maintain that human subjectivity, far from being the source of people's actions and social relations, is the effect of the latter. It is only in our social relations that we assume 'subject positions'. Moreover, subjective identity is multifaceted and 'overdetermined', that is to say it is built up out of many different relations which only partly overlap with one another. For instance, the same man may be simultaneously a productive worker, a trade union member, a supporter of the SDP, a consumer, a racist, a home-owner, a wife-beater and a Christian. No one of these 'subject positions' can be logically derived from any of the others. No one of them is the 'essence' underlying the others.

Laclau and Mouffe develop from Gramsci the concept of hegemony as a new logic in which political action no longer expresses the 'economic-corporate' interests of particular classes but expands across class lines to form a 'historical bloc', a 'collective will' of popular forces united in struggle. At the same time they reject Gramsci's own view that hegemony necessarily involves the leadership of a fundamental class, treating this as a residue of classist thinking incompatible with the new logic implicit in the concept. They themselves see hegemony as a particular form of articulation (linkage) between different social agents. [. . .]

It would have to oppose the Right's current and successful yoking together of 'liberty' and 'democracy' with the free market economy, balloting of trade union members and popular resentments of 'welfare statism' and bureaucracy, by an alternative articulation in which 'liberty' and 'democracy' are connected instead with such things as women's and black people's rights, freedom for all within the economy, the right to local self-government. The work of articulation is not therefore, as has sometimes been asserted, merely 'ideological' or 'cultural', although it is these things too. It also takes place across material institutions and practices. It is political work in the fullest sense.

Hegemony and Socialist Strategy is a brilliant *tour de force* of scholarship and argument. Nevertheless its revisionism raises as many problems as it solves. In dethroning the working class as privileged agent of socialist change and admitting instead a 'polyphony of voices' of equal intensity the book leaves a big question mark over how *socialism*, as opposed to some form of mixed economy, will actually be achieved. In crude terms, what is one actually going to *do* about the private property of one's middle-class partners in a hegemonic alliance? Moreover, by taking the element of class leadership out of the Gramscian notion of hegemony and turning it into a purely consensual relationship among equals, Laclau and Mouffe are hard pressed to specify how all these struggles can be held together in one hegemonic articulation without either pulling apart or without one of them becoming dominant over the others. Their notion of an open plural democracy depends crucially on maintaining an unstable equilibrium between different social agents without lapsing either into authoritarian centralisation or fragmentation. An attractive idea, but hard to see how it would work.

4

THEORY AND SOCIALIST STRATEGY†

Stanley Aronowitz

Like Forgacs, Stanley Aronowitz is broadly sympathetic to the thrust of Laclau and Mouffe's critique of classical Marxism, as well as the need for such a critique to take place, but ultimately doubtful of its practicality in terms of political action. Aronowitz feels that Laclau and Mouffe have been so keen to prove their pluralist credentials that they have emptied socialism of any kind of moral authority. Further, that their tendency to assume that 'authority' equals 'authoritarianism' (a criticism just as applicable to poststructuralist thought in general, it should be said) is less than helpful when it comes to confronting abuses of political power in the real world. Overall, Aronowitz finds Laclau and Mouffe's theory of a 'radical democratic politics' too abstract to form the basis for left-wing political action (he bemoans the lack of historically specific case studies in this respect), although he does agree that the pair succeed in raising the right kinds of issues if Marxism is ever to regenerate itself.

The global left is embroiled in two concurrent but separate debates. The first concerns the so-called 'crisis in marxism', the second is a much more recent controversy: what is the status of socialism both as an alternative to capitalism considered historically, and as a social movement. The crisis in marxism is not new; it has reappeared periodically since the turn of the twentieth century and possesses a different character than the issues surrounding socialism. First of all, since marxism considers itself a critical or positive science (depending on tendency), its links to socialist politics, which have a distinctly 'ideological' character, are indirect. One may argue that the new self-examination of marxism has been detonated by the conjuncture of economic and political developments, but the nature of the questions asked and the answers provided are connected to the specific discourses of science. Put another way, the sociological and ideological aspects of the crisis of marxism as a science do not exhaust the issues. [. . .] Suffice it here to point out that while it is not new, every reincarnation adds more challenges to the marxist scientific paradigm. For example, none of the previous

† From S. Aronowitz, 'Theory and Socialist Strategy', *Social Text*, 1986/7, pp. 1–16 (pp. 1–3, 10–16).

periods in this debate subjected socialism to such scrutiny as is currently the norm, or challenged the role of the working class as a vital component of any possible emancipatory project. Thus socialism suffers today from the first global challenge to at least three of its fundamental claims:

1. to be the *determinate* alternative to the prevailing capitalist world order;
2. that the societies that constitute the 'really existing' socialisms represent a historical advance over advanced capitalist countries, and that under conditions of world economic and political crisis of the capitalist order the movements toward socialism are clearly on the political agenda; and
3. that socialism as an ideology subsumes other oppositional social movements and can accommodate their demands within its program.

Ernesto Laclau and Chantal Mouffe have added their voices to these debates. What distinguishes *Hegemony and Socialist Strategy* from other contributions are two critical differences. First, theirs is the boldest, if not the first, attempt to marshal the entire corpus of French post-structuralist philosophy as methodological and epistomological critiques of historical materialism. They have not only provided an external critique in the light of events, but have attempted to refute marxism from within as a form of essentialism. Further, they have proposed an alternate paradigm in which the primacy of the economic, indeed the existence of the social as an axiom of political and social theory, is denied. Second, this is the premier effort to carry the apparatus of post-structuralism, particularly the work of Derrida and Foucault, in the examination of socialism as the defining vision of a putative radical or revolutionary movement. They have affirmed the key tenets of democracy, especially its radical version, as unfinished business in those societies of which they are a part. Democracy constitutes itself as the alternative, of which socialism is a subordinate aspect in their discourse. Ideas such as pluralism, when placed in the context of Laclau and Mouffe's political theory, separate themselves from liberalism. Thus, unlike the spate of post-marxisms of the late 1970s, this is a *left* critique of marxism that tacitly accepts Marx's own attack against representative democracy and the 'free' market as proposed by nineteenth-century liberals.

Laclau and Mouffe have proposed a libertarian model of democratic society that rests on the power of social movements rather than political parties to transform civil society. Given the political backgrounds of the authors, their adoption of a 'social movements' perspective is undoubtedly linked to the character of the post-war reliance of the socialist movements, including the communists, on the electoral arena for representing their programme. Consequently, the rise of bureaucratic leftism, so vividly portrayed by Claude Lefort and Cornelius Castoriadis, raised serious questions concerning the status of the established European left as an alternative to late capitalism. Rather, implied by the parliamentary focus of the left is a deep desire to integrate themselves as part of the forces of order, not against them.

Hegemony and Socialist Strategy is deeply influenced by the action-critique of 'new' historical agents, particularly feminists and ecologists but also the ultra left splits from the communist and socialist parties for whom the declarations of the Italian

Communists that they are a party of order represent the death of the mainstream socialist movement. More concretely, the agendas of both feminist and ecologically based movements challenge the hegemony of the traditional working class in their respective national contexts. Laclau and Mouffe's renunciation of the idea of working-class hegemony is also a critique of the practical strategy of seeking parliamentary reforms adopted by the parties of the left. For them, it is not only an historical question (the working-class movement has declined in social weight since the end of the 1950s, for example), but a matter of the formulation of the question of historical agency itself. The heart of this book is the discourse concerning agency, but . . . it succeeds only in raising the question, not in providing a solid alternative theory. [. . .]

I will argue that they have succeeded in making their case against some varieties of marxism, but that their post-structuralist critique of historical materialism, although fascinating, contains large caveats that they cannot overcome without revising their framework. I will also argue that while their political theory is suggestive and some-times exciting, it suffers from a lack of specificity – it must, therefore, be considered a series of *hypotheses* rather than a real theory. [. . .]

Derrida admits that it is impossible to avoid logocentrism since these structures are embedded in language and, of course, language is inseparable from thought (cf. Derrida in Macksey and Donato, eds, *The Structuralist Controversy*). Therefore, Derrida's philosophy is a provocation, not a system that can hope to replace Hegel or, indeed, any philosophy of totality that promises to transcend immediate conditions. Whether the expressive totality of the hegelians in which subject-object identity is the result of a long, contradictory historical process or the structured totalities which acknowledge difference and especially discursive formations but insist on the idea of a *structure of dominance* that holds everything (provisionally) together (one such structure is the economy, another the unconscious), *making sense of the world entails determination*. Even Foucault, whose arguments parallel those of Laclau and Mouffe, faces the paradox of determinacy/indeterminacy when he *does* history instead of talking about it. Although renouncing the historical *a priori* of the political economy, natural History, or clinical medicine as a 'condition for the reality of statements', did not Foucault enter the history of moral/ethical discourse as a condition and carry this *a priori* between and within centuries? It is not a question of posing political economy as a condition *against* the so-called marginal 'superstructural' discourses that Foucault explores. I merely want to assert the ubiquity of essentialism. Indeed, Foucault almost becomes a functionalist when articulating a periodic *episteme* in terms of its discursive practices, while brilliantly succeeding in obliterating the distinction between language and object. His history is infused with interest which is by means innocent.

Foucault may be regarded as a historian of the moral economy of Western Europe. He examines 'rules that define a discursive practice' which are 'caught up in the very things they connect'. But the normative intention is not in the least disguised. For rules of human action are always normative, their 'meaning' derived from the power relations of which they are a part. So Foucault, who demands that we recognise the historicity of every social relation and the embeddedness of power in speech and vice versa, must still assert a tacit logic in his history – discourse as determination. Moreover, Foucault's historiography is not constituted by pure dispersion in that it contains its own unity of method. Foucault's 'rules' are positivities for examining the social. The object of historical inquiry is knowledge that constitutes itself as a science, but can be shown to be just another discursive practice implying power/domination. 'Instead of exploring the consciousness/knowledge/science axis (which cannot excape subjectivity), archaeology explores the discursive practice/knowledge/science axis' (cf. Foucault, *Power/Knowledge*). Thus, the subject is not implied by the term '*savoir*' as opposed to '*connaissance*' because knowledge here does not entail a notion of ideas corresponding either to a 'reality' independent of knowledge or possessing truth separate from the conditions of its production. Logically, these rules enunciated as such pose themselves, perhaps unwittingly, as alternatives to political economy which starts from an examination of the mode of production of material life, the relations that arise from the division of the social product, and the processes and conflicts over accumulation. These are different procedures in form, but the algorithmic substance is similar.

Laclau and Mouffe's reflexivity does not extend to the paradox of doing social 'archaeology' as opposed to social theory. Even the most critical archeology constitutes its object of knowledge as a critique of other possible objects; its discourses imply hierarchies of determination. We may choose certain discursive practices as crucial for specific historical '*epistemes*' in which case we have not abandoned the notion of determination, only *a priori* transhistorical judgement. That is, we might argue (as I would) that the efficacy of political economy on the methodological plane may correspond to specific social formations situated in determinate positions, and would surely be included in any menu of discourses for an inquiry seeking explanation. The task would be to articulate the characteristic categories of political economy (class, commodity, surplus value, profit, etc.) with those that may be specified concerning the political, cultural or any other discursive formation. The problem with the Foucaultian algorithm is its exclusions. Class, commodity and so forth simply disappear as proper objects of interrogation. In their passion to separate their own discourse from that of marxism, Laclau and Mouffe have cogently argued against traditional marxist hegemonies but have left little room for the categories of political economy.

'Whereof one cannot speak, thereof one must be silent', says Wittgenstein in his *Tractatus*. This, together with its corollary, 'The limits of my language mean the limits of my world', signify the death of the extra-linguistic. Language loses its character as representation/expression and becomes the sole constitutive of what we mark as the social or, indeed, the natural. Foucault and Derrida have adapted these *dicta* absent the concern, still present in Wittgenstein, with meaning. Foucault says in an interview published in *Power/Knowledge* that nature cannot be comprehended apart from the signifying practices that recuperate 'it' within discourse. In other words, nature may be understood only in its constructed context, only as it is articulated within culture. This has been a fecund advance from traditional materialist epistomology that insists on a realist theory of science and a reflection theory of knowledge. For what we have gained by discourse theory is that science/knowledge is liberated from the ideological connotation of its neutrality. We understand all knowledge in the context of power, not just social knowledge or politics which Althusser calls ideology. Thus, discourse is never far from the play of domination and resistance. Yet, just as Foucault's rules for historical investigation contain the tacit disappearance of political economy and especially the production of material life (now relegated to the realm of technical rationality which loses its contestatory power), so the reduction of social relations to discursive formations eliminates natural history, condemning it as 'essentialist'.

Since Engels and Marx placed human communities in the context of natural history and, in Engels' case, subjected them to the rules of natural scientific investigation, many tendencies within the marxist movement have laboured to free social relations from the burden of scientific marxism, a feature of which was to insist that human societies were 'organisms' that obeyed laws analogous to physics or, to be more exact, eighteenth-century physics. Lukács' celebrated attack on Engels borrowed heavily from neo-Kantian *Geisteswissenschaft*, which asserted that social relations could only be understood through the interaction of the observer and the observed, a process that strictly precluded the 'objectivity' of the social. For Lukács, it was a matter of remaining faithful to Marx's criticism of traditional materialism. *History and Class Consciousness* tries to comprehend society 'subjectively, as sensuous human activity', that is as a series of practices rather than 'an object of contemplation'. (The reference is, of course, to Marx's *Theses on Feuerbach*, especially the second thesis.) His epistemological critique of the later Engels entailed a rupture with the scientism of the Second International, in which social transformation had the force of natural law that occurred independently of human intervention.

Laclau and Mouffe join contemporary post-structuralism in announcing the death of the *a priori* subject and implicitly associate themselves with Lacan's reading of Freud – the most important twentieth-century theorist of the relatively unsocialised body. Lacan's emblematic pronouncement that the unconscious is structured 'like a language' at once made Freudian theory compatible with French linguistic philosophy and removed the most daunting obstacle to the hegemony of the various analytic perspectives that have dominated twentieth-century philosophy and social theory. For sexuality in Freud's hands could be harnessed only partially by means of its articulation as both utterance and discourse. The remainder, the excess, the surplus which escaped language's imperious tentacles disrupted social ordering. Yet, for him there was no question of the complete constitution of the human subject through discourse since the limits of language did not limit the world (cf. Freud, *Civilization and its Discontents*; Lacan, *Ecrits*).

In another register, Ernst Bloch posits the 'not yet conscious' mysteries that reveal themselves in dreams or remain at the gestural level, never articulated but incorporated into action. Bloch retains the impulse of the non-articulated intuition, will, desire, that for him explains much of the processes of social change. At times, like the Frankfurt School, he situates desire in art or, speaking politically, in youth for whom desire is the motor of development. Clearly, for Bloch, the 'new' cannot be merely a concatenation of discourses but attests to the presence of subjects constituted by the not yet conscious against which the prevailing order rails. Bloch's intervention, like Freud's, raises the question of the efficacy of rationalism as a method that explains historical events/transformations. Adopting the neo-romantic concept that time is a social rather than a natural category, and rejecting the rationalisation of the unconscious, Bloch tries to posit the subject as an indeterminate from the perspective of the social order precisely because it is constituted by a different 'now' than prevailing technologically mediated civilisation. Further, he argues that the not yet conscious is situated as a pre-linguistic field in which desire struggles for articulation in *opposition* to the boundaries of prevailing discourses.

What, from Laclau and Mouffe's perspective, are we to make of the Chernobyl catastrophe and other nuclear disasters? Plainly, the mentality that permits the development of nuclear energy and weapons is formed by discourses in which 'nature' becomes constituted entirely through technology. But the events themselves attest to a revolt of dominated nature. Whether the external world obeys laws independent of human intervention may be debated. But incontestible is its moment of autonomy, that it is a 'subject' the ignorance of whose regularities portend dire consequences for humanity. This is precisely the contention of the ecology movement. Their critique of the arrogance embodied in technological societies, with their post-enlightenment discourses, has barely been heard by socialists – libertarian, authoritarian or democratic. Laclau and Mouffe have still to absorb the experiences of the confrontation with the outcomes of these technologies, genetic engineering and even some ordinary industrial practices such as chemistry which have, in the past decade, become occasions for a new look at the notion of the primacy of practice over its object. It may be that the floating signifier, discourse without object and related doctrines of cultural primacy are by no means simple literary flourishes. Semiotic *philosophy*, as opposed to its descriptive procedures, is merely the cultural expression of the doctrine of the domination of nature which has become a destructive material force in contemporary history.

The importance of *Hegemony* consists in its pathbreaking attempt to make the literary, philosophical critique of post-structuralism political. Theirs remains an engaged discourse, although not to any existing party or political ideology. It is a 'political imaginary' that is 'radically libertarian and infinitely more politically ambitious than the classic left'. They seek to extend the democratic revolution 'to the whole of civil society and the state', as an alternative to the varieties of state socialism, legatees in their view of the jacobin (read elitist) traditions of the French Revolution that aim 'merely' to transform the ownership and control of the means of production, leaving civil society and the repressive state apparatus more or less intact. For Laclau and Mouffe, the democratic revolution is prior to socialism, which, in any case, no longer presents itself as the determinate negation of capitalism. Further, the workers' movements, contrary to the expectation by marxists that they would seek to transform relations of production, have defined their political imaginary within these relations, a sign that the classical left 'subject' of historical change has refused its assigned role.

Renouncing a general theory of politics, Laclau and Mouffe place their own democratic hopes in the new social movements that have emerged in the past two decades or which might appear in the future. But for them the feminist, ecology or any other of the new social movements do not become 'transcendent guarantors' of liberation. With Claude Lefort, they suggest that the 'site of power is an empty space' filled in an indeterminate manner by those radical democratic discourses that succeed in entering the field of hegemonic practices. None of them enjoys a place of privilege owing to some condition that in advance assures them of premier place in the pantheon of political antagonisms.

Thus, the liberal notion of democratic pluralism is transformed as a political category to mean the autonomisation of disparate discourses and struggles and their equivalence – equality in the social sphere. Laclau and Mouffe are so concerned to show the incipient authoritarianism in marxism that such notions of moral, discursive or any other kind of authority have no place. For they share the confusion of authority with authoritarianism that sometimes afflicts many forms of libertarian thought. This confusion prevents them from engaging the issue of what happens when a social movement gains power, not only within a civil society or the state, but also how its moral authority may enable it to set the agenda for left politics.

One would have to undertake a concrete investigation of the recent experiences of countries such as South Africa, Brazil and Poland, each of which has forged an alliance between an insurgent workers movement and the Church, to grasp the idea of authority without entailed domination. For the workers' movements of these countries function within a set of social antagonisms where their particular demands as workers conjoined with the more generalised demand for freedom from dictatorship. In these cases, a militant working class, acting as *a* but perhaps not *the* subject, has succeeded in exercising moral authority with other social movements, including the democratic movement of intellectuals. Since the workers' movements in these industrialising countries entered a less than empty space of power because a repressive state held nearly all of the reins, democratic demands dominate the political imaginary of these workers' movements as well as other social movements. In Brazil, mass strikes in 1978–79 resulted in the formation of a broadly based Workers' Party that has challenged the traditional opposition to the military regime because it has abandoned the democratic front strategy of the old Brazilian left in favour of a radical democratic politics. In Poland, state socialism confronts the democratic workers' movement. And, in both countries, the Catholic Church has intervened on the side of the workers. The Brazilian Church calls for the return of civil society to 'base communities', while trying to force the state to relinquish authority over such institutions as education, health care, and the workplace. The social movements in Brazil are allied with the Workers' Party or the democratic front. Even the labour movement is divided in its affiliations. However, there is no question that the struggle for hegemony within society entails the appearance of new subjects, preeminently workers.

The common characteristics of these situations are fairly plain: in each country the authoritarian state combined with multinational corporations to invent a model of development based, in part, on the proletarianisation of the countryside without the benefit of the bourgeois democratic revolution. In effect, a working class is constituted without rights. So far, the pattern of development is similar to the period of industrial revolution in Britain and other European countries. However, instead of a situation where the struggle for workers' and other democratic rights conflicts with a prevalent democratic ideology embodied in a parliamentary state, the authority offers only mass consumerism, a fordist solution with which it expects to forestall workers' demands for trade union autonomy and political participation.

The working class is not only constituted as a separate economic category by heavy investments, policies of agricultural migration, etc., but it is also constituted discursively as a class by the globalisation effect of economic development. The bourgeoisie of Brazil, the Communist Party of Poland and the Afrikaner white minority of South Africa want to create a nationalist movement without a popular base in the developing proletariat. Consequently, the democratic workers' demands correspond to those of intellectuals in all these cases (church based in part, university based in part). The coalition becomes simultaneously anti-capitalist and democratic in Brazil and South Africa while anti-new class in Poland. The structure of democratic opposition, while differing in forms, is remarkably similar in many other ways among the three movements.

This account differs from a traditional marxist understanding of class and class struggle. The Brazilian democratic movement arose under specific conditions that differed from the Polish case. In each of them, the configuration of political struggle was determined by the conjuncture of the different forms of repressive states' rapid industrialisation, the history of revolutionary and socialist discourses as well as the concrete circumstances which produced an insurgent working-class movement, not the least of which was the presence of charismatic leaders within the metallurgical industries and within the black South African miners, typically the flagship sectors of advanced industrial economies. There is no question that subjects were formed in these conjunctures, overdetermined, accidental to a large degree, and fraught with consequences that were largely unintentional. Having said all this, it is clear that hegemony constituted as moral and intellectual leadership has become a social category in these situations. In these instances, the role of intellectuals is at once crucial and ambiguous. For the Brazilian labour movement works with intellectuals but is by no means subordinate to them. The intellectuals of the Church and the secular marxist academics constitute quite separate discursive formations in the complex alliance that is the Workers' Party, but on every level of ideological struggle, the metal workers have articulated their own position including the vision of the new society they seek – in Laclau and Mouffe's terms, their political imaginary. Needless to say, their political imaginary differs from those articulated by intellectuals not linked directly to the labour movement.

In sum, a rigorous application of the principle of *historical specificity* in the articulation of radical democratic politics of the type Laclau and Mouffe affirm helps to confront discourse theory with its own *a prioris*. One wishes the textual emphasis of their work could have been supplemented with case studies. Such studies would have encountered moments of hegemony without domination which would have corrected Laclau and Mouffe's confusion between authoritarianism and authority, the Subject with a complex of subjects, and restored political economy, natural history and other despised discourses of the last century to a place in the multiple positions that constitute the social. Nevertheless, *Hegemony and Socialist Strategy* deserves careful reading. It raises most of the questions that have languished on the margins of traditional left discourse, particularly Leninist circles and even among democratic socialists. It is precisely in the wake of the current crisis that their book offers an opportunity to lay aside the legacy of an all but discredited past and start over.

5

POST-MARXISM?†

Norman Geras

If Forgacs and Aronowitz represent, broadly speaking, the sympathetic response to Hegemony and Socialist Strategy, *Norman Geras can be considered to lead the cause of the opposition. The following extract is taken from a long, and at times vitriolic, attack on Laclau and Mouffe in the pages of* New Left Review *(163): an attack which generated a reply from the targets themselves in a following issue of the same journal. Geras finds the picture of Marxist history painted by Laclau and Mouffe to be crude and reductive, and* Hegemony and Socialist Strategy *to be a book almost entirely without merit. Laclau and Mouffe's project is more properly to be described as 'ex-Marxist' than post-Marxist, and indeed the term 'post-Marxist' is for Geras a mere affectation, with no intellectual coherence to it. There is more than a suggestion in Geras's response that Laclau and Mouffe have not acted in good faith.*

BEYOND MARXISM

I want to discuss Ernesto Laclau and Chantal Mouffe's *Hegemony and Socialist Strategy: Towards a Radical Democratic Politics* – which styles itself 'post-Marxist'.[1] This is not because I consider the book to be theoretically worthwhile in any substantive respect. I do not. Indeed, it is a product of the very advanced stage of an intellectual malady, in a sense I shall presently explain; and it is theoretically profligate, dissolute, in ways I shall also seek to demonstrate, more or less any ideational combination or disjunction being permitted here, without regard for normal considerations of logic, of evidence or of due proportion. But the book is interesting nevertheless for at least two reasons. The first is that, as Ellen Meiksins Wood has said, it is 'beautifully paradigmatic': it brings together virtually all the key positions of a sector of the European left moving rightwards;[2] and the second is the post-Marxist claim itself.

This has, let it be noted, relative, at least, to the likes of Bernstein's 'revision' of Marxism, a certain plain-speaking accuracy. The authors announce a clear break. They

† From N. Geras, 'Post-Marxism?', *New Left Review*, 163, May/June 1987, pp. 40–82 (pp. 42–6, 52–9).

are now beyond Marxism. There is a bit more to be said about it, however. For, they do also insist on reminding us that Marxism is where they have come from. Whilst allowing that their present conclusions could have been arrived at by other paths and ones 'alien to the socialist tradition' – to which one can only say: verily! – they are mindful of their own past and have chosen, therefore, to proceed from 'certain intuitions and discursive forms' within it.[3] Could they be mindful too in this of links they are for the time being content to preserve? I shall suggest, in any event, that the tendency in recent Marxism most germane to the construction of their current outlook is merely the bad side of something which was two-sided in the hands of its originator. And then there is the exact meaning in which they may be said now to be 'beyond' Marxism. At the point in time, thought and politics they have so far reached, the post-Marxist tag no doubt has a nicer ring to Laclau and Mouffe's ears than would the alternative, 'ex-Marxist'. It evokes an idea of forward movement rather than a change of colours, what purports to be an advance or progress, and all decked out in the finery of discourse theory. My contention will be that at the heart of this post-Marxism there is an intellectual vacuum, a term I use advisedly: both a theoretical and a normative void, with some very *old* viewpoints, prejudices and caricatures around it.

I mount, then, what is in a certain sense a defence of Marxism; in a certain sense only, because it is to be doubted that anyone not already a Marxist will be persuaded to become one just by virtue of what I have to say here. But my purpose is more limited. It is to show that if there are good reasons for not being, or for ceasing to be, a Marxist, so-called post-Marxism isn't one of them.

Let us try to orient ourselves. These are some standard Marxist positions rejected in Laclau and Mouffe's book. In the first place: that objective, or structural, class position is the primary historical determinant of social and political identities and alignments; that the relations of production (or economic structure) enjoy(s) explanatory primacy; that politics and ideology are, correspondingly, secondary; that the metaphor of base and superstructure is a theoretically viable one.[4] Then: that the working class has an objective interest in socialism; that it is valid to speak of the *objective* interests of a class; that there are structural tendencies towards unification of the working class, for all the factors which fragment and divide it; and that as compared with other potentially radical social forces, it has a special – what these writers, in a noteworthy usage, like to call a 'privileged' – connection with the struggle for socialism.[5] Denied also: that socialism itself, the abolition of capitalist production relations, is the crucial strategic goal within the project of emancipatory social transformation (rather than, as Laclau and Mouffe now see it, just a dimension of 'radical democracy', or of 'the democratic revolution') and defines the fundamental moment, the decisive point of revolutionary rupture, in this epochal process of transformation.[6] And even, finally: that society and history can be rendered intelligible by some unifying principle or principles, or within a unified framework, of explanation and knowledge (something rejected however, it must be emphasised in this case, only incompletely and without the trouble of intellectual consistency, since with this as with every other assertion of relativism, its advocates necessarily contradict themselves so soon as they venture explanatory categories of their own).

Now, I think it fair to say that there is nothing in this catalogue of denials that could really surprise anyone. They are all thoroughly familiar. With the possible exception only of the last of them, they will be readily assented to by ordinary, old-fashioned *non*-Marxists. To discover what could be *post*-Marxist here, we must proceed a bit, therefore.

EXPRESSIVE TOTALITY

We will find, at least, something taken from one school of Marxism and taken further, so to say. Across its several particular propositions and negations, Laclau and Mouffe's argument is organised around a single all-embracing constructional principle. This is the division between the *simple* and the *complex*, or the *closed* and the *open*. On one side, there is simplicity, a desire for theoretical closure; on the other side, the recognition of complexity and openness. That is how the intellectual universe is divided.

In attempting to understand social and historical processes, there are those – the Marxist tradition in its entirety, but other thinkers as well – who reduce the complexity, diversity, multiformity, disparateness, plurality and opacity of it all to the simple, the single, the unified, the transparent. Thereby they theorise a closure. Determined from, and intelligible by reference to, one foundation or origin, society becomes a closed totality, is conceived, in the word of a less familiar idiom, as *sutured*. Because of this, of 'the conviction that the social is sutured at some point, from which it is possible to fix the meaning of any event', Marxism is deficient.[7] *Hegemony and Socialist Strategy* is replete with the language of its deficiency: 'reductionist problematic' for obvious reasons, 'monist' and 'profoundly monist', because of the idea of the unique foundation, 'essentialist discourse' ('essentialist core', 'essentialist vision', 'essentialist conception', 'orthodox essentialism'), because this foundation is an essence of the social, and 'economist paradigm', because it is the economy; 'classism', because of the primary role accorded to its constituent classes, 'stagist paradigm', because of the necessary stages through which it evolves, 'rationalism' and 'rationalist paradigm', because of the belief in the transparent intelligibility of the social whole, and still more, on account of the closed or fixed or *a priori* conceptual basis. And then a variety of combinations: like 'essentialist monism', and 'classist economism', and 'economist stagism'; 'essentialist apriorism' also; 'essentialist fixity'; 'the internal rationality and intelligibility of a closed paradigm', 'a purely classist and closed view of the world', 'the sutured space of a rationalist paradigm', and so on.[8]

But there are those, on the other hand, Laclau and Mouffe themselves particularly, who insist on facing up to social complexity, diversity and the rest and, to this end, on 'the open, non-sutured character of the social',[9] which has no essence except negatively speaking: 'we must begin by renouncing the conception of "society" as founding totality of its partial processes. We must, therefore, consider the openness of the social as the constitutive ground or "negative essence" of the existing.'[10] In other terms: 'the mere idea of a centre of the social has no meaning at all.'[11] Unification and closure are, here, accordingly impossible: 'The moment of the "final" suture never arrives'.[12]

Nourished though it plainly has been from other sources as well, readers of

Althusser's writings will easily recognise within this polar contrast an old friend and familiar foe, by name the 'spiritual' or 'expressive' totality. The concept was used by him in the effort to remove Marx's mature work out of the shadow of Hegel, in whose thought, Althusser argued, the apparent complexity of the social whole was *merely* apparent since its multiple aspects were always traceable and therefore reducible in the end to an original common essence, itself a moment or stage in the development of the world spirit. The diverse and manifold appearances of the Hegelian totality were expressions of this unique spiritual essence, which was present and more or less legible in them all. The outwardly complex thus gave way to the essentially simple.[13] Against every such simplifying tendency, Althusser himself emphasised the reality of 'overdetermination'; and Laclau and Mouffe in turn – as they put it, 'radicalizing' this last concept[14] – now propose openness and the like. But a crucial shift has taken place. The concepts in question were deployed by Althusser to inscribe a line within Marxism between what he saw as its authentic and its deviant forms. Laclau and Mouffe redraw the line between the whole of Marxism, this erstwhile mentor of theirs included, all vitiated beyond the hope of any remedy, and the theoretical outlook they have come now to favour. [. . .]

AN IRREDUCIBLE DUALISM

The same impoverishing view of Marxism . . . emerges more systematically in the account we are given of the tradition, writer by writer. I shall briefly summarise the main lines of this account. Its secret, however, is disclosed at the very start, in the Introduction to *Hegemony and Socialist Strategy*. The concept of hegemony, it is announced there, denotes a relation incompatible with, rather than complementary to, the basic Marxist categories. This concept, which will be central to the theoretical construction the authors will for their part propose, which they want, in one movement, both to take and to free from the conceptual armoury of Marxism, introduces, so they argue, a social logic of contingency opposed to the necessitarian logic that is Marxism's own.[15] The theme begets another, unavoidably. If hegemony and notions similar to it are incompatible with Marxist categories, then the presence of such notions in the thought of any particular Marxist must be the sign of an incoherence. They may be there, but they are not there with full theoretical legitimacy. However they may testify to the knowledge, insight, perspicacity or innovativeness of the thinker in question, they can do no credit to Marxism itself. In fact, they testify to the crisis, not the creativity, of the paradigm. The name of this theme, of this incoherence and crisis, is *dualism*. Let us try to get the measure of it, beginning, where Laclau and Mouffe do, with Rosa Luxemburg.

In the great movement of mass actions which she summed up in the expression, 'the mass strike', Luxemburg saw the possibility of a revolutionary unification. Their rolling, more or less spontaneous course would tend to transcend the division between economic and political aspects of the struggle, to generalise partial into more far-reaching and comprehensive demands, to overcome the aforementioned fragmentation of the working class. The conception so far, according to the authors of *Hegemony and Socialist Strategy*, had much in its favour. Not only did it take as its point of departure the manifest realities of proletarian diversity and dispersion. It envisaged, also, a unifying process whose type is symbolic, because having to do with the flow, and overflow of *meanings* as between one struggle and another. Said to be 'the highest point' of her analysis, this set Luxemburg's thought at a 'maximum distance' from Second International orthodoxy, far along the way towards recognising the scope and nature of social contingency. But she could not go right through to the end. Had she done so, she would have had no reason to suppose the result of the unifying process to be a *class* unity. 'On the contrary, the very logic of spontaneism seems to imply that the resulting type of unitary subject should remain largely indeterminate.' Why could this subject not be a 'popular or democratic' one? What held her back, limiting 'the innovatory effects' of the logic of spontaneism, was her belief in objective laws of capitalist development. The two things, that logic and these laws, made up an 'irreducible dualism'. Here it is that we come upon the disjunction already discussed: either pure economic necessity or permanent fragmentation.[16]

The details will be different but the pattern always the same. From Kautsky to Gramsci, Max Adler to Louis Althusser, it will be dualism (and, of course, 'essentialism'), engulfing all of Marxist thought and not only that. Karl Kautsky, like Luxemburg well aware of the fragmentary tendencies and interests within the German working class, makes the party into a 'totalizing instance'. The vehicle of scientific Marxist theory, and vouchsafing thereby a mediating role to intellectuals, it constitutes 'an articulating nexus that cannot simply be referred to the chain of a monistically conceived necessity'; there is a space here for '*the autonomy of political initiative*'. However, this space, with Kautsky, is minimal, just the initial relation of exteriority between socialist theory and the working class. For, theory itself is the guarantor of an eventually unfolding necessity and conceives political identities, reductively, fixedly, as governed by the relations of production.[17] Antonio Labriola, on the other hand, proposes that the objective laws of history are morphological only, valid for the broad, underlying tendencies and no more; and so makes use also of 'other explanatory categories' in order to grasp the complexity of social life. But as he cannot derive these, dialectically, from the morphological ones, since that would be 'to extend the effects of neccessity' back out again to embrace the whole, such categories – mark this – are '*external to Marxist theory*'. His proposal too, then, 'could not but introduce a dualism'.[18] In turn, Austro-Marxism goes rather far in restricting the scope of historical necessity, expanding that of 'autonomous political intervention', bringing, indeed, 'a strictly discursive element into the constitution of social objectivity'. Adler on Kant, Bauer on nationality, Renner on law – all contribute. But they fail, again, 'to reach the point of breaking with dualism and eliminating the moment of "morphological" necessity'.[19]

Even those who reach the point, at least, of breaking with Marxism and are warmly commended for their astuteness in so doing, do not evade the long arm of this judgement. Though their treatment is not directly relevant to the account we are given of Marxism itself, it is relevant indirectly in showing just how difficult escape here can be. I will not, therefore, disrupt the sequence of this intellectual history by omitting them.

Eduard Bernstein actually makes 'the break with the rigid base/superstructure distinction that had prevented any conception of the autonomy of the political'; achieves a 'rupture with orthodox determinism'. With him, 'the moment of political articulation' cannot, as it can with Kautsky, be reduced to movements of the infrastructure. Alas, this does not carry Bernstein far enough to avoid a form of dualism. He continues to allow, alongside the space of the free ethical subject, some residual space and truth to the causalities of orthodoxy. Worse still, he has replaced the 'essentialist connections' of orthodoxy with 'essentialist presuppositions' of his own: 'in this case, the postulate of progress as a unifying tendency'. The latter provides new '*totalizing contexts* which fix a priori the meaning of every event'.[20] Georges Sorel, by contrast, does *not* subscribe to an evolutionist belief in progress, recognising possibilities of disintegration and decay. He sees Marxism, initially, as an ideological and moral force for the formation and orientation of a new social agent, the proletariat. Then, accepting the revisionist critique, he comes to substitute the notion of social *mélange* for that of objective totality and to conceive classes, not as structural locations, but as *blocs*, constituted through will, action, and open contestation with antagonists. This culminates in the idea of the general strike as a constitutive myth, with its components of sentiment, fiction and violence as solidarising factors. In all, Sorel not only creates an area for contingency, as have the others, but tries also 'to think the specificity' of its logic. Has *he* made it, then? Has he escaped from the ubiquitous dualism? He has not. His 'politically or mythically reconstituted subject' is a class subject.[21]

TROTSKY, LENIN, GRAMSCI

Returning to Marxism's own story, we arrive with Russian Social Democracy at hegemony proper, a venture, at first too hesitant, across class boundaries. Marxism's problem in Russia, the problem of the Russian revolution, was not any longer only that of the political formation of a proletarian unity out of pre-existing diversity. It was the devolution to the working class of tasks of the bourgeois revolution, owing to the weakness of the Russian bourgeoisie and in departure from the orthodox schema of stages. The theoretical result in the debates of the time was a novel relation (between proletarian agent and bourgeois tasks) called hegemony; 'a space of indeterminacy', expanding in scope from the Mensheviks through Lenin to a maximum in Trotsky. Having discovered and named this relation, however, the Russian Marxists contrived to make it 'invisible' again, reproducing within the theory of hegemony, it can by now be no surprise to learn, 'the spurious dualism' of the Second International. This was because the specifically Russian 'narrative' continued to be conceptually subordinate to the orthodox one – even in Trotsky, the theory of permanent revolution to the schema of stages – with the second providing a level and order of 'essences' that gave meaning to the first. What was connected in the hegemonic relation remained external to and unaffected by it: though devolving upon a proletarian agent, bourgeois tasks remained bourgeois; the identity of the agent, despite this new breadth of its tasks, was still seen as determined by its structural position, and class identity in general as 'constituted on the basis of the relations of production'.[22] The point, in fact, turns out to have

compromised all of Leninism. To be sure, the Leninist tradition did emphasise h
the conditions of uneven development in the imperialist era made hegemonic relatic
indispensable to the revolutionary struggle by complicating the map of pure class
antagonisms; and hence insisted on the function of leadership within a class *alliance*,
a decisively political bond across structurally defined locations. But this relation was
still conceived as an external one, leaving unaltered the class identities making up the
alliance. Their interests were not formed, just *represented*, there. Instead of 'the efficacy
of the political level in constructing social relations', consequently, politics was but 'a
bare stage', the players upon it scripted from elsewhere.[23]

It was only Gramsci, according to Laclau and Mouffe, who 'radically subverted' the
foundations of this long dualist epic, moving beyond the notion of an external alliance
of classes. By a broadening of the perspective from the political to the intellectual
and moral plane – the terrain of ideology – Gramsci could think in terms of the
forging of a *historical bloc*, which was 'a higher synthesis, a "collective will"', with a set
of shared ideas and values across different class positions. Here, the hegemonic link
was not concealed but 'visible and theorized', and the base/superstructure distinction
transcended, and the guarantee of laws of history dispensed with. The social agents
were no longer, strictly, classes, but such 'collective wills'. In Gramsci's analysis,
we are told, 'the field of historical contingency has penetrated social relations more
thoroughly than in any of the previous discourses: the social segments have lost those
essential connections which turned them into moments of the stagist paradigm'; there
is 'a new series of relations among groups which baffles [sic] their structural location
within the . . . schema of economism'. But then again, perhaps not. For, Gramsci's
conception was 'ultimately incoherent', not yet quite beyond 'the dualism of classical
Marxism', inwardly 'essentialist' after all. His problem? – 'the unicity of the unifying
principle, and its necessary class character'. For him, that is to say, 'there must always
be a *single* unifying principle in every hegemonic formation, and this [could] only be a
fundamental class'. Determination by the economy had been reaffirmed.[24]

What, finally, of Althusser? Althusser is hoist with his own petard. With the concept
of overdetermination he is said to have reached out potentially towards the understanding of a specific and irreducible type of complexity, a *symbolic* one in fact, entailing
'a plurality of meanings'. It implied that society could have no essence, since there was
no possibility of fixing upon its ultimate 'literality' or sense. But 'a growing closure led
to the installation of a new variant of essentialism.' Determination in the last instance
by the economy, actually incompatible with the concept of overdetermination, was
the thesis responsible for this; 'exactly the same dualism' was its result.[25]

THE ESSENCE OF THE STORY

Now, there is more than one way of looking at this tale of Marxism Laclau and Mouffe
have told. The first is as a simple sort of intellectual game. I call it simple because the
basic rules of it are clear and easy to grasp. You take some Marxist, any Marxist will
do, and begin by showing how in deference to complicated historical realities he or she
departed from a rigidly, an absolutely, determinist economism. This will not be difficult

to show since even the most economistic of them has allowed some efficacy, however small, to political and/or other non-economic instances, but in any case the distance he or she has travelled that way will give a measure of his theoretical insight, her recognition of contingency or indeterminacy, their relative success in groping towards an adequate idea of hegemony, and so on. You then nail the thinker in question for 'essentialism'. To do that, you need only catch them out in the use of a central Marxist category. Which Marxist category it is precisely – objective laws of capitalism, class or class interest, the forces or the relations of production – and its exact role and weight in the writer's thought, are matters of indifference. It is its bare presence there that counts. At some point, finally, you should work in a reference to the resulting dualism. As we shall see, certain features of the game are not quite so straightforward, indeed rather strange. But this much anyone can learn to play. You may try it with some other Marxist writers – Herbert Marcuse, say, or Isaac Deutscher – analyses of whom in this mode we have thankfully been spared.

A second angle of vision follows directly from this first. As it is no trouble to catch a Marxist at the use of Marxist concepts, such being what composes his or her Marxism, the reproach of 'essentialism' levelled here at writers in the tradition is just the reproach that they remained Marxists, nothing more. To show, for example, that notwithstanding her ideas about spontaneity, Luxemburg, and despite emphasising the importance of political alliances, Lenin, and even within his theory of hegemony, Gramsci, continued to deploy a structural concept of class, only tells those interested what they already know. It does not demonstrate, as would be needed for the charge of 'essentialism' to have any bite, that Luxemburg, Lenin or Gramsci took the concept as explaining and resolving everything; show a conceptual inflation of class on their part into the originative source of all social and historical processes. Integral to Laclau and Mouffe's own argument, on the contrary, is that in the generality of Marxist writing the basic structural categories of Marxism were *not* used as all-explanatory and sufficient. For their users, then, they were not everything. But they were something. And more than that, of course, they were something crucially important. To say 'essentialism' merely on this account, however, is to be willing to find the vice wherever there are organising explanatory concepts, where there is any kind of categorial priority. It is a long, firm step into the darkness.

Is more confirmation of such nihilism wanted than is provided by the repeated triggering in the text, at every conceivable sort of encounter with a basic Marxist category, of one of the manifold terms pertaining to 'essence' and 'suture'? If so, it is surely given by the fate at Laclau and Mouffe's hands of their chosen non-Marxists. Bernstein went so far as to repudiate historical materialism in its fundamentals. Nevertheless, we are cautioned, he believed in progress and this tended to endow other beliefs of his with a certain overall meaning. Sorel, then: he renounced both historical materialism and faith in progress. He clung, however, to the notion of the class subject. But, on the authors' account, this was scarcely any longer a structural concept of class. Well . . . but it *was* still class! The word, as we know, can be written with a capital 'c' and behind the definite article. If Laclau and Mouffe mean to say no more than that class is unimportant, or at least not so important as Sorel in his way and the Marxists in theirs understood it to be, or that a confidence in progress such as Bernstein had is ill-founded, then naturally they have every right to try to make both the one case and the other, as indeed any case they may think they can give good reasons to prove. Their constant cry of 'essentialism', however, evokes some deeper kind of error, associated with conceptual unity or priority in themselves. As such, it resembles nothing so much as an obfuscatory curse.

Third, in the light of their completed history of Marxism, we are better placed to judge the claim Laclau and Mouffe make at the beginning of *Hegemony and Socialist Strategy*, that they 'have tried to recover some of the variety and richness of Marxist discursivity'.[26] I come back to the matter of richness in just a moment. As to variety, certainly there is some: Lenin is not Kautsky, Trotsky and Luxemburg are different from Gramsci, and this is reflected in what the authors tell us of them. But one is entitled to ask whether the variety has not proven, in the event, to be of a somewhat superficial kind. From beginning to end, all these writers were in exactly the same sort of fix, making repeated but vain attempts to get beyond unity and necessity towards plurality and contingency. Could a more simplistic story be imagined? One is not merely entitled but, in the given intellectual context, bound to ask whether this is not a reduction – of the breadth, the panorama, the continent, of Marxist thought. Laclau and Mouffe may have happened for once, but this time unwittingly and unwillingly, upon a genuine 'essentialist' essence: in their own words, when excoriating 'orthodoxy' for one of its several sins – reduction of the concrete, be it noted, to the abstract – upon 'an *underlying reality* to which the ultimate sense of every concrete presence must necessarily be referred, whatever the level of complexity in the system of mediations.'[27] Can a better instance of what they are talking about be cited than the story they have recounted of, and the game they have played with, Marxism? It is hard to think of one. Few, if any, of the Marxists they have taken to task made class so exhaustively the explanation of human existence as they have made 'essentialism' the explanation and meaning of the development of Marxist thought in its entirety.

One bad Althusserian chicken has come home to roost, here, with a vengeance. Whilst putting a considerable intellect at the service of defending historical materialism, Althusser in some ways also showed scant respect, scholarly or just human, for the tradition to which he himself belonged, a great many Marxist lives and ideas; subsuming the specificity and detail of them, their effort to grapple with difficult problems, under a simple, dichotomous division of the intellect and on the wrong side of it. This could not but affect some of those influenced by him and inheriting in a less auspicious political time such easy and too clever disrespect for other Marxisms, both precursive and contemporary. If so many Marxist thinkers, so much of Marxist theorising, fell beyond the line of intellectual salvation, must that not be because Marxism itself was deficient, inherently? Even in differing from him with this conclusion, they inherited from Althusser, also, something of the passion for closed certainties which he and they liked and like to castigate in others. Only, where he had sought to distinguish just one single, anti-reductionist truth from amongst all the varieties of Marxism, they have found all the varieties of Marxism to be distinct from the one anti-reductionist truth.

A RICHNESS IMPOVERISHED

Fourth, and the crux of the matter, we can see now how Laclau and Mouffe's is an impoverishing account of Marxist thought. To see it in all clarity though, we must look into the face of a conundrum. The two of them think nothing of the logical feat of charging Marxism with being both monist and dualist at the same time. Just where we might have expected a stern 'either . . . or', we get a conjunction: monism and dualism both. Actually, the connection is even stronger. More than a conjunction it is a species of entailment. *Because* it was monist, so the argument is, Marxism has had to be dualist. Unpacking this a bit: because in 'aspiration' or 'profoundly'[28] – let us just say *in essence* – Marxism was monist whilst the world itself was not, Marxist theoreticians trying to come to terms with the world have had to utilise categories extraneous – *really* – to the theory they espoused and become dualists. This describes, once again, an uncomfortable Marxist predicament, a dilemma whose teasing shape we earlier had occasion to notice. Should one make use of any other concepts, then either they are linked 'dialectically' to those of class, the relations of production and so on, and the monism remains unbroken, or they are not thus linked and, consequently, are 'external' to Marxist theory.[29] It is either Kautsky or it is Labriola. The economist rigidity of a Plekhanov may be avoided only for the incoherence of a Gramsci to be the result.[30] Since all the more creative Marxist thinkers have tended towards this latter (dualist) choice, bringing into their discourse a logic of the contingent or idea of the symbolic, as it may be, that was foreign to the basis of their Marxism, it can be said that where the more orthodox were reductionists, the more creative were eclectics. And even they were reductionists. For, at the heart of their eclecticism the reductionism still lurked: in the phrase applied to Gramsci, an 'inner essentialist core';[31] a monism within a dualism. In this place, truly, there can be no salvation, other than by taking leave of Marxism altogether.

But it should be clear, in any event, how the effect of it all is radically to reduce the scope and content, the wealth, of actual Marxist thought: not the shrivelled thing Laclau and Mouffe give out as being its essence; actual Marxist thought as thought by actual Marxists. Much of this has simply been denatured, a whole swathe of arguments, themes, concepts and theory been transmuted and deranged. These are not, as one might previously have thought them, part of the development or deepening, the extension and inner differentiation – part of the richness, precisely – *of* Marxism. They are, so it transpires, incompatible with its monist and reductionist core. Richness of Marxist 'discursivity', therefore, they may be, if the term just refers loosely to the writings of people who happened to be Marxists. But they are a departure, strictly speaking, from Marxist *theory*, so many external supplements more or less *ad hoc*. They betoken not the richness but the poverty of it, and the resulting crisis, the dualism, the incoherence.

NOTES

1.   Ernesto Laclau and Chantal Mouffe, *Hegemony and Socialist Strategy: Towards a Radical Democratic Politics* (hereafter HSS), Verso, London 1985, p. 4. Except where indicated otherwise, all emphasis in quotations is Laclau and Mouffe's.

2. Ellen Meiksins Wood, *The Retreat From Class*, Verso, London 1986, p. 47.

3. HSS, pp. 3–4.

4. See, e.g., HSS, pp. 20–1, 58, 67–8, 109, 174.

5. HSS, pp. 82–7.

6. HSS, pp. 156, 176–8, 192.

7. HSS, p. 177.

8. These expressions appear at HSS, pp. 21 (and 67), 4, 18, 88 (and 97), 69, 71, 70 (and 76), 76 (and 104), 76, 177, 68, 3, 100, 13–4, 55, 57 (and 61), 177, 177, 16, 68, 99. There is also, for good measure: 'classist categories', 'a monist perspective', 'dogmatic rationalism', 'class reductionism', 'a classist terrain', 'essentialist paradigms', 'essentialist assumption', 'essentialist solutions' – at pp. 11, 27, 34, 52 (and 85), 62, 77, 109, 134. And still the list is far from being complete.

9. HSS, p. 138.

10. HSS, p. 95.

11. HSS, p. 139.

12. HSS, p. 86. This echoes Althusser's well-known formula, 'From the first moment to the last, the lonely hour of the "last instance" never comes.' See Louis Althusser, *For Marx*, London 1969, p. 113.

13. See *For Marx*, pp. 101–4, 202–4; Louis Althusser and Étienne Balibar, *Reading Capital*, London 1970, pp. 93–7; and my 'Althusser's Marxism: An Account and Assessment', in Norman Geras, *Literature of Revolution*, Verso, London 1986, pp. 108 ff. For an excellent assessment of Althusser's thought, see Gregory Elliott, *Althusser – The Detour of Theory*, Verso, London, 1987.

14. HSS, pp. 87, 97.

15. HSS, pp. 3, 7.

16. HSS, pp. 8–14.

17. HSS, pp. 19–21, 25.

18. HSS, pp. 25–7.

19. HSS, pp. 27–9.

20. HSS, pp. 29–36.

21. HSS, pp. 36–41.

22. HSS, pp. 48–54.

23. HSS, pp. 55–62, 65.

24. HSS, pp. 65–9.

25. HSS, pp. 97–9.

26. HSS, p. 4.

27. HSS, p. 22.

28. HSS, pp. 4, 18.

29. See text to n. 18 above.

30. For Plekhanov, see HSS, pp. 23–4.

31. HSS, p. 69.

6

POST-MARXISM WITHOUT APOLOGIES†

Ernesto Laclau and Chantal Mouffe

Laclau and Mouffe's reply to Norman Geras's critique of their project to redefine Marxism reveals the deep divisions that are opening up on the left in the wake of the new theoretical movements, and the threat they pose to existing paradigms of thought and analysis. The authors of Hegemony and Socialist Strategy *are entirely unrepentant about their championship of these movements, consigning thinkers like Geras (those 'fading epigones of Marxist orthodoxy' as they dismissively style them) to the dustbin of history. Above all, Laclau and Mouffe confirm their desire to go 'beyond' Marxism. Not to do so is, they argue, to treat it more like a religion than a theory which has the capacity to evolve: and evolution is very much the name of the game in their view. Geras's objections to the principles of a 'radical democratic politics' are brushed aside as those of a mere 'sectarian' who is out of touch with the real world, where Marxism's track record as a political theory is somewhat less than exemplary (as so often, Stalin provides a handy stick with which to beat one's 'classical' adversary). One might almost say that Laclau and Mouffe's concern is to rescue Marxism (or at the very least its spirit) from its defenders.*

Why should we rethink the socialist project today? In *Hegemony and Socialist Strategy* we pointed out some of the reasons. As participating actors in the history of our time, if we are actually to assume an interventionist role and not to do so blindly, we must attempt to wrest as much light as possible from the struggles in which we participate and from the changes which are taking place before our eyes. Thus, it is again necessary to temper 'the arms of critique'. The historical reality whereof the socialist project is reformulated today is very different from the one of only a few decades ago, and we will carry out our obligations as socialists and intellectuals only if we are fully conscious of the changes and persist in the effort of extracting all their consequences at the level of theory. The 'obstinate rigour' that Leonardo proposed as a rule for intellectual work should be the only guideline in this task; and it leaves

† From E. Laclau and C. Mouffe, 'Post-Marxism Without Apologies', *New Left Review*, 166, November/December 1987, pp. 79–106 (pp. 79–81, 97–106).

no space for complacent sleights of hand that seek only to safeguard an obsolete orthodoxy.

Since we have referred in our book to the most important of these historical transformations, we need do no more here than enumerate them: structural transformations of capitalism that have led to the decline of the classical working class in the post-industrial countries; the increasingly profound penetration of capitalist relations of production in areas of social life, whose dislocatory effects – concurrent with those deriving from the forms of bureaucratisation which have characterised the Welfare State – have generated new forms of social protest; the emergence of mass mobilisations in Third World countries which do not follow the classical pattern of class struggle; the crisis and discrediting of the model of society put into effect in the countries of so-called 'actually existing socialism', including the exposure of new forms of domination established in the name of the dictatorship of the proletariat.

There is no room here for disappointment. The fact that any reformulation of socialism has to start today from a more diversified, complex and contradictory horizon of experiences than that of fifty years ago – not to mention 1914, 1871 or 1848 – is a challenge to the imagination and to political creativity. Hopelessness in this matter is only proper to those who, to borrow a phrase from J. B. Priestley, have lived for years in a fools' paradise and then abruptly move on to invent a fools' hell for themselves. We are living, on the contrary, one of the most exhilarating moments of the twentieth century: a moment in which new generations, without the prejudices of the past, without theories presenting themselves as 'absolute truths' of History, are constructing new emancipatory discourses, more human, diversified and democratic. The eschatological and epistemological ambitions are more modest, but the liberating aspirations are wider and deeper.

In our opinion, to rethink socialism in these new conditions compels us to undertake two steps. The first is to accept, in all their radical novelty, the transformations of the world in which we live – that is to say, neither to ignore them nor to distort them in order to make them compatible with outdated schemas so that we may continue inhabiting forms of thought which repeat the old formulae. The second is to start from this full insertion in the present – in its struggles, its challenges, its dangers – to interrogate the past: to search within it for the genealogy of the present situation; to recognise within it the presence – at first marginal and blurred – of problems that are ours; and, consequently, to establish with that past a dialogue which is organised around continuities and discontinuities, identifications and ruptures. It is in this way, by making the past a transient and contingent reality rather than an absolute origin, that a *tradition* is given form.

In our book we attempted to make a contribution to this task, which today starts from different traditions and in different latitudes. In almost all cases we have received an important intellectual stimulus from our reviewers. Slavoj Zizek, for example, has enriched our theory of social antagonisms, pointing out its relevance for various aspects of Lacanian theory.[1] Andrew Ross has indicated the specificity of our line of argument in relation to several attempts in the United States to address similar problems, and has located it within the general framework of the debate about post-

modernity.[2] Alistair Davidson has characterised the new Marxist intellectual climate
of which our book is part.[3] Stanley Aronowitz has made some interesting and friendly
criticisms from the standpoint of the intellectual tradition of the American Left.[4]
Phillip Derbyshire has very correctly underlined the theoretical place of our text in
the dissolution of essentialism, both political and philosophical.[5] David Forgacs has
posed a set of important questions about the political implications of our book, which
we hope to answer in future works.[6]

However, there have also been attacks coming – as was to be expected – from the
fading epigones of Marxist orthodoxy. In this article we will answer the criticisms of
one member of this tradition: Norman Geras.[7] [. . .]

THE HISTORY OF MARXISM

Let us move now to Geras's criticisms of our analysis of the history of Marxism. The
centrality we give to the category of 'discourse' derives from our attempt to emphasise
the purely historical and contingent character of the being of objects. This is not a
fortuitous discovery which could have been made at any point in time; it is, rather,
deeply rooted in the history of modern capitalism. In societies which have a low
technological level of development, where the reproduction of material life is carried
out by means of fundamentally repetitive practices, the 'language games' or discursive
sequences which organise social life are predominantly stable. This situation gives rise
to the illusion that the being of objects, which is a purely social construction, belongs
to things themselves. The idea of a world organised through a stable ensemble of
essential forms is the central presupposition in the philosophies of Plato and Aristotle.
The basic illusion of metaphysical thought resides precisely in this unawareness of the
historicity of being. It is only in the contemporary world, when technological change
and the dislocating rhythm of capitalist transformation constantly alter the discursive
sequences which construct the reality of objects, that the merely historical character
of being becomes fully visible. In this sense, contemporary thought as a whole is, to
a large extent, an attempt to cope with this increasing realisation, and the consequent
moving away from essentialism. In Anglo-American thought we could refer to the
pragmatist turn and the anti-essentialist critique of post-analytic philosophy, starting
from the work of the later Wittgenstein; in continental philosophy, to Heidegger's
radicalisation of phenomenology and to the critique of the theory of the sign in post-
structuralism. The crisis of normative epistemologies, and the growing awareness
of the non-algorithmic character of the transition from one scientific paradigm to
another, point in the same direction.

What our book seeks to show is that this history of contemporary thought is *also*
a history internal to Marxism; that Marxist thought has also been a persistent effort
to adapt to the reality of the contemporary world and progressively to distance itself
from essentialism; that, therefore, our present theoretical and political efforts have a
genealogy which is internal to Marxism itself. In this sense we thought that we were
contributing to the revitalisation of an intellectual tradition. But the difficulties here are
of a particular type which is worth discussing. The article by Geras is a good example.

We learn from it, with amazement, that Bernstein and Sorel 'abandoned' Marxism – and in Geras this has the unmistakable connotation of betrayal. What can we think about this ridiculous story of 'betrayal' and 'abandonment'? What would one make of a history of philosophy which claimed that Aristotle betrayed Plato, that Kant betrayed Leibnitz, that Marx betrayed Hegel? Obviously, we would think that for the writer who reconstructs history in that way, the betrayed doctrine is an object of *worship*. And if we are dealing with a religious object, any dissidence or attempt to transform or to contribute to the evolution of that theory would be considered as apostasy. Most supporters of Marxism affirm its 'scientific' character. Science appears as separated by an absolute abyss from what mortal men think and do – it coincides with the distinction between the sacred and the profane. At a time when the philosophy of science is tending to narrow the epistemological gap between scientific and everyday languages, it seems deplorable that certain sectors of Marxism remain anchored to an image of science which is more appropriate to popular manuals from the age of positivism.

But this line of argument does not end here. Within this perspective the work of Marx becomes an *origin* – that is to say, something which contains within itself the seed of all future development. Thus, any attempt to go beyond it *must* be conceptualised as 'abandonment'. We know the story very well: Bernstein betrayed Marx; European social-democracy betrayed the working class; the Soviet bureaucracy betrayed the revolution; the Western European Communist parties betrayed their revolutionary vocation; thus, the only trustees of 'Revolution' and 'Science' are the small sects belonging to imaginary Internationals which, as they suffer from what Freud called the 'narcissism of small differences', are permanently splitting. The bearers of Truth thus become fewer and fewer.

The history of Marxism that our book outlines is very different and is based on the following points.

1. Classical Marxism – that of the Second International – grounded its political strategy on the increasing centrality of the working class, this being the result of the simplification of social structure under capitalism.
2. From the beginning this prediction was shown to be false, and within the bosom of the Second International three attempts were made to respond to that situation: the Orthodox Marxists affirmed that the tendencies of capitalism which were at odds with the originary Marxist predictions were transitory, and that the postulated general line of capitalist development would eventually assert itself; the Revisionists argued that, on the contrary, those tendencies were permanent and that Social Democrats should therefore cease to organise as a revolutionary party and become a party of social reforms; finally revolutionary syndicalism, though sharing the reformist interpretation of the evolution of capitalism, attempted to reaffirm the radical perspective on the basis of a revolutionary reconstruction of class around the myth of the general strike.
3. The dislocations proper to uneven and combined development obliged the agents of socialist change – fundamentally the working class – to assume

democratic tasks which had not been foreseen in the classical strategy, and it was precisely this taking up of new tasks which was denominated 'hegemony'.

4. From the Leninist concept of class alliances to the Gramscian concept of 'intellectual and moral' leadership, there is an increasing extension of hegemonic tasks, to the extent that for Gramsci social agents are not classes but 'collective wills'.

5. There is, then, an internal movement of Marxist thought from extreme essentialist forms – those of Plekhanov, for example – to Gramsci's conception of social practices as hegemonic and articulatory, which virtually places us in the field, explored in contemporary thought, of 'language games' and the 'logic of the signifier'.

As we can see, the axis of our argument is that at the same time that essentialism disintegrated within the field of classical Marxism, new political logics and arguments started to replace it. If this process could not go further, it was largely due to the political conditions in which it took place: under the empire of Communist parties which regarded themselves as rigid champions of orthodoxy and repressed all intellectual creativity. If today we have to carry out the transition to post-Marxism by having recourse to a series of intellectual currents which are outside the Marxist tradition, it is to a large extent as a result of this process.

AN ATEMPORAL CRITIQUE

We will reply point by point to Geras's main criticisms of our analysis of the history of Marxism. First, he suggests that we have designed a very simple game, choosing at random a group of Marxist thinkers and separating the categories they inherited from classical Marxism from those other aspects of their work in which, confronted with a complex social reality, they were forced to move away from economic determinism. We are then alleged to have given medals to those who went furthest in this direction. This is, obviously, a caricature. In the first place, our main focus was not on economic determinism but on essentialism (it is possible to be absolutely 'superstructuralist' and nevertheless essentialist). In the second place, we did not consider 'any Marxist' at random but narrated an *intellectual history*: one of *progressive* disintegration within Marxism of the originary essentialism. Geras says nothing of this history. However, the image he describes fits his own vision well: for him there is no internal history of Marxism; Marxist categories have a validity which is atemporal and it is only a question of complementing them here and there with a bit of empiricism and good sense.

Second, we are supposed to have contradicted ourselves by saying that Marxism is monist and dualist at the same time. But there is no contradiction here: what we asserted was that Marxism becomes dualist as a result of the failure of monism. A theory that starts by being pluralist would run no risk of becoming dualist.

Third, Geras alleges that we have presented ourselves as the latest step in the long history of Marxism, and so fallen into the error, criticised by Althusser, of seeing in the past only a pre-announcement of oneself. Here, at least, Geras has posed a relevant intellectual question. Our answer is this: any history that deserves its name and is not a mere chronicle must proceed in the way we have proceeded – in Foucault's terms, history is always history of the present. If today I have the category 'income distribution', for instance, I can inquire about the distribution of income in ancient times or in the Middle Ages, even if that category did not exist then. It is by questioning the past from the perspective of the present that history is constructed. Historical reconstruction is impossible without *interrogating* the past. This means that there is not an *in-itself* of history, but rather a multiple refraction of it, depending on the traditions from which it is interrogated. It also means that our interpretations themselves are transitory, since future questions will result in very different images of the past. For this very reason, Althusser's critique of teleological conceptions of the past is not applicable in our case; we do not assert that we are the *culmination* of a process that was pre-announced, as in the transition from the 'in itself' to the 'for itself'. Although the present organises the past, it can have no claim to have disclosed its 'essence'.

Finally, at several points Geras questions our treatment of texts by Trotsky and Rosa Luxemburg. In the case of Trotsky, we are said to have made use of 'tendentious quotations'. What we actually said was that:

1. Pokrovsky posed a *theoretical* question to Trotsky: namely, whether it is compatible with Marxism to attribute to the State such a degree of autonomy from classes as Trotsky does in the case of Russia.
2. Trotsky, instead of answering *theoretically*, gave an account of Russian development and attempted to deal with the specific *theoretical* aspect of Pokrovsky's question only in terms of the contrast between the greenness of life and the greyness of theory ('Comrade Pokrovsky's thought is gripped in a vice of rigid social categories which he puts in place of live historical forces', etc.).[8]

Thus the type of question that Pokrovsky's intervention implied – one referring to the degree of autonomy of the superstructure and its compatibility with Marxism – is not tackled by Trotsky at any point. The reader can check *all* the passages of Trotsky to which Geras refers and in *none* of them will he or she find a *theoretical* discussion concerning the relationship between base and superstructure. As for the idea that we demanded from Trotsky a theory of relative autonomy when we had affirmed its impossibility in another part of our book, we have already seen that this last point is a pure invention by Geras.

In the case of Rosa Luxemburg it is a question not of misquotations but of simplifications – that is, we are supposed to have reduced everything to the 'symbol'. Geras starts by enumerating five points, with which it would be difficult to disagree because they are simply a summary of Rosa Luxemburg's work on the mass strike. Our level of analysis is different, however, and does not contradict any of the five points in Geras's summary. The fifth point, for instance, reads: 'economic and political dimensions of the overall conflict interact, intersect, run together.'[9] A further nine-point enumeration then explains what this interaction is, and we would not disagree with it either since it merely gives examples of such interaction. What our text asserts – and what Geras apparently denies without presenting the slightest argument – is that through all these examples a specific social logic manifests itself, which is the logic of the symbol. A meaning is symbolic when it is a *second* meaning, added to the primary one ('rose', for example, can symbolise 'love'). In the Russian Revolution, 'peace', 'bread' and 'land' symbolised a variety of other social demands. For example, a strike for wage demands by any group of workers will, in an extremely repressive political context, also symbolise opposition to the system as a whole and encourage protest movements by very different groups; in this way an increasing relation of overdetermination and equivalence is created among multiple isolated demands. Our argument was that:

1. This is the mechanism described by Rosa Luxemburg in *The Mass Strike*.
2. It is, for her, the central element in the constitution of the unity between economic struggle and political class struggle.
3. Her text is conceived as an intervention in the dispute between syndicalist and party theoreticians about the relative weight of economic and political struggle.

Since Geras does not present any argument against these three theses, it makes little sense to prolong this discussion.[10]

RADICAL DEMOCRACY

As is usual in sectarian literature, when it comes to talking about politics Geras has remarkably little to say. But we do need to deal with his assertion that it is an axiom that socialism should be democratic.[11] The fact is that for any person who does not live on Mars, the relation between socialism and democracy is axiomatic only in Geras's mind. Has Geras ever heard of Stalinism, of the one-party system, of press censorship, of the Chinese Cultural Revolution, of the Polish coup d'état, of the entry of Soviet tanks into Prague and Budapest? And if the answer is that nothing of the kind is *true* socialism, we have to be clear what game we are playing. There are three possibilities. The first is that Geras is constructing an ideal model of society in the way that the utopian socialists did. Nothing, of course, prevents him from doing so and from declaring that in Gerasland collective ownership of the means of production and democracy go together; but in that case we should not claim to be speaking about the real world. The second possibility is to affirm that the authoritarian states of the Soviet bloc represent a transitory and necessary phase in the passage towards communism. This is the miserable excuse that 'progressive' intellectuals gave to support the worst excesses of Stalinism, from the Moscow trials onwards. The third possibility is to assert that these states are 'degenerate forms' of socialism. However, the very fact that such 'degeneration' is possible clearly indicates that the relation between socialism and democracy is far from being axiomatic.

For us the articulation between socialism and democracy, far from being an axiom, is a political project; that is, it is the result of a long and complex hegemonic construction, which is permanently under threat and thus needs to be continuously redefined. The first problem to be discussed, therefore, is the 'foundations' of a progressive politics. For Geras this presents the following difficulty: has not our critique of essentialism eliminated any possible basis for preferring one type of politics to another? Everything depends on what we understand by 'foundation'. If it is a question of a foundation that enables us to decide with apodictic certainty that one type of society is better than another, the answer is no, there cannot be such a foundation. However, it does not follow that there is no possibility of reasoning politically and of preferring, for a variety of reasons, certain political positions to others. (It is comical that a stern critic of 'either/or' solutions such as Geras confronts us with exactly this type of alternative.) Even if we cannot decide algorithmically about many things, this does not mean that we are confined to total nihilism, since we can reason about the *verisimilitude* of the available alternatives. In that sense, Aristotle distinguishes between *phronesis* (prudence) and *theory* (purely speculative knowledge). An argument founded on the apodicticity of the conclusion is an argument which admits neither discussion nor any plurality of view-points; on the other hand, an argument which tries to found itself on the verisimilitude of its conclusions, is essentially pluralist, because it needs to make reference to other arguments and, since the process is essentially open, these can always be contested and refuted. The logic of verisimilitude is, in this sense, essentially *public and democratic.* Thus, the first condition of a radically democratic society is to accept the contingent and radically open character of all its values – and in that sense, to abandon the aspiration to a single foundation.

At this point we can refute a myth, the one which has it that our position is incompatible with humanism. What we have rejected is the idea that humanist values have the metaphysical status of an essence and that they are, therefore, prior to any concrete history and society. However, this is not to deny their validity; it only means that their validity is constructed by means of particular discursive and argumentative practices. The history of the production of 'Man' (in the sense of human beings who are bearers of rights in their exclusive human capacity) is a recent history – of the last three hundred years. Before then, all men were equal only in the face of God. This history of the production of 'Man' can be followed step by step and it has been one of the great achievements of our culture; to outline this history would be to reconstruct the various discursive surfaces where it has taken place – the juridical, educational, economic and other institutions, in which differences based on status, social class or wealth were progressively eliminated. The 'human being', without qualification, is the overdetermined effect of this process of multiple construction. It is within this discursive plurality that 'humanist values' are constructed and expanded. And we know well that they are always threatened: racism, sexism, class discrimination, always limit the emergence and full validity of humanism. To deny to the 'human' the status of an essence is to draw attention to the historical conditions that have led to its emergence and to make possible, therefore, a wider degree of realism in the fight for the full realisation of those values.

THE TRANSFORMATION OF POLITICAL CONSCIOUSNESS

Now, the 'humanisation' of increasingly wider areas of social relations is linked to the fundamental process of transformation of political consciousness in Western societies during the last two hundred years, which is what, following Tocqueville, we have called the 'democratic revolution'. Our central argument is that socialism is an integral part of the 'democratic revolution' and has no meaning outside of it (which, as we will see, is very different from saying that socialism is axiomatically democratic). In order to explain our argument we will start from an analysis of the capitalist–worker relation. According to the classical Marxist thesis, the basic antagonism of capitalist society is constituted around the extraction of surplus-value by the capitalist from the worker. But it is important to see where the antagonism resides. A first possibility would be to affirm that the antagonism is inherent in the very form of the wage-labour–capital relation, to the extent that this form is based on the appropriation by capital of the worker's surplus labour. However, this solution is clearly incorrect: the capitalist–worker relation considered as form – that is to say, insofar as the worker is considered not as flesh and blood but only as the economic category of 'seller of labour power' – is not an antagonistic one. Only if the worker *resists* the extraction of his or her surplus-value by the capitalist does the relation become antagonistic, but such resistance cannot be logically deduced from the category 'seller of labour power'. It is only if we add a further assumption, such as the 'homo oeconomicus' of classical political economy, that the relation becomes antagonistic, since it then becomes a zero-sum game between worker and capitalist. However, this idea that the worker is a profit-maximiser in the same way as the capitalist has been correctly rejected by all Marxist theorists.

Thus, there is only one solution left: that the antagonism is not intrinsic to the capitalist relation of production as such, but rather, that it is established *between* the relation of production and something external to it – for instance, the fact that below a certain level of wages the worker cannot live in a decent way, send his or her children to school, have access to certain forms of recreation, etc. The pattern and the intensity of the antagonism depend, therefore, to a large extent, on the way in which the social agent is constituted *outside the relations of production*. Now, the further we are from a mere subsistence level, the more the worker's expectations are bound up with a certain perception of his or her place in the world. This perception depends on the participation of workers in a variety of spheres and on a certain awareness of their rights; and the more democratic-egalitarian discourses have penetrated society, the less will workers accept as natural a limitation of their access to a set of social and cultural goods. *Thus, the possibility of deepening the anti-capitalist struggle itself depends on the extension of the democratic revolution. Even more: anti-capitalism is an internal moment of the democratic revolution.*[12]

However, if this is right, if antagonism is not intrinsic to the relation of production as such but is established between the relation of production and something external to it, then two consequences follow. The first is that there are no apriori privileged places in the anti-capitalist struggle. We should remember that for the Second International – for Kautsky, particularly – the idea of the centrality of the working class was linked to:

1. a vision of the collapse of capitalism as determined by the contradiction between forces and relations of production which would lead to increasing

social misery – that is to say, to the contradiction *between* the capitalist system as a whole and the vast masses of the population; and

2. to the idea that capitalism would lead to proletarianisation of the middle classes and the peasantry, as a result of which, when the crisis of the system came about, everything would be reduced to a simple showdown between capitalists and workers.

However, as the second process has not taken place, there is no reason to assume that the working class has a privileged role in the *anti-capitalist* struggle. There are many points of antagonism between capitalism and various sections of the population (environmental pollution, property development in certain areas, the arms race, the flow of capital from one region to another, etc.), and this means that we will have a variety of anti-capitalist struggles. The second consequence is that the potential emergence of a radical anti-capitalist politics through the deepening of the democratic revolution, will result from global political decisions taken by vast sectors of the population and will not be linked to a particular position in the social structure. In this sense there are no *intrinsically* anti-capitalist struggles, although a set of struggles, within certain contexts, could *become* anti-capitalist.

DEMOCRATIC REVOLUTION

If everything then depends on the extension and deepening of the democratic revolution, we should ask what the latter itself depends on and what it ultimately consists of. Marx correctly observed that capitalism only expands through permanent transformation of the means of production and the dislocation and progressive dissolution of traditional social relations. Such dislocation effects are manifest, on the one hand, in commodification, and on the other hand, in the set of phenomena linked to uneven and combined development. In these conditions, the radical instability and threat to social identities posed by capitalist expansion necessarily leads to new forms of collective imaginary which reconstruct those threatened identities in a fundamentally new way. Our thesis is that egalitarian discourses and discourses on rights play a fundamental role in the reconstruction of collective identities. At the beginning of this process in the French Revolution, the public space of citizenship was the exclusive domain of equality, while in the private sphere no questioning took place of existing social inequalities. However, as Tocqueville clearly understood, once human beings accept the legitimacy of the principle of equality in one sphere they will attempt to extend it to every other sphere of life. Thus, once the dislocations generated by capitalist expansion became more general, more and more sectors constructed the legitimacy of their claims around the principles of equality and liberty. The development of workers' and anti-capitalist struggles during the nineteenth century was a crucial moment in this process, but it was not the only or the last one: the struggles of the so-called 'new social movements' of the last few decades are a further phase in the deepening of the democratic revolution. Towards the end of the nineteenth century Bernstein clearly understood that future advances in the democratisation of the State and of society would depend on autonomous initiatives starting from different points within the social fabric, since rising labour productivity and successful workers' struggles were having the combined effect that workers ceased to be 'proletarian' and became 'citizens', that is to say, they came to participate in an increasing variety of aspects of the life of their country. This was the start of the process that we have called the 'dispersion of subject positions'. Bernstein's view was, without any doubt, excessively simplistic and optimistic, but his predictions were fundamentally correct. However, it is important to see that from this plurality and dislocation there does not follow an increasing integration and adaptation to the system. The dislocatory effects that were mentioned above continue to influence all these dispersed subject positions, which is to say that the latter become the points which make possible a new radicalisation, and with this, the process of the radical democratisation of society acquires a new depth and a new impulse. The result of the process of dispersion and fragmentation whose first phases Bernstein described, was not increasingly conformist and integrated societies: it was the great mobilisations of 1968.

There are two more points which require discussion. The first refers to liberalism. If the radical democratisation of society emerges from a variety of autonomous struggles which are themselves overdetermined by forms of hegemonic articulation; if, in addition, everything depends on a proliferation of public spaces of argumentation and decision whereby social agents are increasingly capable of self-management; then it is clear that this process does not pass through a direct attack upon the State apparatuses but involves the consolidation and democratic reform of the liberal State. The ensemble of its constitutive principles – division of powers, universal suffrage, multi-party systems, civil rights etc. – must be defended and consolidated. It is within the framework of these basic principles of the political community that it is possible to advance the full range of present-day democratic demands (from the rights of national, racial and sexual minorities to the anti-capitalist struggle itself).

The second point refers to totalitarianism. Here Geras introduces one of his usual confusions. In trying to present our critique of totalitarianism, he treats this critique as if it presupposed a fundamental identity between communism and fascism. Obviously this is not the case. Fascism and communism, as types of society, are totally different. The only possible comparison concerns the presence in both of a certain type of political logic by which they are societies with a *State Truth*. Hence, while the radical democratic imaginary presupposes openness and pluralism and processes of argumentation which never lead to an ultimate foundation, totalitarian societies are constituted through their claim to master the foundation. Evidently there is a strong danger of totalitarianism in the twentieth century, and the reasons are clear: insofar as dislocatory effects dominate and the old structures in which power was immanent dissolve, there is an increasing tendency to concentrate power in one point from which the attempt is made 'rationally' to reconstruct the ensemble of the social fabric. Radical democracy and totalitarianism are, therefore, entirely opposite in their attempts to deal with the problems deriving from dislocation and uneven development.

To conclude, we would like to indicate the three fundamental points on which we consider it necessary today to go beyond the theoretical and political horizon of Marxism. The first is a philosophical point which relates to the partial character of

Marx's 'materialism', to its manifold dependence on crucial aspects of the categories of traditional metaphysics. In this respect, as we have tried to show, discourse theory is not just a simple theoretical or epistemological approach; it implies, by asserting the radical historicity of being and therefore the purely human nature of truth, the committment to show the world for what it is: an entirely social construction of human beings which is not grounded on any metaphysical 'necessity' external to it – neither God, nor 'essential forms', nor the 'necessary laws of history'.

The second aspect refers to the social analyses of Marx. The greatest merit of Marxist theory has been to illuminate fundamental tendencies in the self-development of capitalism and the antagonisms that it generates. However, here again the analysis is incomplete and, in a certain sense, parochial – limited, to a great extent, to the European experience of the nineteenth century. Today we know that the dislocation effects which capitalism generates at the international level are much deeper than the ones foreseen by Marx. This obliges us to radicalise and to transform in a variety of directions Marx's conception of the social agent and of social antagonisms.

The third and final aspect is political. By locating socialism in the wider field of the democratic revolution, we have indicated that the political transformations which will eventually enable us to transcend capitalist society are founded on the plurality of social agents and of their struggles. Thus the field of social conflict is extended, rather than being concentrated in a 'privileged agent' of socialist change. This also means that the extension and radicalisation of democratic struggles does not have a final point of arrival in the achievement of a fully liberated society. There will always be antagonisms, struggles, and partial opaqueness of the social; there will always be history. The myth of the transparent and homogeneous society – which implies the end of politics – must be resolutely abandoned.

We believe that, by clearly locating ourselves in a post-Marxist terrain, we not only help to clarify the meaning of contemporary social struggles but also give to Marxism its theoretical dignity, which can only proceed from recognition of its limitations and of its historicality. Only through such recognition will Marx's work remain present in our tradition and our political culture.

NOTES

1. Slavoj Zizek, 'La société n'existe pas', *L'Ane*, Paris, October–December 1985.
2. Andrew Ross, in *m/f* 11/12, 1986.
3. Alastair Davidson, in *Thesis Eleven*, No. 16, Melbourne, 1987.
4. Stanley Aronowitz, 'Theory and Socialist Strategy', *Social Text*, Winter 1986/87.
5. Philip Derbyshire, in *City Limits*, 26 April 1985.
6. David Forgacs, 'Dethroning the Working Class?' *Marxism Today*, May 1985.
7. Norman Geras, 'Post-Marxism?', *New Left Review* 163, May–June 1987.
8. L. Trotsky, *1905*, London 1971, p. 333.
9. Geras, p. 60.
10. One further point concerning Rosa Luxemburg. Geras sustains (fn., p. 62) that we deny that Rosa Luxemburg had a theory of the mechanical collapse of the capitalist system. This is not so. The point that we make is rather that nobody has pushed the metaphor of the mechanical collapse so far as to take it literally; and that, therefore, all Marxist writers of the period of the Second International combined, in different degrees, objective laws and conscious intervention of the class in their theorizations of the end of capitalism. A second

point that we make in the passage in question – and here yes, our interpretation clearly differs from Geras's – is that it is because the logic of spontaneism was not enough to ground the class nature of the social agents, that Luxemburg had to find a different grounding and was forced to appeal to a hardening of the objective laws of capitalist development. Fully to discuss this issue would obviously require far more space than we have here.

11. Geras, p. 79.

12. We would like to stress that, in our view, the various anti-capitalist struggles are an integral part of the democratic revolution, but this does not imply that socialism is *necessarily* democratic. The latter, as a form of economic organisation based upon exclusion of private ownership of the means of production, can be the result, for example, of a bureaucratic imposition, as in the countries of Eastern Europe. In this sense, socialism *can be* entirely external to the democratic revolution. The compatibility of socialism with democracy, far from being an axiom, is therefore the result of a hegemonic struggle for the articulation of both.

II

POST-MARXISM/POST-*MARXISM*: POSTSTRUCTURALIST AND POSTMODERNIST INTERVENTIONS

7

THE DESIRE CALLED MARX†

Jean-François Lyotard

There are few more vicious attacks on Marxism than that contained in the pages of Jean-François Lyotard's Libidinal Economy *(1974), and in particular that in the chapter entitled 'The Desire called Marx'. In what he was later to call his 'evil book, the book of evilness that everyone writing and thinking is tempted to do', Lyotard breaks irrevocably with his Marxist past. Lyotard had been involved with Marxist groups, such as* Socialisme ou Barbarie *(dedicated to conducting a critique of Marxist theory from within) in the 1950s and 1960s, but as he makes utterly clear here, he is no longer even remotely concerned with conducting a dialogue with Marxism. Instead, he mocks, abuses, and belittles it (as well as its founder) in a highly provocative fashion that infuriated his erstwhile colleagues on the left, many of whom broke off relations with Lyotard as a result. The main thrust of Lyotard's argument is that Marxism has to deny the power of the instinctive, sub-rational side of human behaviour – those libidinal drives first identified by Freud – in order to maintain the fiction that its particular brand of rational, 'scientific', analysis (its 'political economy') offers the answer to all human problems. Libidinal economy, the polar opposite to political economy, explodes this belief in Lyotard's opinion, since it reveals that there is always an excess of energy (expressed in those various drives) that can never be brought under total control by any socio-political system. Marx himself is somewhat maliciously portrayed by Lyotard as a victim of the working of just such an excess in his own, notoriously incomplete and sprawling, writings and researches. As its biting, sarcastic tone unmistakably declares, in cases like* Libidinal Economy *we are most definitely in a* post-Marxist *terrain. Lyotardean postmodernism, at least, is not interested in any kind of accommodation with Marxism.*

LIBIDINAL MARX

We must come to take Marx as if he were a writer, an author full of affects, take his text as a madness and not as a theory, we must succeed in pushing aside his theoretical

† From J.-F. Lyotard, *Libidinal Economy*, trans. Iain Hamilton Grant, London: Athlone Press, 1993 (pp. 95–104, 111–14).

barrier and stroking his beard without contempt and without devotion, no longer the false neutrality which Merleau-Ponty advised in the past for someone who, he said, has now become a classic and must be treated no differently than Hegel or Aristotle – no, stroke his beard as a complex libidinal volume, reawakening his hidden desire and ours along with it. There is no need to criticise Marx, and even if we do criticise him, it must be understood that it is in no way a critique: we have already said and repeated that we laugh at critique, since it is to maintain oneself in the field of the criticised thing and in the dogmatic, indeed paranoiac, relation of knowledge. Marx's desire interests us, not for itself, but inasmuch as it informs the themes of writings which metamorphose into themes of social and political 'practices'. Marx must be introduced, the big fat Marx, and also the little Marx of the Epicurean and Lutheran studies, this entire continent, into the atlas of libidinal cartography – or rather the reverse: to start crossing this strange country with our affections and disaffections, letting our attachments and our deceptions circulate, refining our analysis here, neglecting it there, because we have neither the hope nor the intention of setting up a portrait of the work, of giving an 'interpretation' of it. We do not interpret, we read, and we effect by writings. We have, for a long time, having read Marx, operated by means of practices (since this is the word left us by the Greeks as a disastrous heritage). We say this not to render the libidinal use we make of the Old Man more justifiable or less shameful; rather to situate these 'practices' in the sphere of what rightly belongs to interpretation. A Marxist political practice is an interpretation of a text, just as a social or Christian spiritual practice is the interpretation of a text. So much so that practices are themselves texts, insofar as they are interpretations. And this is precisely what we desire not to do here. We no longer want to correct Marx, to reread him or to read him in the sense that the little Althusserians would like to 'read *Capital*': to interpret it according to 'its truth'. We have no plan to be true, to give the truth of Marx, we wonder what there is of the libido in Marx, and 'in Marx' means in his text or in his interpretations, mainly in practices. We will rather treat him as a 'work of art'. We will take some inconstestable detail, considered minor, and which in fact it is in regard to the manifest themes of the work; quite certain, however, that it is not so for the libidinal geography of the continent.

We note even this, libidinal economist friends: we feel almost obliged, as you've just heard, to make some sort of a declaration of intentions, a little solemn, vaguely epistemological (as little as possible, nevertheless, take note), at the shores of this continent. No other continent would extract such declarations from us – although they remain somewhat stupid and certainly useless. We could say that it is through suspicion and intimidation, warned as we are by a militant past of, when laying a hand on Marx, even and indeed especially if it were to screw with him, we are closely watched by the paranoiacs calling themselves Marxist politicians and in general all the Whites of the left. We would therefore prudently warn: it is in this state of mind, this state of heart, this state of body that we approach the Old Man.

But the libidinal 'truth' of our preamble lies elsewhere. It already states the essential which is this: the Old Man is also a young woman to us, a strange bisexual assemblage. The *dispositifs* which channel their impulsions into theoretical discourses, and will give rise to organisms of power, the very ones which will harden into the German Party, the Bolshevik Party, these *dispositifs* are of course 'compromise-formations', they are so many attempts to stabilise the forces on the libidinal front, mediations – oh how 'alienated', as he loved to say – interposed between the fluxes of desire and the regions into which they travel. This happens not only in certain themes, or at least in certain 'minor' motifs, some of which we will pick out, its position is established first of all in something quite astonishing: the perpetual *postponement* of finishing work on *Capital*, a chapter becoming a book, a section a chapter, a paragraph a section, by a process of cancerisation of theoretical discourse, by a totally pulsional proliferation of a network of concepts hitherto destined on the contrary to 'finalise', to 'define' and to justify a proletarian politics, hence by the racing of a discursive machinery explicitly, however, laying claim to rationality (theoretical-practical). Is the *non-finito* a characteristic of rational theory? We are able to support this, in these post-relative days; but for Marx (and therefore for Engels the impatient!), it must rather have been a bizarre, worrying fact.

We say that this postponement, which results in the 'Economy' never being completed,[1] and in the calculations of *Capital*, Book 3 being false,[2] already demonstrates a whole *dispositif*, a libidinal monster with the huge fat head of a man full of warrior's thoughts and petty quarrels, and with the soft body of young amorous Rhénane – a monster which never achieves the realisation of its unity, because of this very incapacity, and it is this 'failure' which is marked in the interminable theoretical suspense. What we have here is not exactly the centaur, the master of politicians as Chiron was the master of Achilles; rather, it would be the hermaphrodite, another monster in which femininity and masculinity are indiscernibly exchanged, thereby thwarting the reassurance of *sexual difference*. But it is exactly this which is in question in the 'Economy', and we maintain, dear comrades, the following thesis: the little girl Marx, offended by the perversity of the polymorphous body of capital, requires a great love; the great prosecutor Karl Marx, assigned the task of the prosecution of the perverts and the 'invention' of a suitable lover (the proletariat), sets himself to study the file of the accused capitalist.

What happens when the person assigned to the prosecution is as fascinated by the accused as he is scandalised by him? It comes about that the prosecutor sets himself to finding a hundred thousand good reasons to prolong the study of the file, that the enquiry becomes meticulous, always more meticulous, that the lawyer submerged in the British Museum in the microscopic analysis of the aberrations of capital is no longer able to detach himself from it, that the organic unity, that this swarming of perverse fluxes that is supposed to have to produce (dialectically), never stops moving away, escaping him, being put off, and that the submission of petitions is kept waiting interminably. What was happening then throughout the thousands of manuscript pages? The unification of Marx's body, which requires that the polymorphous perversity of capital be put to death for the benefit of the fulfilment of the desire for genital love, is not possible. The prosecutor is unable to *deduce* the birth of a new and beautiful *(in)organic body* (similar to that of precapitalist forms) which would be child-socialism, from the pornography of capitalism. If there is a body of capital, this body is *sterile*, it engenders nothing: it exceeds the capacity of theoretical discourse as unification.

'I do not want to be resigned to sending just anything,' Marx wrote to Engels who presses him (31 July 1865), prior to having the whole work in his sight. 'Whatever defect they may have, it is to the advantage of my writings that they constitute an artistic whole, and I can only achieve this result in my own way and by never having them printed until I have them before me *in their entirety*.' These writings on their own, however, never constitute this *visible artistic whole whose* model is an (in)organic body, organic insofar as it is a complete and fecund totality, inorganic insofar as it is not biological, but theoretical here (the same unitary model which will be desired and 'recognised' in precapitalist forms or in socialism, this time on the socio-economic plane).

The young innocent Little Girl Marx says: you see, I am in love with love, this must stop, this industrial and industrious crap, this is what makes me anxious, I want the return to the (in)organic body; and it has been taken over by the great bearded scholar so that he may establish the thesis that *it cannot stop*, and so that he may testify, as the counsel to the poor (amongst which is the Little Girl Marx), to his revolutionary conclusions; so that he may perform the obstetrics of capital; and so that he may give, *to her*, this *total body* he requires, this child, at least this child of words which would be the anticipated double (the younger child born first) of the child of flesh: of the proletariat, of socialism. But alas, he does not give her this child. She will never have this 'artistic whole' before her, these writings 'in their entirety'. She will have suffering growing before her and in her, because her prosecutor will discover in the course of his research, insofar as it is endless, a strange *jouissance*: the same *jouissance* that results from the instantiation of the pulsions and their discharge in *postponement*. The *jouissance* of infinity. This 'perversity' of knowledge is rightly called (scientific) research, and intensity there is not, as it is in orgasm, 'normal', the intensity of discharge instantiated in a genital couple, but is the intensity of an inhibition, of a putting into reserve, of a postponement and of an investment in means. So much so that the prosecutor charged with obtaining proof of the pornographic ignominy of capital repeats, in his enquiry and even in his preparation and pleading, this same 'Don't come yet' – so to speak – which is simply another modality of *jouissance*, which is found in the libidinal *dispositif* of capital. While, as concerns the content, it is always in search of the lovable body which he-she desires, the form of this research already contains its denial and its impossibility.

This is why the attention which this body is able to command, and to which it must have the right, provokes the *bad temper* of the paradoxical defender of the poor. When the refugees from the Commune fled to London and the International was fully preoccupied with them, while in short something like the subversive 'reality' of this proletarian-socialist body, supposedly much sought after, comes to explode in the eyes of the world (and, it seems, in the eyes of the author of the 'Address to the Committee of the International' dated 30 May 1871), what does Marx find to write, on 9 November of that same year, to Danielson, his Russian translator, who is awaiting the corrections to the text of the first chapter? 'It is, without any doubt, quite useless to *await* a revision of the first chapter, for my time has for some months been so taken up (and on this point there is little hope of improvement in the near future) that I am unable to pursue my theoretical labours any more. It is certain that one fine morning

I will put an end to all this, but there are circumstances where one is morally bound to busy oneself with *things much less attractive* than study and theoretical research.' Not very attractive, says the equivocal prosecutor, your fine proletarian body, again we catch a glimpse of the infamous prostitution of capital . . .

But, you say, this suspension of theoretical labour on capital, this is not for one second a pleasure in the sense of a security, an irresponsibility, it is on the contrary the result of a libidinal transaction, it is the price that the young amorous Girl-Marx's desire for the reconciled body is made to pay by the fat-headed Accuser-Marx with the shattered social body: ah, you dream of the relation of non-domination between men and things, and between men themselves, and between men and women! All right then, show the consistency of the dream, demonstrate that reality too, dreams this dream. That is to say: *you also pay*, pay in word-products, in articulations, in structured arguments, endlessly. Wasn't this said, in substance, in the peripheries of the work, in 1844: the proletariat is Christ, and his real suffering is the price of his redemption, and this is why it is not enough that a particular wrong is done him, a shopkeeper's wrong, a pathetic limitation of his profit-margin, for example, no, his redemption requires a total suffering, therefore a total wrong, as the proletariat will be for Marx, once and for all, and as Marx will be once and for all for the proletariat required by the desire named Marx: Christ the proletariat, Marx his witness-martyr? *Theoretical* discourse being his cross, his torture?

Certainly, we may put it this way, in terms of a religious metaphor. But it misses the essential, because it presupposes exactly what turns out to be in question in Marx's desire, it presupposes this *body of reference* as a sacrifice, body of capital for the martyr of the proletariat, body of the proletariat for Marx's martyr, without which sacrifice and martyr go up in smoke, and are no more than phantasms of guilt. In other words, the sacrificial metaphor is not libidinally neutral, it is not economically correct, it is topically 'correct', it requires a principle (be it imaginary, which none the less requires a 'symbolic' medium) of unification and inscription in comparison to which pain and pleasure, here those of Marx's research, may be counted, registered. And what if it was precisely this referential instance which Marx's inspection turned out to lack, this body of *Ratio*, of the account? What if what would prolong the research interminably were not, as 'psychoanalytic' or 'Nietzschean' crassness wouldn't fail to say, Karl Marx's 'masochist' desire or 'bad conscience', but the vertigo of a terrible discovery (always hidden): that *there is no-one* to keep the accounts of suffering and *jouissance*, and that this, too, is the domination of money-capital?

If we restrict ourselves to a 'critique' (which means, of course, *non-critique*) of whatever *guilt* or ressentiment there is in the assemblage of the desire named Marx and generally named *militant*,[3] we will *de facto* remain in the *religious metaphor*, we will replace the religious metaphor with an *irreligious metaphor*, still religious then, in which judgements will be discovered at work according to good and evil in reference to a 'new' god, which will be desire: movement will be good, investment evil; action as innovation and the force of the event will be good, reaction reiterating identity, evil. And how will we then describe the 'Marx' or 'militant' libidinal *dispositif*? We turn to the passion for expiation and ressentiment. Every reversal (of the 'first' into the 'last', but just as much of the dominant into the equal) which forms the figure of the revolution implies, we say, the intention of a price to (be) charged. If Marx authorised himself to set himself up as the proletariat's advocate, and petition against their exploiters, if he can declare to them: this is why it is you who will pay the price, it is, we say again, on condition that he had marked down the suffering, the expiation and the ressentiment on his own body and that he himself suffers and pays. Is this not the law which gives *the right to the desire for revolution*, in the sphere of ressentiment: that the militant had formed his own body into a monstrous composition, so that the woman-proletariat would obtain the most durable man-prosecutor and the greatest total pain, that all revolutionary ressentiment will be played out between Little Girl Marx and Old Man Marx on its body?

Far from emancipating ourselves through such a critique of what we detest, religion, ressentiment, guilt, morality, we will only invert its signs; Marx wants an (in)organic body, does his desire enslave it to a genital model? We want a schizophrenic model and an unstable body. Marx wants to charge? We want generalised gratuity. Marx accuses? We exonerate. Marx-the-proletariat suffers and redeems? We joyfully love all that appears. Etc. A new morality, a new religion, is in fact merely a very ancient ethnics, itself strongly 'reactive', since the party of movement and existence has always existed *at the core* of religions, at least of those taking authority from a revelation, to act as a counter-poison in belief and in the *systems* of belief, every time that its adversary, the party of order and structure, has ended up wearying the faithful and even the priests. Do we want to be merely the saviours of a fallen world, then, the hearts of a heartless world, prophets (cruel, very cruel, as the programme goes) for a humanity without words? Do we bring new values then? In denouncing militant ressentiment, we are doing nothing other than *valorising a certain sort of libidinal dispositif*, in fact the admirable viscosity of the fluxes ceaselessly setting up and wiping out on the great libidinal film; we affirm its *exclusive value*: but the exclusive value is called truth. Therefore we affirm: schizo-desire, there's truth! How then does the *dispositif of our affirmation* differ from that by which the ancient statements (love is the truth; renunciation is the truth; knowledge is the truth; socialism is the truth) were affirmed? Doesn't their reactive element lie in their *power of exclusion*? Are we too not going to exclude? How pitiful!

This, then, is not how the libidinal *dispositif* named Marx should be described, merely *described*; not as the effect of ressentiment. Our rule should be never to describe anything as effect; we should describe everything as *capable of effects*. Now there is, in the interminable postponement of the prosecution's revolutionary summation in Marx, a certain effective force; theoretical discourse ceases to be presented according to its closure even though this is what it *seeks*. What Marx perceives as failure, suffering (and maybe even lives through as ressentiment) is the mark on his work of a situation which is precisely the same as that of capital, and which gives rise to a strange success as much as to an awful misery: the work cannot *form a body*, just as capital cannot form a body. And this absence of organic, 'artistic' unity gives rise to two divergent movements always associated in a single vertigo: a movement of flight, of plunging into the bodiless, and thus of continual invention, of expansive additions or affirmations of new pieces (statements, but elsewhere musics, techniques, ethics) to the insane patchwork – a movement of *tension*. And a movement of institution of an organism, of an organisation and of organs of totalisation and unification – a movement of reason. Both kinds of movement are there, effects as force in the *non-finito* of the work just as in that of capitalism.[4]

Marx's inability to catch up with his book (a delay which is equally an 'advance' upon it, a form of temporal dislocation in any case), rather than being considered as an effect of masochism or guilt, should be compared with the way in which Sterne makes a theme of this delay in *Tristram Shandy*. In each case, the following configuration is involved: to fabricate a discourse, whether narrative or theoretical, implying a new, unprecedented organisation of space and time, the writer (narrator, theoretician) uses space and time. With Sterne, this use (or this usury) is inscribed in the narrative itself, and devours it: the place and the duration occupied by the 'narrative act' little by little invade those which should be given over to the narration of the story and render this latter impossible, or at least transform it into the narrative of this invasion and this impossibility. With Marx, the effect that the 'act of elaboration' has on the space-time of theoretical discourse is not explicitly marked in this latter, and the final impossibility of the domination of the duration and location in a discourse (which is here theoretical and no longer narrative, but which nevertheless refers to a supposed 'story' taken as a reference) does not give rise to Sterne's desperate humour, to a style. With Marx, the expression of this despair remains repressed, caught and hidden between his activity of fabricating apodictic final statements and the statements, not even assertive, which he publishes in another text, those of confessions, letters, abandoned or withdrawn manuscripts, lecture notes, plans. But this despair gives rise, in whatever way, to theoretical suspense, it opens the void of: Wait until I have finished.

This void is that of the mediator alienating the subject (Marx, Sterne) and the object (the book), to speak in Marx's language; it is that of inhibition, which leads desire from its primary object towards the *means* of its realisation; it is that of capital, which loves production rather than the product, and for which the product is only the means of producing; it is that of the 'communist' party, which loves not the revolution, but the means by which they are *able* to make it happen, which in their hands is only a pretext to the machinery for capitalising the desire for revolution. Therefore, this void is that in which the mechanisms of power are constructed; but it is also the *supple* viscosity of capitalism as fragments of the body, as connected-disconnected singularities, as amnesia, decentred and anarchic, as harlequinade, as metamorphoses without inscription, as the undoing of totalities and totalisations, as ephemeral groupings of unforeseen affirmations.

THERE IS NO SUBVERSIVE REGION

Let's repeat it over and again, we are not going to do a critique of Marx, we are not, that is to say, going to produce the theory of his theory: which is just to remain within the theoretical. No, one must show what intensities are lodged in theoretical signs, what affects within serious discourse; we must steal his affects from him. Its force is not at all in the power of its discourse, not even in inverse proportion to it, this would still be a little too dialectical an arrangement; no, its force erupts here and there, independently of the consistency of the discourse, sometimes in a forgotten detail, sometimes in the very midst of a solid conceptual mechanism, well articulated and rooted – but of course always in intelligent signs. What would a critique of Marx be (apart from the fact that there are already a hundred thousand such critiques)? We must inevitably say of him: oh he remained alienated, oh he brought out the symbolic system (this is Baudrillard), oh he is still religious (this would rather be us), oh he remained an economist (this was Castoriadis). Quite obviously he *remained* this, *forgot* that, is *still* such and such a thing – something which the critic is supposed to *no longer* be, to have *superseded*. Well, we have superseded nothing and we have nothing to supersede, we do not climb onto Marx's back here, 'armed with double spectacles, some Lilliputian stands on the extremity of the giant's posterior [it was Aristotle actually], announces amazedly to the world what an astoundingly new view is offered from his *punctum visus*, and ridiculously endeavours to demonstrate that the Archimedian point . . . on which the world hinges, can be found, not in the pulsating heart but in the firm and solid area on which he stands' – so the Little Girl Marx, Alice, wrote in the annotations to her doctoral thesis.[5]

Of course he remained *religious*. But what do we want-desire? A true atheism? Certainly not! A beyond of both religion and atheism, something like Roman parody, and consequently, we would not at all be content to have 'demonstrated' that Marx's politics and political economics are full of religiosity, reconciliation and hope – although we are constrained to do so and it is impossible to avoid this sort of knowledgeable discourse. We are, however, aware that this is set out in such a way that there is no trace of the emotions which induce it, and that, in consequence, its very position is reassuring, perhaps allowing only a certain anguish, apparently the only noble affect, to filter through, but not love, not anger, not some disconcerting surprise. It would make us happy to be able to retranscribe, into a libidinal discourse, those intensities which haunt Marx's thought and which, in general, are dissimulated in the brass-tacks solemnity of the discourses of economy and politics. We will show, therefore, how in Marx's own terms, political economy is a libidinal economy. . . . look at the English proletariat, at what capital, that is to say *their labour*, has done to their body. You will tell me, however, that it was that or die. *But it is always that or die*, this is the law of libidinal economy, no, not the law: this is its provisional, very provisional, definition in the form of the cry, of intensities of desire; 'that or die', i.e. that and dying from it, death always in it, as its internal bark, its thin nut's skin, not yet as its *price*, on the contrary as that which renders it unpayable. And perhaps you believe that 'that or die' is an *alternative*?! And that if they choose that, if they become the slave of the machine, the machine of the machine, fucker fucked by it, eight hours, twelve hours, a day, year after year, it is because they are forced into it, constrained, because they cling to life? Death is not an alternative to it, it is a part of it, it attests to the fact that there is *jouissance* in it, the English unemployed did not become workers to survive, they – hang on tight and spit on me – *enjoyed* [*ils ont joui de*] the hysterical, masochistic, whatever exhaustion it was of *hanging on* in the mines, in the foundries, in the factories, in hell, they enjoyed it, enjoyed the mad destruction of their organic body which was indeed imposed upon them, they enjoyed the decomposition of their personal identity, the identity that the peasant tradition had constructed for them, enjoyed the dissolution of their families and villages, and enjoyed the new monstrous *anonymity* of the suburbs and the pubs in the morning and evening.

And let's finally acknowledge this *jouissance*, which is similar, Little Girl Marx was clear on this point, in every way to that of prostitution, the *jouissance* of anonymity, the *jouissance* of the *repetition of the same* in work, the same gesture, the same comings and goings in the factory, how many penises per hour, how many tonnes of coal, how many cast-iron bars, how many barrels of shit, not 'produced', of course, but *endured*, the *same parts of the body* used, made use of, to the total exclusion of others, and just as the prostitutes' vagina or mouth are hysterically *anaesthetised*, through use, through being used, so the worker's ear as described and analysed by Tomatis, who, next to an alternator functioning at 20,000 Hz, peacefully writes his letters and hears the finest noises; and when Tomatis makes his audiogramme study, he notices that the resonant range corresponding to the alternator functioning at 20,000 Hz, is neutralised, *mute*. Hence a hysterical treatment of a fraction of the auditory body, whore assemblage, the libidinal use demanded, of course, by the 'conditions of labour', which are also, however, those of prostitution. It goes without saying, of course, that we say this without any condemnation, without any regret, on the contrary by discovering that there has been, and perhaps still is, the extraordinary dissimulated-dissimulating force of the worker, force of resistance, force of *jouissance* in the hysterical madness of the conditions of labour which the sociologists would call *fragmented* without seeing what libidinal intensities these fragments can convey *as fragments*.

How can we continue to speak of alienation when it is clear that for everybody, in the experiences he *has* (and that more often than not he cannot properly *have*, since these experiences are allegedly shameful, and especially since instead of having them, he is these experiences) of even the most stupid capitalist labourer, that he can find *jouissance* and a strange, perverse intensity, what do we know about it? – when it is clear that not one 'productive' or 'artistic' or 'poetic' metamorphosis has ever been accomplished, nor will be, by a unitary and totalised organic body, but that it is always at the price of its alleged dissolution and therefore of an inevitable stupidity that this has been possible; when it is clear that there has never been, nor even will be such a *dissolution* for the good reason that there has never been nor ever will be such a body bound up in its unity and identity, that this body is a phantasy, itself fairly libidinal, erotic and hygienic = Greek, or erotic and supernatural = Christian, and that it is by contrast with this phantasy that all alienation is thought and *resented* in the sense of ressentiment which is the feeling aroused by the great Zero as the desire for return. But the body of primitive savages is no more a whole body than that of the Scottish miners of a century ago, there is no whole body.

Finally, you must also realise that such *jouissance*, I am thinking of that of the proletariat, is not at all exclusive of the hardest and most intense *revolts*, *Jouissance* is *unbearable*. It is not in order to regain their dignity that the workers will revolt, break the machines, lock up the bosses, kick out the deputies, that the victims of colonisation will set the governors' palaces on fire and cut the sentries' throats, no, it is something else altogether, there is no dignity; Guyotat has so admirably put this into writing with regard to Algeria.[6] There are libidinal positions, tenable or not, there are positions invested which are immediately disinvested, the energies passing onto other pieces of the great puzzle, inventing new fragments and new modalities of *jouissance*, that is to say of intensification. There is no libidinal dignity, nor libidinal fraternity, there are libidinal contacts without communication (for want of a 'message'). This is why, amongst individuals participating in the same struggle, there may exist the most profound miscomprehension, even if they are situated in the same social and economic bracket. If some Algerian fights for four years out in the brush or for a few months in the urban networks, it is because his desire has become the desire to kill, not to kill in general, but to kill an invested part, still invested, there's no doubt about it, of his sensitive regions. Would he kill his French master? More than that: he would be killed as the obliging servant of this master, to disengage the region of his prostitute's consent, to seek other *jouissances* than prostitution as a model, that is to say as the predominant modality of investment. Nevertheless, instantiating itself in murder, perhaps his desire remained still in the grip of the punitive relation that he meant to abandon, perhaps this murder was still a suicide, a punishment, the price due to the pimp, and still servitude. But during this same struggle for independence, some other 'moderate', even centrist, Algerian, decided on compromise and negotiation, he sought quite another disposition of *jouissance*, his intelligence dismissing such a death and swearing in calculation, already nourishing contempt for the body and exalting words as negotiation demands, hence also his own death as the death of flesh in general, not as the prostitute body, a very acceptable death to the Western talker. Etc.

Now these disparities, which are heterogeneities of investment in the erotic and deadly fluxes, are of course also found within any social 'movement' whatsoever, whether minute, on the scale of a factory, or immense, when it spreads to a whole country or continent. But apart from the movements of open revolt, notice that these singular 'hysterical' *jouissances*, for example, or those we might call 'potential', so akin to modern scientificity, or again those by which a 'body' is installed within the increased reproduction of capital, where it is entirely subordinated to the measurement of time saved and time advanced – and indeed all these instantiations (brutally sketched here), even when the capitalist machine is humming in the apparent general boredom and when everyody seems to do their job without moaning, all these libidinal instantiations, these little *dispositifs* of the retention and flow of the influxes of desire are *never unequivocal* and cannot give rise to a sociological reading or an unequivocal politics, to a decoding into a definable lexis and syntax; punishment incites both submission and revolt, power, the fascination of pride and autodepreciative depression, every 'discipline' demands passion and hate, even if these are only the *indifference* in Marx's sense, of whomever performs it. Hence ambivalence, said Baudrillard. And we say: much more than that, something else besides this condensed house of love and disgust or fear, which in general will be vulnerable to the attack of a semiotic or hermeneutic analysis of affects; no interpreter is afraid of polysemia; but at the same time and indiscernibly something which is a functioning or *dysfunctioning* term in a system, and something which is abruptly implacable joy and suffering; at once ambivalent signification and tension, dissimulated into one another. Not only the *and/or*, but the silent comma: ',.

NOTES

1. M. Rubel shows this in his introduction to Volume II of the Pléiade edition of the *Oeuvres*.
2. This is Böhm-Bawerk's classic critique. See Eugen Böhm-Bawerk, *Critique of Marx* (London: Merlin, 1975). See also Piero Sraffa, *Production of Commodities by Means of Commodities* (Cambridge: Cambridge University Press, 1960), and S. Latouche's discussion of these theses in *Epistémologie et économie* (Paris: Anthropos, 1973), pp. 539–51.
3. See F. Fourquet's text, 'Généalogie du Capital II – L'Idéal historique', *Recherches*, 14, Revue de CERFI (January 1974), especially ch. IV.
4. See n. 3; here we encounter the discoveries made by Patrice Loraux in a study in progress.
5. Karl Marx, 'Notes to the Doctoral Dissertation', in *Writings of the Young Marx*, ed. and tr. by Loyd D. Easton and Kurt H. Guddat (New York: Doubleday, 1967), p. 64.
6. Pierre Guyotat, *Tombeau pour 500 000 soldats* (Paris: Gallimard, 1967).

8

A MEMORIAL OF MARXISM†

Jean-François Lyotard

Lyotard returned to his attack on the Marxist tradition in 'A Memorial of Marxism'. Published in English as an appendix to his late book Peregrinations *(1988), 'A Memorial' recounts Lyotard's Marxist past in the 'Socialisme ou Barbarie' movement in terms of his friendship with the French Marxist historian, and 'Socialisme ou Barbarie' colleague, Pierre Souyri. Lyotard charts his progressive sense of disenchantment with Marxist thought over the course of the 1950s and 1960s in this piece, which has a certain elegaic quality to it (no doubt out of respect for the recently deceased Souyri), although it is no less uncompromising in its rejection of Marxism than* Libidinal Economy *was. Ultimately, Lyotard regards the differences between himself and Souyri (who becomes something of a representative of all that was best in classical Marxism in this reading) as irreconcilable, to the point where their respective political positions are incommensurable (what Lyotard calls a* 'différend'). *Once Lyotard loses faith in Marxist doctrines (particularly their claims to universality), there no longer exist any grounds for debate between himself and a classical Marxist.*

In 1966, I resigned from 'Pouvoir Ouvrier', one of the two groups resulting from the schism of 'Socialisme ou Barbarie' in 1964. In September, I sent Souyri a copy of my letter of resignation, 'so that it cannot be said that the one with whom I entered the group was the last to know that I am leaving it'. Admitted together in 1954 to take part in the practical and theoretical activities of the group that published the journal *Socialisme ou Barbarie*, we had during those twelve years devoted our time and all our capacities for thinking and acting to the sole enterprise of 'revolutionary critique and orientation' which was that of the group and its journal. We had even kept up the habit, developed after our first meeting in late 1950, of getting together on our own, or writing to each other, in order to debate as much as necessary all the political questions which we happened to confront through experience or reading. Nothing else, with the exception of love, seemed to us worth a moment's attention during those years.

† From J.-F. Lyotard, *Peregrinations: Law, Form, Event*, New York: Columbia University Press, 1988 (pp. 47–62). ['A Memorial of Marxism', trans. Cecile Lindsay, 1982.]

He answered me in October in a letter .full of painful humour. He affirmed that our divergences dated from long before, divergences so deep that he considered it pointless to try to resolve them. He attributed to me the project of elaborating a new philosophy of history, one which he felt he had every reason to fear would be eclectic and idealistic, even though I might be unaware of it. He added: 'The problems we confront are, in my eyes, neither ill-posed nor insoluble within the framework of Marxist concepts'. There followed several lines in which he pastiched the grand political style. My future seemed to him, in sum, to be necessarily peaceful; a stage of my life was ending, I was leaving the service of the revolution, I would do something else, I had saved my skin. As for him, he knew himself to be bound to Marxist thought as though to his fate, without, however, being unaware that it was no longer, and perhaps had not for a long time been, 'the thought that reality seeks'. He prepared himself for the perhaps pointless solitude that the search for truth required of him.

We saw each other again, never as political men engaged in common or parallel undertakings, even in '68, but rather as long-lost friends. These encounters were the occasion for cheerful and bitter reminiscences, shared like a common good and scorned like a vain remedy for divorce. Sometimes brief and violent conflicts erupted: on terrorism, on the situation of capitalism, on the 'final solution', on the scope of the opposition movement . . . Neither of us wanted to pretend, concede, or flatter – but neither wanted either to break off irrevocably. We did not confront head on what confronted us, but the conversation, as though carried by a constant wind, pushed every subject toward that reef, and it was necessary to tack in order to avoid it, while still signalling that one had seen it and had done nothing more than contain one's anger. I felt myself scorned for the direction I had taken, as I knew we had scorned the intellectuals and politicians who had retired from class combat or who were blind to its stakes. He knew that I felt this, and drew from it no advantage or guilt. On his side, he must have felt both impatience and weariness at sensing that I was irritated by his obstinacy in preserving intact the problem of history and society such as we had received it from Marx, Lenin, Luxemburg, Trotsky, and Pannekoek, and in wanting to resolve it exclusively within the theoretical and practical framework of Marxism.

I believe that our *différend* is of some importance for an understanding of the present. It was not only personal, and it was not only conceptual. What was at stake seemed to be knowing whether 'with' Marxism – and with which Marxism? – one could still understand and transform the new direction taken by the world after the end of the Second World War. This was open to debate, which was most definitely the case in our group, and between us. But in what language should it be debated, and in what language should it be decided? The debate had to do with content: class struggle in modern capitalism, the drop in the rate of profit, imperialism and the third world, the proletariat and the bureaucracy, etc.; but what was at stake was the way of expressing those contents. How could the means of expression known as Marxism put itself into play and debate about itself as though it were just one content among others? The problem was one of logic. A *différend* is not a simple divergence precisely to the extent that its object cannot enter into the debate without modifying the rules of that debate.

Our *différend* was without remedy from the moment that one of us contested or even suspected Marxism's ability to express the changes of the contemporary world. We no longer shared a common language in which we could explain ourselves or even express our disagreements. And yet each of us had in principle sufficient knowledge of the partner's idiom to be able to translate into his own idiom what the other was privately saying to himself about him, and sufficient experience and friendship to know that he was thereby betraying the other. Marxism had probably been for both of us a universal language, capable even of accepting within itself, under the name of dialectical logic, the rupture and opposition of universals which were abstractions, and the paradoxical and infinite movement by which they are concretely realised. We had known, by experience and reflection, and each of us differently, what it is to be enclosed within a particular life and point of view, within a particular language, and to be able to get out only through conflict and paradox. But now it was dialectical logic itself, with its still irrefutable operator, the anti-principle of contradiction, that was in the process of becoming a simple idiom. The machine for overcoming alterity by negating and conserving it, the machine for producing universality out of particularity, had for one of us – for me, as it happened – broken down. In the language of the dialectic since Hegel, this blockage was a portend of my imminent relapse into the thinking of the understanding, and into the logic of identity. I knew this, but the fact was that this risk, and the concomitant danger of political regression of which the Marxists warned, had ceased to frighten me. And what if, after all, the philosopher asked himself, there wasn't any Self at all in experience to synthesise contradictorily the moments and thus to achieve knowledge and realisation of itself? What if history and thought did not need this synthesis; what if the paradoxes had to remain paradoxes, and if the equivocacy of these universals, which are also particulars, must not be sublated? What if Marxism itself were in its turn one of those particular universals which it was not even a question of going beyond – an assumption that is still too dialectical – but which it was at the very least a question of refuting in its claim to absolute universality, all the while according it a value in its own order? But then, in what order, and what is an order? These questions frightened me in themselves because of the formidable theoretical tasks they promised, and also because they seemed to condemn anyone who gave himself over to them to the abandonment of any militant practice for an indeterminate time.

For Souyri, that is, for me when I would try to speak of myself in Souyri's language, the cause for my 'relapse' seemed obvious: I again became that which I had tried in vain to stop being – a good petit-bourgeois intellectual reconstructing in his head for the thousandth time after others a vain palace of ideas, and who, believing he was freeing himself from dialectical logic, only fell all the more inevitably into eclecticism. That his judgement of it was as severe as this, I had every reason to assume; I knew he thought that we have significance only through what we think and do in the immense war between exploiters and exploited, and that in these matters, the affection one has for someone must not be heeded. Certainly, his sympathies, indifferences, and hostilities were not based on his theoretical and political principles; he could keep a tenderness and fidelity for very old friends who had remained communists, or he could frankly dislike comrades from our group. In the domain of thought, however, a person was right or wrong, refutable or irrefutable. Not even the dearest friend was excepted from this rule; he had to hear without reserve what Souyri believed to be true, he had to argue his refutation with reasons and proofs. A general conversation, where ideas that were not yet tried were put to the test, soon took on the form of a dialectical joust, even an eristic exercise. He liked to provoke his interlocutor by confronting him with the arguments of an advocate of revolution. A sensitive and absent-minded man in daily life, he could press on to the point of cruelty in discussion. Half in parody, half in sincere anguish, he thus reminded others and himself that there is no tolerance for the mind that forgets its only goal, the destruction of exploitation by thought and by acts. The dialectic was his way of thinking, a component part of the dialectic he tried to uncover in things. Theoretical experience proceeded for him like a practice of contradiction, just as contradiction formed for him the nervure of historical reality.

But on my side, this perserverance in thinking and acting according to the dialectic, as if for forty years the revolutionary movement had not suffered one failure after another – which Souyri moreover had no trouble admitting because that was the very thing he wanted to understand – seemed to me to be more and more alien to the exigencies of thought. Was one able to think, after these failures, without recognising in them, first of all, the failure of a way of thinking? And in this latter case, did the 'failures' of the revolutionary movement really deserve to be called that? Capitalism had succeeded, after twenty-five years and a war without precedent, in coming out of the crisis of the thirties without the proletariat of the developed countries having seized the opportunity to take power. The revolution of 1917 had on the contrary given birth to new relations of exploitation. That was true and intolerable. But in thus characterising this period of history, did not Souyri's Marxism hide from itself its own failure? Did it not project in the form of an accursed reality its own inability to understand the nature of what was at stake in the contemporary world? If in fact the stakes were not the suppression of relations of exploitation, the failure was only that of the thought that claimed the opposite. (And I knew what Souyri would say to that: if those are not the stakes, then all is vain, and it matters little to me.)

But how to know this? And even, how to discuss it, first of all? This suspicion, which made me drift imperceptibly and which separated me from Souyri, was no more arguable than a withdrawal of affective investment is explainable by reason, so that the essence of the *différend* could not be said. In what language would I have been able to dispute the legitimacy of the Marxist phrase and legitimise my suspicion? In Marxist language? That would have amounted to recognising that that language was above suspicion, and that the Marxist phrase was legitimate by its very position, even though I might contest or refuse it. The idiom was more important than the referent; it seemed to be the very stakes of the *différend*. Now, according to what rules can we debate the rules to adopt for the debate?

Some good souls think that this difficulty can be remedied by means of dialogue. But what are the rules of this dialogue? The same things goes for the dialectic. The drift which separated me from Souyri made me measure the extent to which a *différend* is not a contradiction, even in the dialectical materialist sense. For our *différend* did not, in my eyes, affect mutually exclusive propositions which could each still be expressed by dialectical logic, and which that logic was supposed to synthesise. The alteration affected that logic itself. Perhaps reality did not obey one unique language, I told myself; or rather – and this was worse – the obstacle was not that there could exist several languages in reality, for after all, languages are translatable into one other, and their multiplicity so little hinders the universality of a meaning that the translatability of an expression is instead the touchstone of that universality. No, the multiplicity that constituted an obstacle to dialectical logic had to be analogous to the one that distinguishes the genres of discourse. One might well transcribe a tragedy into a soap opera, a news item, a Broadway comedy; the intelligible schema of the action might well remain identical to itself from one version to another (this can be ascertained, moreover, only if it is formulated in a theory, which is yet another genre of discourse), but in every case what is tragic in the original version is lost. It seemed to me that the discourse called historical materialism caused its referent, historical reality, to speak in the language of class struggle. Now, this latter was a genre of discourse, and it had its rules, of course, but its rules prohibited me, precisely, from treating it as a genre, because it claimed to be able to transcribe all genres – or, what amounts to the same thing, to be able to say everything about its referent.

Our *différend* took on its full amplitude for me when it appeared to me that there was no symmetry between our respective situations. At least I supposed it to be so, and I can only suppose. Souyri must not be having too much trouble, I would say to myself, diagnosing what was happening to me. He did not have to overturn his way of thinking, he still had the ability to make the distinction, which was never fixed, of course – he was not a dogmatist – but which was always possible in principle, between what does and does not merit consideration in the struggle of ideas; between what continues to will the concrete emancipation of the exploited as its end, and what ceases to will it. With the critical Marxism which was his own, he always had at his disposition an apparatus for reading facts as symptoms, and my miniscule adventure, which had no importance, did not in any case escape its jurisdiction.

Such was not the case for the one whom Marxism seemed to abandon. A sort of uneasiness or inhibition came over him at the same time as the reasons to argue began to escape him, and he began to lose the use of the dialectic. What was the point of refuting the other, the Marxist, if the logic of reality was not, as he had believed, governed by contradiction? How could an argument prove that one is more a 'realist' than he? And in the name of what could it be done, if it were not certain that a subject which is the victim of a radical wrong – the proletariat – awaited this refutation in the unconscious of history, like a reparation that was due it? And finally, according to what logic was one to argue, if it were true that between the Marxist phrase and others, the contradiction was not analyzable or dialectisable, like between the true and the false, but rather a difference or a *différend* to be noted, described, meditated, like that between genres which are equally possible and perhaps equally legitimate? What other name could I oppose to that of the proletariat, what other logic to that of the dialectic? I couldn't tell; or rather, I began to think that it was not in fact a question of opposition.

In this way, the *différend* took a paradoxical turn. It filled me with anger, but also left me stupefied. I found myself without words to speak, without words to tell myself what Souyri's attachment to the Marxist mode of thought could mean and be worth. And what is more, I could still, in his place and in his genre of discourse, demolish my own irresolution; but I did not see how, in what genre, in what place, which should have been my own, I could attack *his* certainties. It seemed to me, in an obscure and indistinct way, that I must not hasten to overcome this dissymetry or to reestablish a parity of incomprehension. Only by my not mourning my powerlessness could another way of thinking be sketched out, I thought without justification, just as at sea a swimmer incapable of opposing the current relies on drifting to find another way out.

Thus I did not want or was not able to develop by means of a critique, and bring to a 'theoretical' conclusion, something which was at first only a faint and disagreeable insinuation: the suspicion that our radical Marxism was not the universal language. The page where Souyri's name was inscribed in this language had not been turned. It was not a question, for me, of refuting theses, of rejecting a doctrine, of promoting another more plausible one, but rather of leaving free and floating the relation of thought to that Marxism.

What took place as a result of this prudence was not, initially, what I expected, but rather at first glance the opposite. I did not immediately acquire a new way of thinking, but an occasion soon made me discover that there was in that vaguely outmoded discourse called Marxism – certain of whose expressions were even beginning to be unpronounceable for me, just as the flowers of a rhetoric can wilt – something, a distant assertion, which escaped not only refutation, but also decrepitude, and preserved all its authority over the will and over thought.

This occasion was provided me by the schism which in 1964 brought about the divorce between, on the one hand, a 'tendency' directed most notably by Castoriadis, who was to continue the publication of the journal *Socialisme ou Barbarie*, and on the other hand, a group of comrades, some resolutely 'Old-Marxist', and others who were uncertain but who shared a common mistrust of the 'tendency'. This latter group intended to devote itself to building a proletarian organisation and would continue to publish the monthly newspaper *Pouvoir Ouvrier*. The schism came at the end of a long collective reflection. In 1959, shortly after the discussion on revolutionary organisation had ended in the withdrawal of the minority faction,[1] Castoriadis had submitted for discussion a group of theses which implied not only a profound reorientation of our politics, but also a questioning of the very language in which it was possible to describe and intervene in the contemporary world.[2] I felt myself to be close to these theses, open to their argumentation, because I could believe that they formulated in a clear manner the suspicions and misgivings of which I have spoken.

The theses were the following: that the revolutionary movement can expect nothing from struggles centred on claims of an economic nature, controlled by 'worker' bureaucracies; that the question of labour has ceased to be central when there is 'full employment' in all the developed countries; that the unions have become 'tools of the system'; that 'official political' life now arouses only the apathy of the 'people'; that, apart from production, the proletariat has ceased to appear 'as a class having its own objectives'; that 'the dominant classes have succeeded in controlling the level of economic activity and in preventing major crises'.[3] Those were assertions that were easily verifiable, it seemed, in those periods of regular growth of capitalism in the most developed countries. And it seemed reasonable to conclude that under those conditions, if there were a revolutionary project, it would have to find its mainspring in a contradiction other than the one Marx described in *Capital*. Indeed, how could the elevation of the organic composition of capital, bringing about a drop in the rate of profit, have been able to continue providing the revolutionary perspective with an objective foundation if it was clear that the expected social and economic effects were neutralised by the functioning of modern capitalism?

From Lyon, Souyri communicated to me in December 1959 his 'perplexity' before the 'novelties' presented by Castoriadis. He pronounced himself profoundly hesitant from a theoretical point of view, 'never so hesitant in many years, since the break with Trotskyism'. He needed more time in order to make up his mind, along with additional information and explanations. He cautioned me: 'Are you fully aware of the meaning, in regard to the Marxist "tradition", of the concept that Castoriadis is developing on capitalism? He said enough to frighten me, but not enough to convince me. Those who already have a set opinion are very lucky.' And then suddenly he added: 'Is it necessary to resign? I have reflected, hesitated, debated many contradictory ideas. Finally, everything that opposes me to this group derives from the fact that it does not have a proletarian character.'

I had more reason to be surprised by this abrupt question than by the warning that preceded it: he was asking for a delay for theoretical reflection, and yet he was thinking about resigning then and there for reasons that were not theoretical but rather concerned the group's social composition and organisational functioning. In the course of the years 1960 and 1961, his perplexity gave way to the conviction that the description of modern capitalism presented by Castoriadis was erroneous. The temptation to leave was replaced by the resolve to prevent the group, as much as possible and from within, from hastily taking a stand by voting on the adoption of Castoriadis's theses: 'I find that by asking me to take a stand – and I must not be the only one – they are asking me to decide on a "scientific" problem of crucial importance about which, finally, I know very little. I find it deplorable in this situation to be exchanging epithets like paleo- and neo-Marxist. Polemics can only result in serious and useless disagreements within the group.' As for the content, he declared, in the same letter from January 1960, his 'fear that Castoriadis is taking as an accomplished fact a consolidation of capitalism which is only a tendency destined to confront new contradictions, and that he is confusing an economic *stage* with a durable and stable transformation'.

This conviction was to orient all his work in the years that followed: he reexamined in detail the analyses of the contradictions of capitalism made by the Austro-Marxist theoreticians Hilferding, Luxemburg, Lenin, and Boukharin; he began studying the enormous amount of social and economic literature on the functioning of contemporary monopolistic State capitalism; he set out to elaborate as fully as possible the contradictions that would not fail to result from this functioning. After 1967, he concluded the 'Remarques sur les contradictions du capitalisme', which serve as the Introduction to *Impérialisme et bureaucratie face aux révolutions dans le tiers-monde*, with the following provisional diagnosis:

> Considering the system in its global functioning and concrete configuration, and from the point of view of its intrinsic dialectic, it remains legitimate to posit that the contradictions which are in the process of the developing out of the growth of the present productive forces prepare – on the level of the relations of imperialist domination as well as on the level of the antagonisms of Capital and Labour and of the specific relations between the State and monopolising capital – the disintegration of the relative equilibrium which capitalism has achieved in surmounting the crisis of 1930.[4]

In this text, his conviction shone through that the history in progress and to come was continuing and would continue to obey contradictions that neither the monopolizing groups nor the state bureaucracies could succeed in controlling. After the first great depression (1874–96), overaccumulation had found its 'solution' in the remodeling of capitalism into imperialism; the second (1930–50) had motivated its remodeling into monopoly state capitalism, thanks to the so-called mixed economy. But the new arrangement did not have the means to ward off the next crisis of overaccumulation that would be brought on by the very 'growth' it would have encouraged; this is what the premonitory text of this Introduction explained, fifteen years ago now. I admire today its somber perspicacity, when capitalism, now engaged in a new depression due in particular to overcapitalisation, is indeed blindly searching for, at once, the expedients (perhaps war) and the new structures which will allow it to again put off the date of its ruin.

This was not what I was sensitive to at the time of the schism. For to that, I could object, and did in fact object, that the tableau was probably true, but what difference did it make if there were no revolutionary movement capable, ideologically and organisationally, of orienting the struggles, which would not fail to occur as a result of the new contradictions, toward the radical solution of those contradictions? The movement had never been as weak as at that time, in the early 1960s; crushed by its own offspring, Stalinism, it had never so little realized what might have been, from then on, a radical solution to capitalist contradictions. Souyri asked himself the same question, but it was not for him a matter of objection. To Castoriadis, who would say: there is no longer an objectivity leading to the ruin of capitalism; the problem of the revolution is that of critical subjectivity, Souyri would answer: indeed, that has always been the problem of the revolution, but it has also always been posed in objective conditions which are those of the contradictions of capitalism, and which are independent of that subjectivity. Even when this subjectivity does not become critical, the objective dynamics go their own way, blindly. If revolutionary consciousness is incapable of destroying the capitalistic relations of production, then those relations produce their necessary effects, at first euphoric when their consolidation has just taken place, but soon redoubtable when the contradictions resulting from this very consolidation explode. It is not because we are powerless that capitalism is stabilised to such an extent. If we are unable to make socialism out of it, then it will make without us what it is in its logic to make: misery that is both uncultivated and 'developed' – barbarism.

I could not understand his obstinacy in wanting to understand how capitalism, and with it the entire world that it had attracted into the orbit of its movement, was to perish for lack of a conscious interruption of its course. At stake in this obstinacy was not, at any rate, the preservation of the security which the status quo of proven methods and received doctrines furnishes for the mind. It was suspiciously unjust to call Souyri a paleo-Marxist because he thought that there is a dialectical logic in capitalist objectivity. I suspected that the 'tendency' represented by Castoriadis wanted to bury something with objectivism, and this something is perhaps not matter for refutation or revision or something that can decline, whatever may be the transformations undergone by the reality of the fact of capitalist development. In the conflict between the innovators and Souyri, the concern to protect thought and life from anguish was surely not on the side of the latter.

I am trying today to understand why, in spite of the *différend* which opposed me to Souyri and the sympathy I had for the majority of the theses presented by Castoriadis, I found myself, at the time of the 1964 schism, with Souyri in the group which opposed Castoriadis. And also why, in May 1968, while I was working one morning with some comrades from the Movement of March 22 on the draft of a tract intitled 'Your Struggle Is Ours', when one of the former comrades of 'Socialisme ou Barbarie' who had gone over to the 'tendency', and whom I respected, came to get me from a nearby hall so that I could participate in the elaboration of the Movement's platform, which the Movement had entrusted to the direction of 'Socialisme ou Barbarie' and ICO (*Informations et Correspondance Ouvrières*), I answered him stupidly: No, I don't have confidence in you. All in all, that was not an especially important event, and it was not an especially strong motive; I attach no particular importance to it. It was something like a lapsus.

There was something that did not let itself be corrupted by the wealth of argumentation that the 'tendency', and especially Castoriadis, expended in order to explain and justify the new orientation. Nothing was lacking from the argumentative panoply of these comrades, and yet this saturation revealed a lack, the same one that the philosopher senses on reading certain texts of Hegel: the disappointment coming from exhaustiveness. I am speaking of tone and method, for as to its content, it was rather existential. They were cleaning up Marxism, giving it new clothes. The old contradiction of Capital, judged to be economistic, was thrown out. A new contradiction – social, this time, and almost ethical – between directing and executing was designated as the right one. I certainly believed, along with the comrades of the 'tendency', that the world was changing, but in the framework of capitalistic relations of production, and thus without the disappearance of the extraction of surplus value, exploitation, and necessity. They were disguised as something else, but it had to be that subjection, in respect to a non-dominated objectivity, persist for one part of society, and thus also for the whole. Ethics is born of natural suffering; the political is born from the supplement that history adds to this suffering. We had not left the realm of the political.

But those were platitudes. Who would not have agreed? The 'tendency' protested that it was not claiming the contrary. What, then, was lacking in its argumentation? No one among the opposition that we formed was able to say at that time.

Let us call it complexity, the *différend*, the point of view of class. That was perhaps the thing that my *différend* with Souyri, and paradoxically the retreat of Marxism for me, had revealed as more fundamentally political than any divergence, the thing within which divergences took form. If *Capital* had been the critique, or a critique, of political economy, it was because it had forced the *différend* to be heard where it lay, hidden beneath the harmony, or at least beneath the universal. Marx had shown that there were at least two idioms or two genres hidden in the universal language of capital: the MCM spoken by the capitalist, and the CMC spoken by the wage earner. The speaker of one idiom understood perfectly well the speaker of the other, and each idiom was translatable into the other; but there was between them a difference which operated in such a way that in the transcription of a certain situation, experience, or referent expressed by one in the idiom of the other, this referent became unrecognizable for the first one, and the result of the transcription became incommensurable with the initial expression. The 'same' thing, a day of work, said in the two genres, became two things, just as the 'same' affective situation which is tragic for one of the protagonists can be a melodrama for the other. And as I had discovered in my *différend* with Souyri, this incommensurability was not symmetrical, but rather imbalanced. One of the idioms proposed itself as able to say what the 'same' situation was, to explain how it was indeed a question of the 'same' referent on both sides. It thus presented itself not as one party in a suit, but as the judge, as the science in possession of objectivity, thereby placing the other in the position of stupor or stupidity in which I had found myself, confining the other within the subjective particularity of a point of view that remained incapable of making itself understood, unless it borrowed the dominant idiom – that is, unless it betrayed itself.

Inasmuch as there was in Marxism a discourse which claimed to be able to express without residue all opposing positions, which forgot that *différends* are embodied in incommensurable figures between which there is no logical solution, it became necessary to stop speaking this idiom at all, and I assented to the direction taken by the 'tendency' in this respect, despite Souyri's opposition. But he had known long before me that the question did not reside there. One could certainly make this critique, but all one had refuted by doing so was the dogmatism in Marxism, and not Marxism itself. Some speculative satisfaction was perhaps derived from this, but one surely lost that thing which, rightly or wrongly, remained in Souyri's eyes attached to the name of Marxism.

This thing that I call here the *différend* bears in the Marxist 'tradition' a 'well-known' name which gives rise to many misunderstandings; it is that of practice or 'praxis', the name par excellence that theoretical thought misinterprets. Souyri was not mistaken; he was not confusing Marx with Hegel. If there exists a class practice, and if at the same time the concept does not give rise to practice, it is because universality cannot be expressed in words, unless it be unilaterally. The roles of the protagonists of history are not played out in a single genre of discourse. Capital, which claims to be the universal language, is, by that very fact, that which reveals the multiplicity of untranslatable idioms. Between these latter and the law of value, the *différend* cannot be resolved by speculation or in ethics; it must be resolved in 'practice', in what Marx called critical practice, in an uncertain struggle against the party which claims to be the judge.

NOTES

1. Claude Lefort and the comrades who maintained after 1958 the publication of the bulletin *Informations et liaisons ouvrières*, which subsequently became *Informations et correspondence ouvrières*. Lefort's positions had been stated in a text entitled 'Organisation et parti', published under his name in *Socialisme ou Barbarie*, no. 26 (November–December 1958); those of the majority were published in a text signed by Paul Cardan, entitled 'Prolétariat et organisation', and published in numbers 27 and 28 of the same journal (April–May and July–August 1959).
2. This 'platform' was published in *Socialisme ou Barbarie*, nos. 31 and 32 (December 1960–February 1961) under the title 'Le Mouvement révolutionnaire sous le capitalisme moderne'.
3. The expressions in quotation marks are taken from the introductory resumé of the text mentioned in the preceding note, *Socialisme ou Barbarie*, no. 31, pp. 51 sq.
4. Souyri, *Impérialisme et bureaucratie face aux révolutions dans le tiers-monde* (supplement to *Pouvoir Ouvrier*, January 1968), p. xviii.

9

LIVING WITHOUT AN ALTERNATIVE†

Zygmunt Bauman

The Polish-born, British-resident sociologist Zygmunt Bauman is one of the most penetrating commentators on both Marxism and postmodernism. If Lyotard presents us with a memorial of Marxism, Bauman, in his influential study, Intimations of Postmodernity *(1992), offers us a memorial of communism (and indeed, one of the chapters in the book is entitled 'Communism: A Postmortem'). The nature of the relationship between Marxism and communism is a controversial one, and some Marxists would claim it is at best tenuous, but Bauman's concern here is to examine the implications of the collapse of communism, as some kind of expression of Marxist-socialist ideals, on political life in the Western democracies. The demise of communism is not, Bauman contends, something to be welcomed unreservedly, in that communism's absence as a political alternative serves further to marginalise dissent in capitalist societies. For someone like Bauman, notions like the 'end of history' have a sinister ring. One of the most pressing problems facing a post-Marxist, postmodern world, therefore, is how to create a basis for self-criticism; without that, Bauman feels, the individual will be left totally at the mercy of the market. And as the extract below makes clear, he does not think that the market is the solution to all our socio-political problems.*

———◆———

Communism has died. Some say, of senility. Some say, of shameful afflictions. All agree that it will stay dead for a long, long time.

The official opinion (whatever that means) of the affluent West greeted the news, arguably the least expected news of the century, with self-congratulating glee. The theme of the celebration is well known: 'our form of life' has once and for all proved both its viability and its superiority over any other real or imaginable form, our mixture of individual freedom and consumer market has emerged as the necessary and sufficient, truly universal principle of social organisation, there will be no more traumatic turns of history, indeed no history to speak of. For 'our way of life' the world has become a safe place. The century remarkable for fighting its choices on the

———

† From Z. Bauman, *Intimations of Postmodernity*, London: Routledge, 1992 (pp. 175–86).

battlefield is over, ten years before the appointed time. From now on, there will be just more of the good things that are.

In the din of celebration, the few voices of doubt are barely audible. Some doubts do not dare to be voiced. Some inarticulate worries have not even congealed into doubts fit to be put into words. One can only guess what they are.

Those who deployed communism as a bugbear with which to frighten disobedient children ('look what would become of you if you do not do what I told you to') and bring them to their senses, feel slightly uneasy: where are they to find a substitute for the service the late communism rendered? How to keep people thankful for however little they have if one cannot get credit for defending them from having less still?

Some categories of people have more radical and immediate reasons to be worried. The huge warfare bureaucracy, for instance. It lived off the threat of the communist evil empire, and lived all the better the more it could make the threat look real and terrifying. That bureaucracy presided over, and derived its life juices from, the biggest arms industry that existed in any peacetime of history. That industry did not need actual warfare to thrive: the initial push of the communist threat sufficed to assure continuous, exponential development. After that, it has acquired its own momentum of self-perpetuation and growth. Producers of defensive weapons competed with the merchants of the offensive ones; navies with air forces, tanks with rocketry units. New weapons had to be developed one day because the weapons invented the day before made inadequate or downright obsolete the weapons deployed the day before that. Or new weapons had to be developed just because the laboratories, filled with high class brains and kept constantly at the highest pitch of tension by tempting commissions, prestigious ambitions and professional rivalry, could not stop spawning ever new ideas; and because there were spare or idle technological resources eager to absorb them. And yet this cosy arrangement needed the communist threat to secure the steady inflow of life juices. The weapons industry less than anyone else can survive without an enemy; its products have no value when no one is afraid and no one wants to frighten the others.

And there is another powerful industry that may bewail the passage of the communist enemy: thousands of university departments and research institutes, world-wide networks of congresses, conferences, publishing houses and journals all dedicated in full to 'Soviet and East European Studies' and now, like the warfare bureaucracy, facing the prospect of redundancy. Like all well-established and viable organisations (including the warfare bureaucracy), *sovietology* will certainly attempt to find a new topic to justify its continuing services, and this it can only do through construing new targets to match its impressive human and material resources. And yet one doubts whether the new targets, however defined, would attract as in the past the funds and the benevolence of the powers that be in quantities sufficient to keep the industry at its recent level of material wealth, academic prestige and self-congratulatory mood.

These and similar worries may be quite serious for the interests they affect directly, yet the globality of disaster to which they refer is, to say the least, a matter of contention. There are, however, other consequences of the demise of communism which may have truly global deleterious effects for the survival of the very same 'form of life' whose ultimate triumph they ostensibly augur.

It is widely assumed, particularly in the right-most regions of the political spectrum, that the bankruptcy of the communist system must have delivered a mortal blow not just to the preachers and outspoken devotees of the communist faith, but to any cause, however loosely related to the 'left' tradition of disaffection, critique and dissent, of value-questioning, of alternative visions. It is assumed that the practical discrediting of communism (construed as 'the Other' of *our form of life*, as the *negative* totality which injects meaning into *our positivity*), pre-empts by proxy and disqualifies in advance any doubts about the unchallengeable superiority of the *really existing* regime of freedom and the consumer market; that it discredits, moreover, any suggestion that this regime, even if technically more viable, may be still neither entirely flawless, nor the most just of conceivable orders; that it may be instead in urgent need of an overhaul and improvement. I will argue, however, that the assertion that the collapse of communism threatens the survival of the 'left alternative' and the left critique *alone* is invalid as a non sequitur; that such dangers as truly arise in the world that has abandoned the socialist alternative, ostensibly discredited once and for all by the now universally decried practices of its communist variant, apply to 'our form of life' (that is, to the *really existing* regime of free consumers and free markets) in the same (perhaps even greater) measure than they do to its left critique; and that this circumstance may only render the continuation of critique more imperative than it otherwise would have been.

THE HISTORICAL MEANING OF THE COLLAPSE OF COMMUNISM

What has been buried under the debris of the communist system? A number of totalitarian states, of course – specimens of a regime that left rule-unprotected individuals at the mercy of rule-free powers, and which insulated the self-reproduction of the political power-holders from all and any intervention by the powerless. The demise of the totalitarian state cannot, however, be said to be final or complete, as communism was just one of many political formulae of totalitarianism. Non-communist totalitarianism is neither logically incongruent as a notion nor technically inoperative as a practice. Even a cursory survey of the panoply of extant political regimes would show that to issue a death certificate to totalitarianism just because its communist version has disintegrated would be, to say the least, a premature and unwise decision. Even if every former communist state makes the parliamentary democratic procedure and the observance of individual rights stick (not by itself a foregone conclusion), this would not mean that 'the world has become safe for democracy' and that the struggle between liberal and totalitarian principles heretofore coexisting inside contemporary body politics has been settled. To suggest that the communist utopia was the only virus responsible for totalitarian afflictions would be to propagate a dangerous illusion, one that is both theoretically incapacitating and politically disarming – for the future chances of democracy a costly, perhaps even lethal mistake.

There are, however, other graves hidden under the rubble that are still waiting to be uncovered in full. The fall of communism was a resounding defeat for the project of a *total order* – an artificially designed, all-embracing arrangement of human actions and their setting, one that follows the rules of reason instead of emerging from diffuse and uncoordinated activities of human agents; it was also the downfall of the grandiose dream of *remaking* nature – forcing it to yield ever more of anything human satisfaction may require, while disregarding or neutralising such among its unplanned tendencies as could not be assigned any sensible human benefit; it demonstrated as well the ultimate frustration of the ambitions of global management, of replacing spontaneity with planning, of a transparent, monitored, supervised and deliberately shaped order in which nothing is left to chance and everything derives its meaning and *raison d'être* from the vision of a harmonious totality. In short, the fall of communism signalled the final retreat from the dreams and ambitions of *modernity*.

One of the most conspicuous traits of modernity was an overwhelming urge to re-place spontaneity, seen as meaningless and identified with chaos, by an order drawn by reason and constructed through legislative and controlling effort. That urge gestated (or was it gestated by?) what has become a specifically *modern* state: one that modelled its intentions and the prerogatives it claimed after the pattern of a gardener, a medical man, or an architect: a *gardening* state, a *therapeutic/surgical* state, a *space-managing* state. It was a gardening state, in so far as it usurped the right to set apart the 'useful' and the 'useless' plants, to select a final model of harmony that made some plants useful and others useless, and to propagate such plants as are useful while exterminating the use-less ones. It was a therapeutic/surgical state, in so far as it set the standard of 'normal-ity' and thus drew the borderline between the acceptable and the intolerable, between health and disease, fighting the second to support the first – and in so far as it cast its subjects in the role of the patients: the sites of ailments, yet not themselves agents able to defeat the malady without the instruction of a knowledgeable and resourceful tutor. It was a space-managing state, in so far as it was busy landscaping the wasteland (it was the landscaping intention that cast the operating territory as wasteland), subjecting all local features to one, unifying, homogenising principle of harmony.

Communism and Modernity

As it happened, communism took the precepts of modernity most seriously and set out to implement them in earnest. Indeed, its logic as a system had geared it to perform the gardening/therapeutic/architectural functions to the detriment of all, indeed any, prerequisites or demands unjustified by the reason of the enterprise.

Throughout its history, communism was modernity's most devout, vigorous and gallant champion – pious to the point of simplicity. It also claimed to be its only true champion. Indeed, it was under communist, not capitalist, auspices that the audacious dream of modernity, freed from obstacles by the merciless and seemingly omnipotent state, was pushed to its radical limits: grand designs, unlimited social engineering, huge and bulky technology, total transformation of nature. Deserts were irrigated (but they turned into salinated bogs); marshlands were dried (but they turned into deserts); massive gas-pipes criss-crossed the land to remedy nature's whims in distributing its resources (but they kept exploding with a force unequalled by the natural disasters of yore); millions were lifted from the 'idiocy of rural life' (but they got poisoned by the effluvia of rationally designed industry, if they did not perish first on the way). Raped and crippled, nature failed to deliver the riches one hoped it would; the total scale of design only made the devastation total. Worse still, all that raping and crippling proved to be in vain. Life did not seem to become more comfortable or happy, needs (even ones acknowledged by the state tutors) did not seem to be satisfied better than before, and the kingdom of reason and harmony seemed to be more distant than ever.

What the affluent west is in fact celebrating today is the official passing away of its own past; the last farewell to the modern dream and modern arrogance. If the joyous immersion in postmodern fluidity and the sensuous bliss of aimless drift were poisoned by the residues of modern conscience – the urge to do something about those who suffer and clamour for something to be done – they seem unpolluted now. With communism, the ghost of modernity has been exorcised. Social engineering, the principle of communal responsibility for individual fate, the duty to provide commonly for single survivals, the tendency to view personal tragedies as social problems, the commandment to strive collectively for shared justice – all such moral precepts as used to legitimise (some say motivate) modern practices have been compromised beyond repair by the spectacular collapse of the communist system. No more guilty conscience. No scruples. No supra-individual commitments contaminating individual enjoyment. The past has descended to its grave in disgrace.

THE POLITICAL SIGNIFICANCE OF THE COLLAPSE OF COMMUNISM

The demise of the communist system was also a defeat for the over-ambitious and over-protective state. Indeed it is because the last act of the protracted and tortuous process of demise was so final and dramatic that it is credible to describe ambitious and protective states as *over*-ambitious and *over*-protective. Such a state seemed to draw its last breath at the Vaclavske Namesti and the city square of Timisoara, though it survived, albeit temporarily, Tiananmen Square. What discredited that state more than anything else (*de facto*, if not in theoretical interpretations) is that it revealed an unbelievable inner weakness; it surrendered to an unarmed crowd while ostensibly threatened by nothing more than that crowd's resolute refusal to go home. Such a weakness seems to be a sole property of the communist state, and can be easily, and gladly, ascribed to everything it stood for. Can one imagine a similar effect of a public gathering at Trafalgar Square? Or the Champs Elysées? And can one imagine the gathering?

Because of the factors spelled out above, the subjects of the communist state could have more reasons to express disaffection than the population of most western countries. But – a point not stressed strongly enough, if at all – they also had a greater possibility of making their disaffection effective and of re-forging it into systemic change. The overbearing state had to pay a price for the formidable volume of its concerns and entitlements – and the price was *vulnerability*. To assert the state's right to command and control is to assume responsibility for the effects. The doorstep on which to lay the blame is publicly known and clearly marked, and for each and any grievance it is *the same* doorstep. The state cannot help but cumulate and condense social dissent; nor can it help turning the edge of dissent against itself. The state is the major, and sufficient, factor in forging the variety of often incompatible complaints and bids into a unified opposition – at least for long enough to produce a dramatic showdown. The state that assumes the right to structure society also induces a tendency to political polarisation: the conflicts that otherwise would remain diffuse and cut the population in many directions tend to be subsumed under one overriding opposition between the state and society.

Thus it has not been proved that the illusory nature of state power and its incapacity to survive the mere refusal of obedience is solely the property of the communist state. What has been proved instead is that the communist regime created conditions most propitious to calling the bluff of state omnipotence. Most directly related to the nature of the regime was the possibility that refusal of obedience be synchronised, global and involving if not the total, then at least a sizeable part, of the population.

From the point of view of political sociology, the most important consequence of the present western tendency to de-étatisation of the growing number of previously state-managed areas is the *privatisation of dissent*. With both the global balance of social activities and the logic of the life-process split into finely-sliced and mutually autonomous functions, disaffections arising along separate task-oriented activities have no ground on which to meet and merge. Disaffection tends to generate one-issue campaigns, and dissent is functionally dispersed and either depoliticised or politically diluted. Seldom, if ever, is the grievance directed against the state, the frantic efforts of political parties notwithstanding. More often than not it stops short even of blending into social movements; instead, it rebounds in more disillusionment with collective solutions to individual troubles, and blames the sufferer for unfulfilled potential. The difference between the two systems consists not so much in the size of the sum total of disaffection, as in the propensity of dissent in a communist system to cumulate to the point where the system is de-legitimated, and to condense into a system-subverting force.

It is for this reason that the sham of state omnipotence (sometimes represented in political theory as 'legitimacy'), even if it really were only a sham, would tend to remain invisible. Whether the communist and liberal-parliamentary states (one presiding over the command economy, the other letting loose the market game) do or do not share the inner weakness that only communist states have recently demonstrated, is bound to remain a moot question: it is unlikely to be put to a practical test. Hence the repeated assertions of the 'end of history', of the 'end of conflict', of 'from now on, more of the same' may boast immunity to empirical criticism. However wrong such assertions may *feel*, their detractors can find little in the political life of the apparently victorious system to make their doubts credible.

Indeed, what is often called *western civilisation* seems to have found the philosopher's stone all other civilisations sought in vain, and with it the warranty of its own immortality: it has succeeded in re-forging its *discontents* into the factors of its own *reproduction*. What could be described in other systems as aspects of 'dysfunctionality', manifestations of crisis and imminent breakdown, seem to add to this system's strength and vigour. Deprivation breeds and further enhances the alluring power of market exchange, instead of gestating politically effective discontent: public risks and dangers spawned by 'single task' technologies and narrowly focused expertise supply further legitimation for problem-oriented action and generate demands for more technology and specialised expertise instead of questioning the wisdom of 'problem-limited' thinking and practice; impoverishment of the public sphere boosts the search for, and the seductive power of, private escapes from public squalor and further decimates the ranks of the potential defenders of the common weal. Above all, system-generated discontents are as subdivided as the agencies and actions that generate them. At most, such discontents lead to 'single-issue' campaigns that command intense commitment to the issue in focus while surrounding the narrow area of attention with a vast no-man's land of indifference and apathy. Party-political platforms do not reflect integrated group interests, real or postulated; instead, they are carefully patched together following a scrupulous calculation of the relative popularity (that is, vote-generating capacity) of each single issue in the public attention. Party-political mobilisation of votes does not detract from the volume of voters' apathy; indeed, one may say that the success of mobilisation through single issues is conditional on the voters' inattention to the topics left out of focus.

As a result of all this, the current western form of life, with its market-sponsored production of needs, privatisation of grievances and single task actions, seems to be in a position strikingly different from that of the regionally localised civilisations of yore. It has neither effective enemies inside nor barbarians knocking at the gates, only adulators and imitators. It has practically (and apparently irrevocably) de-legitimised all alternatives to itself. Having done this, it has rendered it uncannily difficult, nay impossible, to conceive of a different way of life in a form that would resist assimilation and hamper, rather than boost, the logic of its reproduction. Its courtly bards may therefore credibly pronounce it universal and *sub specie aeternitatis.*

THE COSTS OF VICTORY

One aspect of the situation in which the western form of life has found itself after the collapse of the communist alternative is the unprecedented freedom this form of life will from now on enjoy in construing 'the other' of itself and, by the same token, in defining its own identity. We do not really know what effects such freedom may bring: we can learn little from history, since it knows of no similar situations. For most of historically formed civilisation, 'the other' had the power of self-constitution. Alternatives appeared as real contenders and resourceful enemies; as threats to be reckoned with, adapted to and actively staved off. Alternatives were sources of at least temporary dynamism even if the capacity for change proved in the end too limited to prevent ultimate defeat. For the better part of the twentieth century, communism seemed successfully to play the role of such an alternative. Even before that, virtually from the beginning of capitalist modernity, such a role was played by socialist move-ments. Vivid display of a social organisation that focused on the ends which capitalist modernity neglected made it necessary to broaden the systemic agenda, and enforced corrections which prevented the accumulation of potentially lethal dysfunctions. (The welfare state was the most conspicuous, but by no means the only, example.) This relative luxury of autonomous, self-constituted critique is now gone. The question is where its functional substitute may be found, if at all.

The most immediate part of the answer is the radically enhanced role of intellectual, rational analysis and critique; the latter would now need to carry on its own shoulders a task shared in the past with the contenders in the political battle of systemic alternatives. What is at stake here is not merely an extension and intensification of the old role of intellectuals. Throughout the modern era, in which states have relied for their operative capacity mostly on ideological legitimation, intellectuals and their institutions – the universities most prominent among them – were first and foremost the suppliers of current or potential legitimating formulae, whether in their conformist or rebellious mode. These goods are not today much in demand, as the state by and large cedes the integrative task to the seductive attractions of the market. (This absence of demand stands behind the process dubbed the 'crisis of universities', the relentless erosion of the cultural role from which they derived their high status in the past.) This loss of state-assisted status, however alarming at the moment, may yet prove a blessing in disguise. Prised from automatically assumed or ascribed legitimising or de-legitimising function, intellectual work may share in a general freedom of cultural creation derived from the present irrelevance of culture for systemic reproduction. (I have discussed this process more extensively in the third chapter of *Freedom*.)[1] This gives intellectual work a chance of considerable autonomy; indeed, a radical shift of balance inside the modern power/knowledge syndrome becomes a distinct possibility.

On the other hand, the waning of the communist alternative lays bare the inner shortcomings of the market-centred version of freedom, previously either de-problematised or played down in confrontation with the less alluring aspects of the system of comparative reference. Less can now be forgiven, less is likely to be placidly endured. An immanent critique of the maladies of freedom reduced to consumer choice will be less easy to dimiss by the old expedient of imputed approval of a discredited alternative, and the inanities the critique discloses will be more difficult to exonerate as 'the lesser of two evils'. Market freedom would need to explain and defend itself in its own terms; and these are not particularly strong or cogent terms, especially when it comes to justifying its social and psychological costs.

The costs are, indeed, enormous. And they can no longer be made less appalling by showing that the attempts which have been made to rectify them elsewhere have increased the total volume of human suffering instead of diminishing it. Those attempts are no longer on the agenda, yet the costs show no sign of abating and call for action no less loudly than before; only the call is now more poignant than ever since inactivity cannot be apologised for by proxy. The continuing polarisation of well-being and life chances cannot be made less repulsive by pointing to the general impoverishment which had resulted elsewhere from efforts to remedy it. The traumas of privatised identity-construction cannot be easily whitewashed by pointing to the stultifying effects of the totalitarian alternative. Indifference only thinly disguised by ostensible tolerance cannot be made more acceptable by the impotence of power-enforced coexistence. The reduction of citizenship to consumerism cannot be justified by reference to the even more gruesome effects of obligatory political mobilization. The ironical dismissal of forward dreaming loses much of its cogency once the now-discredited promotion of 'total order' and gardening utopias ceases to be its most conspicuous and tangible incarnation.

All this points to an opportunity. It does not necessarily guarantee success. (I have discussed above the astonishing ability of the postmodern habitat to absorb dissent and avant-garde-style criticism and to deploy them as the sources of its own renewed strength.) We, the residents of the postmodern habitat, live in a territory that admits of no clear options and no strategies that can even be *imagined* to be uncontroversially correct. We are better aware than ever before just how slippery are all the roads once pursued with single-minded determination. We know how easily the critique of 'market only' freedom may lead to the destruction of freedom as such. But we know as well – or we will learn soon, if we do not know it yet – that freedom confined to consumer choice is blatantly inadequate for the performance of the life-tasks that confront a privatised individuality (for instance, for the self-construction of identity); and that it therefore tends to be accompanied by the renascence of the selfsame irrationalities that grandiose projects of modernity wished to eradicate, while succeeding, at best, in their temporary suppression. Dangers lurk on both sides. The world without an alternative needs self-criticism as a condition of survival and decency. But it does not make the life of criticism easy.

NOTE

1.   Z. Bauman, *Freedom* (Milton Keynes: Open University Press, 1989).

10

MARXIST ANTHROPOLOGY AND THE DOMINATION OF NATURE†

Jean Baudrillard

Baudrillard was a student of the French Marxist sociologist and chronicler of 'everyday life' Henri Lefebvre, but he soon moved away from the Marxist tradition to become, first, one of its most trenchant critics, and then, one of the leading, indeed most notorious, voices in postmodernism. The Mirror of Production *(1973) is one of the works where Baudrillard announces his movement away from Marxism, and in the extract below he takes issue with the conception of 'Nature' in Marxist thought. Baudrillard sees Marxism as holding on to the Enlightenment notion of Nature as something to be brought under humankind's domination and harnessed to the forces of production. Marxism, in other words, is just as committed to the philosophy of the market as modern capitalism is, and its obsession with production, Baudrillard argues, inhibits rather than promotes any revolution in social relations. Marxism is criticised for backdating its obsession with economic matters and material production on to previous societies, and for being, in effect, in thrall to Enlightenment ideology. Marxism, as far as Baudrillard is concerned, is not really a socially radical theory. Baudrillard is well on the way here to the* post-*Marxist perspective that marks out his later career.*

In the eighteenth century, the simultaneous emergence of labour as the source of wealth and needs as the finality of produced wealth is captured at the zenith of Enlightenment philosophy in the appearance of the concept of Nature, around which gravitates the entire rationality of the system of political economy.

As late as the seventeenth century, Nature signified only the totality of laws founding the world's intelligibility: the guarantee of an order where men and things could exchange their meanings [*significations*]. In the end, this is God (Spinoza's '*Deus sive natura*'). Subject and world already have respective positions (as they had since the great Judeo-Christian rupture, to which we will return), but not in the sense of a mastery or exploitation of Nature, or conversely as the exaltation of an original myth.

† From J. Baudrillard, *The Mirror of Production*, trans. Mark Poster, St Louis, MO: Telos Press, 1975 (pp. 53–67).

The rule for the autonomous subject confronting Nature is to form his practice so as to achieve an equilibrium of significations.

All this is shattered in the eighteenth century with the rise and 'discovery' of Nature as a potentiality of *powers* (no longer a totality of *laws*); as a primordial source of life and reality lost and recovered, repressed and liberated; and as a deed projected into an atemporal past and an ideal future. This rise is only the obverse of an event: Nature's entry into the era of its technical domination. This is the definitive split between subject and Nature-object and their simultaneous submission to an operational finality. Nature appeared truly as an essence in all its glory but under the sign of the *principle of production*. This separation also involves the *principle of signification*. Under the objective stamp of Science, Technology, and Production, Nature becomes the great Signified, the great Referent. It is ideally charged with 'reality'; it becomes *the* Reality, expressible by a process that is always somehow a process of labour, at once *transformation* and *transcription*. Its 'reality' principle is this operational principle of an industrial structuration and a significative pattern.[1]

From the outset, this process rests on two separated terms whose separation, however, is complicitous: confronted by Nature 'liberated' as a productive power, the individual finds himself 'liberated' as labour power. Production subordinates Nature and the individual simultaneously as economic factors of production and as respective terms of the same rationality – a transparency in which production is the mirror, directing articulation and expression in the form of a code.

For a long time, even in myth, production has been thought of in the mode of human reproduction. Marx himself spoke of labour as the father and the earth as the mother of produced wealth. This is false. In productive labour man does not make children with Nature. Labour is an objective transformation based on carving out and technically abstracting the subject and the object. Their relation is based only on the equivalence of the two terms as productive forces. What unifies them 'dialectically' is the same abstract form.

Thus Nature gains force as ideal reference in terms of the very reality of its exploitation. Science presents itself as a project progressing toward an objective determined in advance by Nature. Science and Technology present themselves as revealing what is inscribed in Nature: not only its secrets but their deep purpose. Here the concept of Nature appears in all its ambiguity:

1. It expresses only the finality of the domination of Nature inscribed in political economy. *Nature is the concept of a dominated essence* and nothing else. In this sense, it is Science and Technology that fulfill the essence of Nature by indefinitely reproducing it as separated.
2. However, they do this in the name of a finality supposed to be Nature itself.

Hence the same concept operates in both cases: a factor of production and a model of finality; a servile, metaphorical instance of freedom; a detached, metaphorical instance of the totality. And it is by being sublimated and repressed that Nature becomes a metaphor of freedom and totality. Everything that speaks in terms of totality (and-or 'alienation') under the sign of a Nature or a recovered essence speaks in terms of repression and separation. Everything that invokes Nature invokes the domination of Nature.

THE MORAL PHILOSOPHY OF THE ENLIGHTENMENT

All the major concepts (those worthy of a capital letter) depend on the same operation. The 'People', for example, whose ideal reference emerges with the collapse of traditional community and the urban concentration of destructured masses. Marxist analysis unmasked the myth of the People and revealed what it ideally hides: wage earners and the class struggle. On the other hand, Marxism only partially dislocated the myth of Nature and the idealist anthropology it supports. Marx indeed 'denaturalised' private property, the mechanisms of competition and the market, and the processes of labour and capital; but he failed to question the following naturalist propositions:

1. the useful finality of products as a function of needs;
2. the useful finality of nature as a function of its transformation by labour.

The functionality of Nature structured by labour, and the corresponding functionality of the subject structured around needs, belongs to the anthropological sphere of use value described by Enlightenment rationality and defined for a whole civilisation (which imposed it on others) by a certain kind of abstract, linear, irreversible finality: a certain model subsequently extended to all sectors of individual and social practice.

This operational finality is arbitrary in such a way that the concept of Nature it forgets resists integration within it. It looks as if forcefully rationalised Nature reemerges elsewhere in an irrational form. Without ceasing to be ideological, the concept splits into a 'good' Nature that is dominated and rationalised (which acts as the ideal cultural reference) and a 'bad' Nature that is hostile, menacing, catastrophic, or polluted. All bourgeois ideology divides between these two poles.

The same split occurs simultaneously at the level of man, through his idealist simplification as an element of the economic system. Starting with the eighteenth century, the idea of Man divides into a naturally good man (a projection of man sublimated as a productive force) and an instinctively evil man endowed with evil powers. The entire philosophical debate is organised around these sham alternatives, which result simply from the elevation of man to an economic abstraction. Marxism and all revolutionary perspectives are aligned on the optimist vision. They preserve the idea of an innate human rationality, a positive potentiality that must be liberated, even in the latest Freudo-Marxist version in which the unconscious itself is reinterpreted as 'natural' wealth, a hidden positivity that will burst forth in the revolutionary act.

This dichotomy also occurs at the level of labour power. When exploited, labour power is good: it is within Nature and is normal. But, once liberated, it becomes menacing in the form of the proletariat. This contradiction is averted by assimilating the proletariat to a demonic, perverse, destructive Nature. Thus the dichotomy in the idea of Nature which expresses the profound separation in the economic order is admirably recuperated at the ideological level as a principle of moral order and social discrimination.

Fetishised for better or for worse, such is the true 'alienation' of Nature and of the corresponding idea of Man. When at the same time he brands Nature and himself with the seal of production, man proscribes every relation of symbolic exchange between himself and Nature. It is this proscribed ambivalence that reemerges in the ambiguity of Nature and in man's own moral contradiction.

Marxism has not disencumbered itself of the moral philosophy of the Enlightenment. It has rejected its naive and sentimental side (Rousseau and Bernardin de Saint-Pierre), its cloying and fantastic religiosity (from the noble savage and the Age of Gold to the sorcerer's apprentice), but it holds onto the religion: the moralising phantasm of a Nature to be conquered. By secularising it in the economic concept of scarcity, Marxism keeps the idea of Necessity without transforming it. The idea of 'natural Necessity' is only a *moral* idea dictated by political economy, the ethical and philosophical version of that bad Nature systematically connected with the arbitrary postulate of the economic. In the mirror of the economic, Nature looks at us with the eyes of necessity.

Marx says, 'Just as the savage must wrestle with Nature to satisfy his wants, to maintain and reproduce life, so must civilised man, and he must do so in all social formations and under all possible modes of production. With his development this realm of physical necessity expands as a result of his wants: but, at the same time, the forces in production which satisfy these wants also increase.'[2] What is not recognised here – and what allies Marx with the foundations of political economy – is that in his symbolic exchanges primitive man *does not gauge himself in relation to Nature*. He is not aware of Necessity, a Law that takes effect only with the objectification of Nature. The Law takes its definitive form in capitalist political economy; moreover, it is only the philosophical expression of Scarcity. Scarcity, which itself arises in the market economy, is not a *given* dimension of the economy. Rather, it is what *produces and reproduces* economic exchange. In that regard it is different from primitive exchange, which knows nothing of this 'Law of Nature' that pretends to be the ontological dimension of man.[3] Hence it is an extremely serious problem that Marxist thought retains these key concepts which depend on the metaphysics of the market economy in general and on modern capitalist ideology in particular. Not analysed or unmasked (but exported to primitive society where they do not apply), these concepts mortgage all further analysis. The concept of production is never questioned; it will never radically overcome the influence of political economy. Even Marxism's transcending perspective will always be burdened by counter-dependence on political economy. Against Necessity it will oppose the mastery of Nature; against Scarcity it will oppose Abundance ('to each according to his needs') without ever resolving either the arbitrariness of these concepts or their idealist overdetermination by political economy.

The political order is at stake here. Can the quantitative development of productive forces lead to a revolution of social relations? Revolutionary hope is based 'objectively' and hopelessly on this claim. Even for Marcuse in *The End of Utopia*, the due date of revolution is at hand given our technological potentials: quantitative change is possible as of now. Even when the situation has clearly drifted enormously far from revolution and the dominant social relations support the very development of productive forces in an endless spiral, this dialectical voluntarism, for which Necessity exists and must be conquered, is not shaken. Scarcity exists and must be abolished; the Productive Forces exist and must be liberated; the End exists and only the means need be found. All revolutionary hope is thus bound up in a Promethean myth of productive forces, but this myth is only the space time of political economy. And the desire to manipulate destiny through the development of productive forces plunges one into the space time of political economy. The wish to abolish scarcity is not furthered by restoring an integrated productivity. The *concept* of Scarcity itself, the concept of Necessity, and the concept of Production must be exploded because they rivet the bolt of political economy. No dialectic leads beyond political economy because it is the very movement of political economy that is dialectical.

LYCURGUS AND CASTRATION

Parallel to the concepts of Necessity, Scarcity, and Need in the (vulgar or dialectical) materialist code, the psychoanalytic concepts of Law, Prohibition and Repression are also rooted in the objectification of Nature.

Vernant cites the story of Lycurgus.[4] Lycurgus kills his son Dryas or, in other versions, cuts off his foot believing he is trimming a vine. In another story, Phylacus makes his son impotent while trimming a tree or butchering livestock, Hence the violence against nature (the rupture of exchange with and symbolic obligation toward it) is immediately expiated. All the myths of a vengeful, bad, *castrating* nature take root here. And this is no mere metaphor, as the story clearly indicates. The rupture is immediately the foundation of *castration*, of the Oedipus complex (in this case parental, since the father emasculates the son), and of Law. For only then does Nature appear as an implacable necessity, 'the alienation of man's own body.' Marx adopted this Law of Necessity along with the Promethean and Faustian vision of its perpetual transcendence, just as psychoanalysis adopted the principle of castration and repression, prohibition and law (in the Lacanian version, by inscription in the order of the Signifier). But in no sense is it a fundamental structure. Neither Law nor Necessity exist at the level of reciprocity and symbolic exchange, where the break with nature that leads to the irreversibility of castration – and consequently to the entire becoming of history (the operational violence of man against nature) and of the unconscious (the redemption of the symbolic debt owed for this operational violence) – has not occurred. In this sense law, which is called the foundation of the symbolic order and of exchange, results instead from the rupture of exchange and the loss of the symbolic. This is why there is properly neither Necessity nor Scarcity nor Repression nor the Unconscious in the primitive order, whose entire symbolic strategy aims at exorcising the apparition of Law.[5]

Under the sign of Necessity and Law, the same fate – sublimation – awaits Marxism and psychoananalysis. We have seen how materialism's reference to 'objective'

Necessity led it to fantasise in its revolutionary perspectives the reverse schemes of Freedom and Abundance (the universality of needs and capacities) which are only the sublimated counterparts of Law and Necessity. Similarly, the analytic reference to the Unconscious, product of repression and prohibition, leads to the same step (today psychoanalysis is being short-circuited on a very large scale, and this turning away cannot be called accidental): an ideal reference to a 'liberation' of the Unconscious and to its universalisation by removing repression.[6] In this case as well, an ideal-revolutionary sublimation of a *content* results from accepting an essential *form* given as irreducible. But this form is merely the specific abstraction of an order that has cancelled symbolic relation in favour of operational violence, symbolic exchange in favour of the Law of castration and value – or, better, it has cancelled the actualisation of the death impulse and the ambivalence in exchange in favour of a productive Eros split into a symbolic violence of the Unconscious.

JUDAEO-CHRISTIAN ANTI-PHYSIS

This separation from Nature under the sign of the principle of production is fully realised by the capitalist system of political economy, but obviously it does not emerge with political economy. The separation is rooted in the great Judaeo-Christian dissociation of the soul and Nature. God created man in his *image* and created Nature for man's *use*. The soul is the spiritual hinge by which man is God's image and is radically distinguished from the rest of Nature (and from his own body): 'Uniquely in its Western form, Christianity is the most anthropocentric religion the world has ever known. In absolute contrast to ancient paganism and oriental religions, Christianity not only institutes a dualism of Man and Nature but also affirms that God's will is that man exploit Nature according to his own ends.'[7]

Rationality begins here. It is the end of paganism, animism and the 'magical' immersion of man in nature, all of which is reinterpreted as superstition. ('Rational' Marxism makes the same error by reinterpreting it in terms of the 'rudimentary' development of productive forces.) Hence although science, technology, and material production subsequently enter into contradiction with the cultural order and the dogmas of Christianity, nonetheless their condition of possibility remains the Christian postulate of man's transcendence of nature. This is why a scientific movement does not emerge in Greece. Greek rationality remains based on a conformity with nature radically distinguished from the Christian rationality and 'freedom' based on the separation of man and nature and on the domination of nature.

This separation immediately establishes not a work ethic (of material domination and production) but an ethic of asceticism, suffering, and self-mortification: an 'other-worldly' ethic of sublimation, in Max Weber's expression. Not a productive morality but a fixed order is outlined, in which well-being is to be 'earned'. And this is an *individualist* enterprise. The passage from the ascetic to the productive mode, from mortification to labour, and from the finality of welfare to the secularised finality of needs (with the Puritan transition at the origin of capitalism where work and rational calculation still have an ascetic, intra-worldly character and an orientation toward well-being) changes nothing in the principle of separation and sublimation, repression and operational violence. Well-being and labour are both well within the realm of ends and means. From ascetic practices to productive practices (and from the latter to consumer practices) there is thus *desublimation*; but the desublimation is only a metamorphosis of repressive sublimation. The ethical dimension is secularised under the sign of the material domination of nature.

Christianity is thus on the hinge of a rupture of symbolic exchanges. The ideological form most appropriate to sustain the intensive rational exploitation of nature[8] takes form within Christianity during a long transition: from the thirteenth and fourteenth century when work begins to be imposed as value, up to the sixteenth century when work is organised around its rational and continuous scheme of value – the capitalist productive enterprise and the system of political economy, that secular generalisation of the Christian axiom about nature. But this revolution of the rational calculus of production which Weber noted is not the beginning; it is prefigured in the Christian rupture. Political economy is only a kind of actualisation of this break.

STRUCTURAL LIMITS OF THE MARXIST CRITIQUE

The above discussion poses a serious methodological question [. . .] Basing the intelligibility of the contradictions of political economy on the structural givens of the finished system (capital), Marxist analysis cannot account for these basic coordinates of economic rationality – because the system of political economy tends to project itself retrospectively as a model and subordinates everything else to the genealogy of this model. When Marxism takes up its critique it does not question this retrospective finality. Thus in the strict sense, it analyses only the conditions of the model's *reproduction*, of its production as such: of the separation that establishes it.[9] The analysis of the production of *the economic as finality and as universal principle of reality*, the analysis of the production of the *production principle*, escapes Marxism since it moves only within the structural field of production. By presupposing the axiom of the economic, the Marxist critique perhaps deciphers the *functioning* of the *system* of political economy; but at the same time it reproduces it as a model. By pretending to illuminate earlier societies in the light of the present structure of the capitalist economy, it fails to see that, abolishing their difference, it projects onto them the spectral light of political economy.

Marx affirmed that it is on the basis of a critical return to its own contradictions that (our) culture becomes capable of grasping earlier societies. Thus we must conclude – and thereby grasping the *relativity* of Marxist analysis – that in Marx's time the system of political economy had not yet developed all its contradictions, hence that even for Marx radical critique was not yet possible nor was the real comprehension of earlier societies. Marx himself could not encroach on the system's total logic. Only at a certain stage of development and saturation of the system can critique go to its *roots*. In particular, the fundamental determinations of the economic (form production and form representation), the break they establish in relation to symbolic exchange, and the way a radical revolution of social relations is sketched starting from them can be read only after political economy has invaded all fields of social and individual practice, far beyond the field of material production. It is useless to question Marx about these matters. Analysing one phase and only one phase of the general process, his critique goes only so far and can only be extrapolated regarding the remainder. Marxism is the projection of the class struggle and the mode of production onto all previous history; it is the vision of a future 'freedom' based on the conscious domination of nature. These are extrapolations of the economic. To the degree that it is not *radical*, Marxist critique is led despite itself to reproduce the roots of the system of political economy.

Notes

1. This is why each product of labour will always be both a commodity and the *sign* of operable Nature and of its operation. In the framework of political economy, each product, besides its use value and exchange value, signifies and verifies the operationality of Nature and the 'naturalness' of the process of production. This is why the commodity always has a value-sign, a coded value element. (It is not a question here of connotations of meaning that are grafted on during the stage of consumption. It is at the level of production itself that the commodity signifies, that it *represents* the principle of production and operationalisation of Nature.) And, in the exchange of products, it is not only economic values but the code, this fundamental code, that circulates and is reproduced. Similarly, in the institution of labour power, man becomes not only economically operational but also the effect-referential of this operationality-sign.
2. *Capital* (Moscow: Foreign Languages Publishing Press) III, pp. 799–800.
3. Cf. Marshall Sahlins, 'La première société d'abondance', *Les Temps Modernes* (October, 1968), pp. 641–80.
4. *Mythe et pensée chez les Grecs* (Paris: Maspero, 1966), p. 205.
5. And the incest taboo? Already this all-powerful concept has lost its legitimacy. Cf. Deleuze and Guattari, *Capitalisme et schizophrénie: L'Anti-Oedipe* (Paris: Minuit, 1972), and also M. C. and E. Oritgues, *L'Oedipe africain* (Paris: Plon, 1966). etc.
6. That is, to the universalisation of a positivised libido and Eros that are 'liberated' as value, by which revolutionaries rejoin all the culturalist neo-Freudians in an optimistic, moralising vision. But the other, strictly Freudian perspective (normally connoting 'pessimism') is based on the economic interpretation (the Nirvana principle and a resolution of tensions). Although this interpretation takes the problem of death into account, it contradicts all traditional humanism (idealist or revolutionary), resting instead on a conception of man in terms of instincts. This 'materialist' vision is also moral and is secretly directed by Law, an instance of sublimation and repression, and hence the finality of a resolution of these instincts either in the transgression of this Law (the pleasure principle) or in repression (Nirvana principle). In neither case can a resolution of Law be envisioned.
7. *Science* (Paris), March, 1967.
8. Yet it was repeatedly intersected by contradictory, heretical currents, which in their protest were always attached to 'naturism': a rehabilitation of nature, a beyond of Christianity most often expressed only by a nostalgia for the origins of Christianity. From St Francis of Assisi with his Christ-like angelicism (all creatures praise God, etc.) – but St Francis was a sort of fire fighter for the Catholic Church quenching the flames of the Cathar and pantheist heresies that threatened to engulf the whole Western world – to Spinoza with his subtle and impious pantheism (God is everywhere in Nature, thus he is nowhere) and all the Adamite sects that preached the refusal of labour and the resurrection of the body, and dreamt of abolishing the very finality of the Christian order (its principle of transcendence and sublimation) in their immediate demand for the end of the whole world and for 'Paradise now'. Against all these naturalist, pantheistic, mystical, libertarian and millenarian heresies, the Church always defended, along with the original break with nature, a morality of effort and merit, of labour and works, which was coupled with the evolution of the order of production and connected with the political dimension of power.

9. Likewise, structural linguistics cannot account for the emergence of language as a *means of communication*: it can only analyse its functioning, and thus its reproduction, as such. But this destination of language, which linguistics takes as an axiom, is merely an extraordinary reduction of language (and hence of the 'science' that analyses it). And what operates in this 'science', in the last instance, is the reproduction of this arbitrary model of language. Similarly, the structural analysis of capital only leads back to its principle of logical reality (in which 'science' itself participates).

11

DESERTIFICATION†

Jean Baudrillard

In the 1980s and 1990s Baudrillard has become something of a media celebrity, achieving a certain notoriety for his iconoclastic views. Books like America *(1986) and* Cool Memories *(1987), with their self-consciously glossy, coffee-table format, have helped to cement his reputation as one of the most deliberately provocative – and marketable – of postmodern thinkers.* America *describes a journey around the USA in which Baudrillard deliberately seeks to shed his 'European' desire to explain and analyse cultural phenomena, instead of just experiencing them in uncritical fashion. The goal is to reach a state of 'desertification', where the self has been stripped down to its bare essentials: a condition which suggests a Zen Buddhist approach to existence. In effect, what Baudrillard is outlining in* America *is a post-Marxist aesthetic, where value judgement is to be utterly avoided.* America, *and the concept of desertification in particular, is indicative of where the logic of the more radical forms of* post-Marxism *can lead, and could hardly be further from the classical Marxist desire to reduce all cultural phenomena to the workings of a teleological dialectic.*

American culture is heir to the deserts, but the deserts here are not part of a Nature defined by contrast with the town. Rather they denote the emptiness, the radical nudity that is the background to every human institution. At the same time, they designate human institutions as a metaphor of that emptiness and the work of man as the continuity of the desert, culture as a mirage and as the perpetuity of the simulacrum.

The natural deserts tell me what I need to know about the deserts of the sign. They teach me to read surface and movement and geology and immobility at the same time. They create a vision expurgated of all the rest: cities, relationships, events, media. They induce in me an exalting vision of the desertification of signs and men. They form the mental frontier where the projects of civilisation run into the ground. They are outside the sphere and circumference of desire. We should always appeal to the deserts against

† From J. Baudrillard, *America*, trans. Chris Turner, London: Verso, 1988 (pp. 63–4, 66–71, 123–4).

the excess of signification, of intention and pretention in culture. They are our mythic operator. [. . .]

Death Valley is as big and mysterious as ever. Fire, heat, light: all the elements of sacrifice are here. You always have to bring something into the desert to sacrifice, and offer it to the desert as a victim. A woman. If something has to disappear, something matching the desert for beauty, why not a woman?

Nothing is more alien to American deserts than symbiosis (loose-fitting clothing, slow rhythms, oases) such as you find in native desert cultures. Here, everything human is artificial. Furnace Creek is a synthetic, air-conditioned oasis. But there is nothing more beautiful than artificial coolness in the midst of heat, artificial speed in the middle of a natural expanse, electric light under a blazing sun, or the artificial practice of gambling in lost casinos. Reyner Banham is right: Death Valley and Las Vegas are inseparable; you have to accept everything at once, an unchanging timelessness and the wildest instantaneity. There is a mysterious affinity between the sterility of wide open spaces and that of gambling, between the sterility of speed and that of expenditure. That is the originality of the deserts of the American West; it lies in that violent, electric juxtaposition. And the same applies to the whole country: you must accept everything at once, because it is this telescoping that gives the American way of life its illuminating, exhilarating side, just as, in the desert, everything contributes to the magic of the desert. If you approach this society with the nuances of moral, aesthetic, or critical judgement, you will miss its originality, which comes precisely from its defying judgement and pulling off a prodigious confusion of effects. To side-step that confusion and excess is simply to evade the challenge it throws down to you. The violence of its contrasts, the absence of discrimination between positive and negative effects, the telescoping of races, technologies, and models, the waltz of simulacra and images here is such that, as with dream elements, you must accept the way they follow one another, even if it seems unintelligible; you must come to see this whirl of things and events as an irresistible, fundamental datum.

The distinctions that are made elsewhere have little meaning here. It would be misguided to focus on aspects of an American civility that is often in fact far superior to our own (in our land of 'high culture') and then to point out that in other respects the Americans are barbarians. It would be wrong-headed to counterpose Death Valley, the sublime natural phenomenon, to Las Vegas, the abject cultural phenomenon. For the one is the hidden face of the other and they mirror each other across the desert, the one as acme of secrecy and silence, the other as acme of prostitution and theatricality.

Having said that, there is something mysterious about Death Valley *in itself*. However beautiful the deserts of Utah and California may be, this one is something else again – something sublime. The preternatural heat haze that enshrouds it, its inverse depth – below sea level – this landscape with its underwater features, its salt surfaces and mudhills, the high mountain chains surrounding it, making it a kind of inner sanctuary – a gentle, spectral place of initiation (which comes from its geological depth and the atmosphere of spiritual limbo). What has always struck me about Death Valley is its *mildness*, its pastel shades and its fossil veil, the misty fantasmagoria of its mineral opera. There is nothing funereal or morbid about it: a transverberation in which everything is palpable, the mineral softness of the air, the mineral substance of the light, the corpuscular fluid of the colours, the total extraversion of one's body in the heat. A fragment of another planet (at least predating any form of human life), where another, deeper temporality reigns, on whose surface you float as you would on salt-laden waters. The senses, the mind, and even your sense of belonging to the human race are all numbed by the fact of having before you the pure, unadulterated sign of 180 million years, and therefore the implacable enigma of your own existence. It is the only place where it is possible to relive, alongside the physical spectrum of colours, the spectrum of the inhuman metamorphoses that preceded us, our successive historical forms: the mineral, the organic, salt desert, sand dunes, rock, ore, light, heat, everything the earth has been, all the inhuman forms it has been through, gathered together in a single anthologising vision.

The desert is a natural extension of the inner silence of the body. If humanity's language, technology, and buildings are an extension of its constructive faculties, the desert alone is an extension of its capacity for absence, the ideal schema of humanity's disappearance. When you come out of the Mojave, writes Banham, it is difficult to focus less than fifteen miles ahead of you. Your eye can no longer rest on objects that are near. It can no longer properly settle on things, and all the human or natural constructions that intercept your gaze seem irksome obstacles which merely corrupt the perfect reach of your vision. When you emerge from the desert, your eyes go on trying to create emptiness all around; in every inhabited area, every landscape they see desert beneath, like a watermark. It takes a long time to get back to a normal vision of things and you never succeed completely. Take this substance from my sight! . . . But the desert is more than merely a space from which all substance has been removed. Just as silence is not what remains when all noise has been suppressed. There is no need to close your eyes to hear it. For it is also the silence of time.

And even the foreshortening effect of cinema is present in Death Valley, for all this mysterious geology is also a scenario. The American desert is an extraordinary piece of drama, though in no sense is it theatrical like an Alpine landscape, nor sentimental like the forest or the countryside. Nor eroded and monotonous like the sub-lunar Australian desert. Nor mystical like the deserts of Islam. It is purely, geologically dramatic, bringing together the sharpest, most ductile shapes with the gentlest, most lascivious underwater forms – the whole metamorphism of the earth's crust is present in synthesis, in a miraculous abridged version. All the intelligence of the earth and its elements gathered together here, in a matchless spectacle: a geological epic. Cinema is not alone in having given us a cinematic vision of the desert. Nature itself pulled off the finest of its special effects here, long before men came on the scene.

It is useless to seek to strip the desert of its cinematic aspects in order to restore its original essence; those features are thoroughly superimposed upon it and will not go away. The cinema has absorbed everything – Indians, *mesas*, canyons, skies. And yet it is the most striking spectacle in the world. Should we prefer 'authentic' deserts and deep oases? For us moderns, and ultramoderns, as for Baudelaire, who knew that the secret of true modernity was to be found in artifice, the only natural spectacle that is really gripping is the one which offers both the most moving profundity *and at the same time the total simulacrum of that profundity*. As here, where the depth of time is revealed through the (cinematic) depth of field. Monument Valley is the geology of the earth, the mausoleum of the Indians, and the camera of John Ford. It is erosion and it is extermination, but it is also the tracking shot, the movies. All three are mingled in the vision we have of it. And each phase subtly terminates the preceding one. The extermination of the Indians put an end to the natural cosmological rhythm of these landscapes, to which their magical existence was bound for millennia. With the arrival of pioneer civilisation an extremely slow process gave way to a much quicker one. But this process itself was overtaken fifty years later by the tracking shots of the cinema which speeded up the process even more and, in a sense, put an end to the disappearance of the Indians by reviving them as extras. Thus this landscape has been witness to all the great events both of geology and anthropology, including some of the most recent. Hence the exceptional scenic qualities of the deserts of the West, combining as they do the most ancestral of hieroglyphs, the most vivid light, and the most total superficiality.

Colours there seem rarefied, detached from all substance, diffracted into the air, floating on the surface of things. Hence the spectral, ghostly, and at the same time veiled, translucent, calm, and subtle impression made by these landscapes. And the mirage effect – a temporal mirage too – which comes near to total illusion. The rocks, sands, crystals, and cacti are eternal, but they are also ephemeral, unreal, and detached from their substance. The vegetation is minimal, but indestructible, and each new spring sees a miracle of bloom. By contrast, light itself has substance here. Floating like a powder on the air, it gives all shades of colour that pastel nuance that seems the very image of disincarnation, of the separation of the body from the spirit. In this sense, one may speak of the abstraction of the desert, of a deliverance from the organic, a deliverance that is beyond the body's abject passage into carnal inexistence, into that dry, luminous phase of death in which the corruption of the body reaches completion. The desert is beyond this accursed phase of decomposition, this humid phase of the body, this organic phase of nature.

The desert is a sublime form that banishes all sociality, all sentimentality, all sexuality. Words, even when they speak of the desert, are always unwelcome. Caresses have no meaning, except from a woman who is herself of the desert, who has that instantaneous, superficial animality in which the fleshly is combined with dryness and disincarnation. And yet, in another sense, there is nothing to match night falling in its shroud of silence on Death Valley, seen from broken-down, worn-out motel chairs on the verandah, looking out over the dunes. The heat does not fall off here. Only night falls, its darkness pierced by a few car headlights. And the silence is something extraordinary, as though it were itself all ears. It is not the silence of cold, nor of barrenness, nor of an absence of life. It is the silence of the whole of this heat over the mineral expanses that stretch out before us for hundreds of miles, the silence of the gentle wind upon the salt mud of Badwater, caressing the ore deposits of Telegraph Peak. A silence internal to the Valley itself, the silence of underwater erosion, below the very waterline of time, as it is below the level of the sea. No animal movement.

Nothing dreams here, nothing talks in its sleep. Each night the earth plunges into perfectly calm darkness, into the blackness of its alkaline gestation, into the happy depression of its birth. [. . .]

No desire: the desert. Desire is still something deeply natural, we live off its vestiges in Europe, and off the vestiges of a moribund critical culture. Here the cities are mobile deserts. No monuments and no history: the exaltation of mobile deserts and simulation. There is the same wildness in the endless, indifferent cities as in the intact silence of the Badlands. Why is LA, why are the deserts so fascinating? It is because you are delivered from all depth there – a brilliant, mobile, superficial neutrality, a challenge to meaning and profundity, a challenge to nature and culture, and outer hyperspace, with no origin, no reference-points.

No charm, no seduction in all this. Seduction is elsewhere, in Italy, in certain landscapes that have become paintings, as culturalised and refined in their design as the cities and museums that house them. Circumscribed, traced-out, highly seductive spaces where meaning, at these heights of luxury, has finally become adornment. It is exactly the reverse here: there is no seduction, but there is an absolute fascination – the fascination of the very disapperance of all aesthetic and critical forms of life in the irradiation of an objectless neutrality. Immanent and solar. The fascination of the desert: immobility without desire. Of Los Angeles: insane circulation without desire. The end of aesthetics.

12

PASSAGES TO POSTMODERNITY: THE RECONSTITUTION OF CRITICAL HUMAN GEOGRAPHY†

Edward W. Soja

Postmodernity involves new ideas about the disposition, perception, and mapping of space, and a distinctive 'postmodern geography' has grown up in order to outline these. Edward W. Soja's Postmodern Geographies *(1989) is one of the key texts in this area, and he takes the contemporary crisis in human geography (including 'Marxist geography') as a subject, to be an integral part of the postmodern condition. In the extract below, Soja examines the relationship of Marxist to postmodern geography, through an analysis of the work of some of the leading Marxist geographers of recent times. He notes a disintegration of Marxist categories in the wake of the debate on 'the significance of spatiality' in late twentieth-century social theory (sociology and urban studies, for example): a debate in which postmodernists have been highly active. The ultimate goal for Soja is to create a 'postmodern critical human geography' which would draw upon, but not be bound by, the tradition of Western Marxism. What such a post-Marxist geography would take from Marxism would be its political agenda (the emancipation of the oppressed, and so on), while rejecting its claims to absolute authority. The suspicion of universal theory that is such a distinguishing feature of the postmodern outlook (and such a source of irritation to classical Marxists) is again well to the fore.*

Bringing up to date the development of Marxist geography and its attendant re-theorisation of the historical geography of capitalism is a necessarily eclectic exercise. It can now be said that geographical modes of analysis are more centrally attached to contemporary political and theoretical debates than at any other time in this century. But the attachment derives from many different sources, takes a variety of forms, and resists easy synthesis. It is also still very tentative and limited in its impact, for the spatialisation of critical theory and the construction of a new historico-geographical materialism have only just begun and their initial impact has been highly disruptive, especially for the two modernist traditions that have shaped the development of Marxist geography over the past twenty years.

† From E. W. Soja, *Postmodern Geographies: The Reassertion of Space in Critical Social Theory*, London: Verso, 1989 (pp. 60–75).

Just as contemporary Western Marxism seems to have exploded into a hetero-geneous constellation of often cross-purposeful perspectives, Modern Geography has also started to come apart at its seams, unravelling internally and in its old school ties with the other nineteenth-century disciplines that defined the modern academic divi-sion of labour. The grip of older categories, boundaries, and separations is weakening. What was central is now being pushed to the margins, while the once tactful fringes boldly assert a new-found centrality. The shifting, almost kaleidoscopic, intellectual terrain has become extremely difficult to map for it no longer appears with its familiar, time-worn contours.

This unsettled and unsettling geography is, I suggest, part of the postmodern con-dition, a contemporary crisis filled, like the Chinese pictograph for crisis and Berman's vaporous description of modernity in transition, with perils and new possibilities; filled with the simultaneous shock of the old and the new. To bring back an earlier argument, another culture of time and space seems to be taking shape in this contemporary context and it is redefining the nature and experience of everyday life in the modern world – and along with it the whole fabric of social theory. I would locate the onset of this passage to postmodernity in the late 1960s and the series of explosive events which together marked the end of the long post-war boom in the capitalist world economy. And to identify the most insightful early cartographers of this portentous transition, I would turn again to the prefigurative writings of Lefebvre and Foucault, Berger and Mandel, for it is there that the geography of postmodernisation was most acutely perceived. Although the links between them are not always direct and intentional, the intellectual trajectories of these four foundational postmodern geographers intersect in the contemporary deconstruction and reconstitution of modernity. I will use them once more to help explore the variegated postmodern landscapes of critical human geography.

THE CONVERGENCE OF THREE SPATIALISATIONS

Lefebvre, Foucault, Berger and Mandel all crystallised their assertions of the sig-nificance of spatiality at a crucial historical moment, when the most severe global economic crisis since the Great Depression had signalled to the world the end of the post-war boom and the onset of a profound restructuring that would reach into every sphere of social life and shatter the conventional wisdoms built upon simplistic projections from the immediate past. Although Mandel is not quite so explicit, the other three clearly rotate their arguments around the realisation that it is now space more than time that hides things from us, that the demystification of spatiality and its veiled instrumentality of power is the key to making practical, political, and theoretical sense of the contemporary era.

Juxtaposing these arguments sets in motion a creative convergence between three different paths of spatialisation that I shall call 'posthistoricism', postfordism', and 'postmodernism'. The first of these spatialisations is rooted in a fundamental refor-mulation of the nature and conceptualisation of social being, an essentially ontological struggle to rebalance the interpretable interplay between history, geography, and society. Here the reassertion of space arises against the grain of an ontological historicism that has privileged the separate constitution of being in time for at least the past century.

The second spatialisation is directly attached to the political economy of the material world and, more specifically, to the 'fourth modernisation' of capitalism, the most recent phase of far-reaching socio-spatial restructuring that has followed the end of the long post-war economic boom. The term 'postfordism' is tentatively chosen to characterise the transition from the regime of accumulation and mode of regulation that consolidated after the Great Depression around large-scale, vertically-integrated, industrial production systems; mass consumerism and sprawling suburbanisation; the centralised Keynesian planning of the welfare state; and increasing corporate oligopoly.[1] Here too it can be argued that space makes a critical difference, that revealing how spatial restructuring hides consequences from us is the key to making political and theoretical sense of the changing political economy of the contemporary world.

The third spatialisation is couched in a cultural and ideological reconfiguration, a changing definition of the experiential meaning of modernity, the emergence of a new, postmodern culture of space and time. It is attuned to changes in the way we think about and respond to the particularities – the perils and possibilities – of the contemporary moment via science, art, philosophy, and programmes for political action. Postmodernism overlaps with posthistoricism and postfordism as a theoretical discourse and a periodising concept in which geography increasingly matters as a vantage point of critical insight.

The confluence of these three spatialisations is effectively exemplified in the recent work of Fredric Jameson, perhaps the pre-eminent American Marxist literary critic. In an essay entitled 'Postmodernism, or the Cultural Logic of Late Capitalism', Jameson captures the spatial specificity of the contemporary *Zeitgeist*.

> Postmodern (or multinational) space is not merely a cultural ideology or fantasy, but has genuine historical (and socio-economic) reality as a third great original expansion of capitalism around the globe (after the earlier expansions of the national market and the older imperialist system, which each had their own cultural specificity and generated new types of space appropriate to their dynamics). . . . We cannot [therefore] return to aesthetic practices elaborated on the basis of historical situations and dilemmas which are no longer ours . . . the conception of space that has been developed here suggests that a model of political culture appropriate to our own situation will necessarily have to raise spatial issues as its fundamental organising concern. (Jameson, 1984: 88–9)

Jameson derives much of his conceptualisation of space from the *Raumgeist* of Lefebvre, whom he helped to reach a larger American audience in the early 1980s. But there are other echoes to be heard. Jameson provisionally defines the spatialised model of radical political culture appropriate to the contemporary (postmodern) situation as an 'aesthetic of cognitive mapping', an ability to see in the cultural logic and forms of postmodernism an instrumental cartography of power and social control; in other words, a more acute way of seeing how space hides consequences from us.

He refers specifically to the work of Kevin Lynch (1960) on 'images of the city', but the insinuating connections link back not only to Lefebvre and Berger but also to Foucault. Foucault's 'carceral city' of cells, ranks, and enclosures, for example, is transposed by Jameson on to the landscape of perhaps the quintessential postmodern place, Los Angeles, the production site for some of the most pervasive and persuasive cognitive imagery in the world today.[2] Jameson maps out from Los Angeles and other postmodern landscapes, material and literary, a hidden and insidious human geography that must become the target for a radical and postmodern politics of resistance, a means of tearing off the gratuitous veils that have been drawn over the instrumentality of contemporary restructuring processes.

Foucault's own explicit but more deflected emphasis on spatiality has already been discussed. His archeology and genealogy of knowledge provided an important passageway to the postmodern cultural critique of spatiality and the cartography of power. Instead of abandoning radical politics, as Anderson and others have claimed he did, Foucault added his voice to Lefebvre's in spatialising the political project of the Left. 'The real political task in a society such as ours', Foucault writes, 'is to criticize the working of institutions which appear to be both neutral and independent; to criticize them in such a manner that the political violence which has always exercised itself obscurely through them will be unmasked, so that one can fight them' (see Rabinow, 1984: 6).[3] The 'fight' extends beyond the exploitative institutions of capitalism alone to all 'disciplinary technologies' wherever they are found, even in the realms of existing socialisms. This delineation of spatial struggle is but one step away from Jameson's postmodernism of resistance. It is an expressly geopolitical strategy in which spatial issues are the fundamental organising concern, for disciplinary power proceeds primarily through the organization, enclosure, and control of individuals in space.[4]

Jameson's use of postmodernism as a periodising concept brings us to the Mandelian connection in the contemporary reassertion of space in critical social theory. Jameson draws directly from Mandel's interpretation of *Late Capitalism* (Mandel, 1975) and the changing role of geographically uneven development, in which Mandel makes the key conjunction between periodisation and spatialisation in the macropolitical economy of capitalism. The 'long wave' periodicity of crisis and restructuring defines not only a series of historical eras but simultaneously a sequence of spatialities, a changing regional configuration of 'uneven and combined' capitalist development that can be mapped on to the sequence of modernities discussed in the preceding chapter. This spatio-temporal patterning plays a significant role in Jameson's critique of reactionary postmodernism and in a wide range of contemporary studies of postfordist economic restructuring. It also provides a useful framework through which to examine the changing urban, regional, and international geography of capitalism – what contemporary analysts have begun to describe as capitalism's multi-layered spatial divisions of labour (Massey, 1984).

There is still one more important passage to postmodernity to be explored, one more arena in which the three spatialisations have begun to converge. This is the postmodern deconstruction and reconstitution of Marxist geography itself, a story which will be told again, in many different ways, in every subsequent chapter. Here,

I intend only to introduce and outline a few of the most important contemporary debates and developments.

THE POSTMODERNISATION OF MARXIST GEOGRAPHY

Marxist geography has changed significantly in the 1980s. Its boundaries have broadened and become more flexibly defined so that its influence extends more deeply into the realms of critical social theory than ever before. At the same time, its centre of gravity has become more difficult to locate except as part of a larger project of insistent spatialisation, wherein traditional Marxist categories and definitions of geography are becoming significantly disassembled and rearranged. Adding to the confusion, a new zest for the empirical has turned many Marxist geographers away from open theoretical debate just when the debate has reached a much larger – and more critical – audience. The passage to postmodernity thus seems to be having a distinctively disintegrating effect.

This disintegration should come as no surprise, especially to those attuned to the influential writings of David Harvey, who, more than any other geographer, has shaped and continues to shape the course of Marxist geographical inquiry. As Harvey notes over and over again:

> The insertion of concepts of space and space relations, of place, locale, and milieu, into any of the various supposedly powerful but spaceless social theoretical formulations has the awkward habit of paralyzing that theory's central propositions . . . Whenever social theorists actively interrogate the meaning of geographical and spatial categories, either they are forced to so many ad hoc adjustments that their theory splinters into incoherence or they are forced to rework very basic propositions. (1985b: xiii)

Harvey also links, in his more recent work at least, the disruptive effects of spatialisation with the rigidities of historicism in Western Marxism as well as in the liberal social sciences.

> Marx, Marshall, Weber and Durkheim all have this in common: they prioritise time and history over space and geography and, where they treat of the latter at all, tend to view them unproblematically as the stable context or site for historical action . . . The way in which space relations and the geographical configurations are produced in the first place passes, for the most part, unremarked, ignored . . . Marx frequently admits of the significance of space and place in his writings . . . [but] geographical variation is excluded as an 'unnecessary complication'. His political vision and his theory are, I conclude, undermined by his failure to build a systematic and distinctively geographical and spatial dimension into his thought. (1985c: 141–3)

These passages mark a significant shift of emphasis in Harvey's work and highlight many of the dilemmas currently facing Marxist geography and geographers.

In *Limits to Capital* (1982), Harvey reached out from the heart of Marxist geography to the wider realm of Western Marxism and modern critical social theory, presenting a demonstrative argument for a spatialised Marxism and a spatialised critique of capitalist development. Giving a concrete geography to *Capital* and to capitalism, however, was at once a major *tour de force* and an invitation to theoretical paralysis. *Limits* thus combined, incongruously, both the crowning achievement of formalistic Marxist geography and the opening salvoes for the necessary deconstruction and reconstitution of this very achievement. Recognising this stressful ambivalence and the possibility that he might have to pull the tightly woven rug from under himself, Harvey almost abandoned the project. Encouraged by ex-students and other supporters, however, Harvey completed his masterful synthesis hoping, it would seem, that the disruptive impact of 'inserting' space would not diminish the force of his avowedly historical and geographical materialism.

Looking back at the critical response to *Limits*, Harvey expressed his concern that most readers seemed to be somewhat confused over the message it was presenting. In the preface to *Consciousness and the Urban Experience*, he notes:

> Curiously, most reviewers passed by (mainly, I suspect, out of pure disciplinary prejudice) what I thought to be the most singular contribution of that work – the integration of the production of space and spatial configurations as an active element within the core of Marxist theorizing. That was the key theoretical innovation that allowed me to shift from thinking about history to historical geography and so to open the way to theorizing about the urban process as an active moment in the historical geography of class struggle and capital accumulation. (1985b: xii)

Most Marxist geographers got the message, but they were already convinced and many had begun their own turnarounds from earlier positions antagonistic to the provocative spatialisation of Western Marxism. In her preface to *Spatial Divisions of Labour: Social Structures and the Geography of Production* (1984: x), Doreen Massey writes:

> My basic aim had been to link the geography of industry and employment to the wider, and underlying structures of society . . . The initial intention, in other words, was to start from the characteristics of economy and society, and proceed to explain their geography. But the more I got involved in the subject, the more it seemed that the process was not just one way. It is also the case – I would argue – that understanding geographical organisation is fundamental to understanding economy and society. The geography of society makes a difference in the way it works.

> If this is true analytically, it is also true politically. For there to be any hope of altering the fundamentally unequal geography of British economy and society (and that of other capitalist countries, too), a politics is necessary which links questions of geographical distribution to those of social and economic organisation.

Massey takes her new path into an analysis of the locational particularities of 'spatial structures of production', seeking to open a middle ground of regional political economy freed from both the iron determination of capitalism's laws of motion and the inane indeterminacy of geographical empiricism.[5]

Neil Smith also strays cautiously off the path of Marxist orthodoxy to make a similar argument in the preface to his *Uneven Development: Nature, Capital and the Production of Space* (1984: xi):

> Occupying the common ground between the geographical and political tradi-
> tions, a theory of uneven development provides the major key to determining
> what characterizes the specific geography of capitalism. . . . But one cannot
> probe too far into the logic of uneven development without realizing that
> something more profound is at stake. It is not just a question of what capitalism
> does to geography but rather of what geography can do for capitalism . . . From
> the Marxist point of view, therefore, it is not just a question of extending the
> depth and jurisdiction of Marxist theory, but of pioneering a whole new facet
> of explanation concerning the survival of capitalism in the twentieth century . . .
> Geographical space is on the economic and political agenda as never before. The
> idea of the 'geographical pivot of history' takes on a more modern and more
> profound meaning than Mackinder could have imagined.

The prefatory admissions of Harvey, Massey, and Smith are not always followed to their appropriate denouement in the subsequent texts, for each is hesitant to engage too deeply in the necessarily transformative deconstruction of historical materialism and its despatialising master narratives. But while historicism is shielded from a rigorous and systematic critique, there is a new confidence regarding the theoretical and political significance of space. The need to justify and defend the theoretical assertion of a historical and geographical materialism is much less pressing than it once was. The time has come instead to demonstrate its political and empirical power through the analysis of the 'specific geography of capitalism':

> Geographical space is always the realm of the 'concrete and the particular'.
> Is it possible to construct a theory of the concrete and the particular in the
> context of the universal and abstract determinations of Marx's theory of capi-
> talist accumulation? This is the fundamental question to be resolved. (Harvey,
> 1985c: 144)

But as Mills stated, every cobbler thinks leather is the only thing. The outreach of this more theoretically confident and assertive Marxist geography is still both insufficiently comprehensible and uncomfortably threatening to the modern academic division of labour, with its reified disciplinary compartments and intellectual territoriality. Moreover, the attack is being launched from what many still perceive as a minor disciplinary backwater into the still sanctified domains of the historical imagination. Retaining the *imprimatur* of Marxism is enough to frighten the contemporary FRUMPs (formerly radical upwardly mobile professionals, a term Harvey uses in a recent polemical defence of his position – see Harvey et al., 1987), but to have the theoretical and empirical trials blazed by 'uppity' geographers has been more than the established market could bear. In the 1980s, even some of the most sympathetic and open-minded social analysts have begun to lash back at the determined space invaders, covering their disciplinary flanks against the disruptive effects of the 'postmodern' spatialisation of critical social theory and analysis.

The most immediate and direct response to the intrusions of Marxist geographers has come from sociologists who continue to assume that they are in control of the spatialisation of social theory, as indeed they largely have been, by default, since the late nineteenth century. Radical political economists have listened attentively to Harvey and the new Marxist geography but tend to keep their calculated distance, incorporating only the bare essentials of a spatialised Marxism. Marxist historians, when they recognise what is happening at all, typically respond by extending their best wishes (while tacitly assuming that radical historiography has already done what was necessary concerning geography years ago). But Marxist and radical Weberian sociologists have been more deeply involved in the spatialising project from the beginning and could not simply set it aside once it started to have a paralysing effect on their most cherished sociological propositions and principles. The spatialization of social theory, many felt, was going too far and needed to be appropriately disciplined.

The most prominent figure leading this sociological backlash has been Peter Saunders, whose work *Social Theory and the Urban Question* (1981, second edn 1986) provides an excellent and comprehensive overview of the historical development of urban social and spatial theory. David Harvey, immediately after observing the disintegrative impact of spatialisation on established theoretical propositions in the social sciences (see above), turns to Saunders's first edition of *Social Theory and the Urban Question* to exemplify his argument.

> Small wonder, then, that Saunders (1981: 278), in a recent attempt to save the supposed subdiscipline of urban sociology from such an ugly fate, offers the extraordinary proposition, for which no justification is or ever could be found, that 'the problems of space . . . must be severed from concern with specific social processes'.

Saunders is even more emphatic in the second edition, after having carefully surveyed the recent work of Marxist geographers. Summing up a chapter aimed explicitly at defining 'A non-spatial urban sociology', Saunders writes:

> Ever since the work of Robert Park early in this century, urban sociologists have been developing theoretical insights which have been undermined by the insistent attempt to mould them to a concern with space. It is time to rid ourselves of this theoretical straitjacket. It is time to put space in its place as a contingent factor to be addressed in empirical investigations rather than as an essential factor to be theorized in terms of its generalities. It is time for urban social theory to develop a distinctive focus on some aspect of social organization in space rather than attempting to sustain a futile emphasis on spatial organization

in society. It is time, in short, to develop a non-spatial urban sociology which, while recognizing the empirical significance of spatial arrangements, does not seek to elevate these arrangements to the status of a distinct theoretical object. (1986: 287–8)

Saunders rides fitfully to the rescue, in the nick of time, to put space in its same old place and to reify once more the traditional domain of Modern Sociology. In stripping urban sociology of a theoretical object that has anything to do with space or, for that matter, with the city, Saunders comes perilously close to vaporising urban social theory entirely. In the end, he slips backward into a 'sociology of consumption' as the definitive focus of theoretical and substantive concern, retaining the adjective 'urban' only as 'a matter of convention', a useful way to 'maintain the intellectual continuity of the field' (*Ibid.*, 289).

The debate on the 'specificity of the urban', that is to say, whether specifically urban social and spatial forms can provide an appropriate object for theorisation, has always been a source of confusion and disagreement within the coalition of geographers, sociologists, and political economists that had formed in the 1970s to develop a new critical interpretation of capitalist urbanisation. Much of the confusion arose from the equivocal conceptualisation of the 'urban question' presented by Manuel Castells, the coalition's most influential Marxist sociologist. On the one hand, Castells attacked the overspecifications of the urban from the Chicago School to its alleged 'left-wing' extension in the works of Henri Lefebvre, arguing that there was no specifically urban problematic. Seeing urbanism as a distinctive 'way of life' was an ideological smokescreen obscuring larger societal problems that are expressed in cities but are not confined, epistemologically and politically, to the urban context. On the other hand, Castells conveniently respecified the urban as a theoretical object by focusing on the urban politics of collective consumption and the mobilisation of distinctively urban social movements. While Castells would eventually extract himself from this epistemological trap, Saunders falls back into it in a desperate effort to maintain the 'intellectual continuity' and nominal disciplinary integrity of urban sociology.

The debate on the specificity of the urban was more than an exercise in epistemological gymnastics. From the beginning, it was a disciplinary conflict between radical sociology and Marxist geography over the spatialisation of social theory, over just how far the reassertion of space would be allowed to go. Castells's Althusserian concoction of the urban question deflected the bolder assertions of Lefebvre, who, far from fetishising the urban, was developing a more general argument that social struggle in the contemporary world, be it urban or otherwise, was inherently a struggle over the social production of space, a potentially revolutionary response to the instrumentality and uneven development of the specific geography of capitalism. In other words, the urban social movements and struggles over collective consumption that had become so central to what I am tempted to call 'Late Modern' radical sociology were being seen as part of a larger spatial problematic in capitalist development.

In the 1980s, however, there were new twists being given to these older debates. Marxist geographers such as Harvey, Smith, and others cut through their former ambivalence to join together in developing a transformative historical-geographical materialism, a much more radical project than the earlier call for a spatialised urban political economy. The project has been supported and sustained, as I have previously described, by a host of 'outsiders' as the debate on the significance of spatiality in social theory and social practice became more widespread than ever before. More significantly for the current discussion, new voices were heard from within Modern Sociology calling loudly for the insertion of space at the very heart of social theory – for an even greater spatialisation than had been achieved through the 1970s. The pesky geographers could still be brushed off as obsessive fetishizers, infatuated with their own 'leather'. Sociologists such as Anthony Giddens, John Urry, and a spatially reawakened Manuel Castells were another matter.

Castells's more recent work is marked by two apparent reversals if seen against the conventional portrayal of his earlier contributions to anglophonic urban sociology. The first comes from a softening of his stance against Henri Lefebvre and a greater willingness to accept the importance of an assertively spatial problematic in the interpretation of urban politics and sociology. The ever-slippery Castells never quite completes this reversal, but the following passage from *The City and the Grass Roots* (1983: 4) suggests a greater willingness to accommodate the Lefebvrean project:

> Space is not a 'reflection of society', it *is* society . . . Therefore, spatial forms, at least on our planet, will be produced, as all other objects are, by human action. They will express and perform the interests of the dominant class according to a given mode of production and to a specific mode of development. They will express and implement the power relationships of the state in an historically defined society. They will be realised and shaped by the process of gender domination and by state-enforced family life. At the same time, spatial forms will be earmarked by the resistance from exploited classes, from oppressed subjects, and from dominated women. And the work of such a contradictory historical process on the space will be accomplished on an already inherited spatial form, the product of former history and the support of new interests, projects, protests, and dreams. Finally, from time to time, social movements will arise to challenge the meaning of spatial structure and therefore attempt new functions and new forms.

Castells falls short of the postmodern proclamation that it is now space more than time, geography more than history, that hides consequences from us. But he seems at least more open to the possibility than he once had been.

Castells's second reversal is also not a complete about-face, but runs equally against the grain of conventional portrayals of his contributions to urban studies. It arises from a reinvigorated interest in industrial production and technology and its effects on the urbanisation process. Here Castells is part of a much larger shift of attention in contemporary urban and regional studies and in Marxist geography, that is not so much a denial of the importance of collective consumption issues as a recognition that the dynamics of industrial production and restructuring must be understood first, before we can make theoretical and practical sense of the politics and sociology of consumption. Castells might argue that this is what he has been saying all along, reminding those who criticised his supposed 'consumptionism' of his early works on urban industrialisation (for example, Castells and Godard, 1974). But he is currently pursuing these interests with renewed enthusiasm and insight (see Castells, 1985), alongside a growing group of postfordist, if not also postmodern, industrial and production-oriented urban geographers (see, for example, Scott and Storper, 1986).

Saunders tries hard to deflect the provocative spatial turns of Giddens and Urry, the apparent reversals of Castells, and the emboldened attempts by Marxist geographers to create a historical and geographical materialism, by appealing to the 'theoretical realist' philosophy of social science that Urry helped to develop (see Keat and Urry, 1982), Giddens draws heavily upon, and the geographer, Andrew Sayer (1984), has so carefully codified. Saunders uses his newfound theoretical realism to 'put space in its place' as merely a contingent factor to be addressed in empirical investigations rather than an essential part of social theorisation. In doing so, he attaches the sociological backlash to a larger philosophical and methodological debate that has confusingly shaped the postmodernisation of Marxist geography.

The impact of theoretical realism (Bhaskar, 1975, 1979; Harre, 1970; Harre and Madden, 1975) on the reassertion of space in social theory has been many-sided and far-reaching. With its flexible synthesis of structuralism and hermeneutics, its insistence on situating social theory and social practice in the conjunctural effects of time and space, and its adaptation of a Marxian notion of praxis whilst simultaneously subjecting Marxism to a vigorous 'contemporary' critique, theoretical realism seemed to provide an almost ideal epistemological framework for postmodern critical human geography. If it did not exist, it would have had to be invented! But it has filtered into the spatial discourse of the 1980s with a disruptive ambivalence, both helping and hindering the development of critical spatial theory.

Realist philosophy over the past decade has inspired the most systematic, forceful, and influential assertions of the significance of space in the construction of social theory, primarily via the structuration theory of Anthony Giddens. It has also provoked, largely through the work of Sayer (1982, 1984, 1985), a constrictive countercurrent which argues that Marx, Weber, Durkheim, and others, may have been justified in paying so little attention to space in their abstract theoretical work because 'the difference that space makes' is important only at the level of the concrete and empirical. The proper path for (post-Marxist?) geography to take is thus primarily an empirical one, leaving behind the grander theoretical debates, whether set in the mould of space-time structuration or historical-geographical materialism. More than any other event, this realist counter-assertion – propelled back to the empirical drawing-board by the perplexities for the left arising from the regressive victories of Ronald Reagan and Margaret Thatcher – helped to split the new Marxist geography consensus that had been emerging in the 1980s.

One of the effects of this disintegrative implosion has been to encourage the reactionary sociological backlash against Marxist geography and to move many erstwhile Marxist geographers to join in with plaintive '*mea culpas*'. Another effect has been a strategic Marxist retrenchment, led by David Harvey, to keep alive the project of historical-geographical materialism against the rising anti-theoretical (and frequently anti-Marxist) onslaught. Confrontations between these two rigidifying positions, complicated by growing confusion over exactly who is on what side, continue to fill the pages of *Antipode* and *Society and Space* and absorb perhaps too much of the energies of those involved.[6]

Fortunately, there has recently also begun to develop the glimmerings of a more reconstructive postmodern critical human geography arising from these still ongoing 'Late Modern'[7] confrontations. It continues to draw inspiration from the emancipatory rationality of Western Marxism but can no longer be confined within its contours, just as it cannot be constrained by the boundaries of Modern Geography. It can perhaps best be described as a flexible specialisation, to adopt a term from current research on postfordist industrial organisation and technology. Flexible specialisation in the workplace of critical human geography means a resistance to paradigmatic closure and rigidly categorical thinking; the capacity to combine creatively what in the past was considered to be antithetical/uncombinable; the rejection of totalising 'deep logics' that blinker our ways of seeing; the search for new ways to interpret the empirical world and tear away its layers of ideological mystification. It thus involves a temporary suspension of epistemological formalism to allow the new combinations of history and geography to take shape dialectically and pragmatically, unburdened by the biases of the past but guided nonetheless by the testing ground of praxis.

This emerging postmodern critical human geography must continue to be built upon a radical deconstruction, a deeper exploration of those critical silences in the texts, narratives, and intellectual landscapes of the past, an attempt to reinscribe and resituate the meaning and significance of space in history and in historical materialism. Spatial deconstruction aims to 'reverse the imposing tapestry' of the past, to use Terry Eagleton's words (Eagleton, 1986: 80), exposing the dishevelled tangle of threads that constitutes the intellectual history of critical social thought. This task has only just begun and is already meeting with fierce resistance, especially from those identified by Foucault as 'the pious descendants of time'. Spatial deconstruction must therefore also be sufficiently flexible to parry the reactionary thrusts of historicism and avoid the simplistic defence of anti-history or, even worse, a new and equally obfuscating spatialism. The objective is, after all, a politically charged historical geography, a spatio-temporal perspective on society and social life, not the resurrection of geographical determinism.

Deconstruction alone is not enough, however, no matter how effectively the critical silences are exposed. It must be accompanied by an at least tentative reconstruction grounded in the political and theoretical demands of the contemporary world and able to encompass all the scales of modern power, from the grand strategies of global geopolitics to the 'little tactics of the habitat', to again borrow from Foucault. This re-constituted critical human geography must be attuned to the emancipatory struggles of all those who are peripheralised and oppressed by the specific geography of capitalism (and existing socialism as well) – exploited workers, tyrannised peoples, dominated women. And it must be especially attuned to the particularities of contemporary restructuring processes and emerging regimes of 'flexible' accumulation and social regulation, not merely to display a newfound empirical prowess but to contribute to a radical postmodernism of resistance.

Flexible specialisation is again a necessary accompaniment to this strategic reconstruction of critical human geography, whether it be focused on the interpretation of the new technology and restructured organisational forms of the postfordist political economy, the cultural logic of postmodernism in art and ideology, or the ontological struggles of a posthistoricist critical theory. These three pathways of spatialisation and potentially radical spatial praxis must be combined as compatible, not competitive, fields and viewpoints. Similarly, the new zest for the empirical, even under the pretence of its political practicality, must not close off theoretical debate and discussion, for there is nothing so practical as good spatial theory.

Flexible deconstruction and reconstitution will not be easy, for it must contend not only with a continuing 'Late Modern' resistance carrying with it the privileged baggage of the past, but must also deal with a rising neo-conservative postmodernism flexing its muscles in the present, monopolising the debate on what now must be done to meet the challenges of a new modernity. Neo-conservative postmodernism is using deconstruction to draw even more obfuscating veils over the instrumentality of restructuring and spatialisation, reducing both history and geography to meaningless whimsy and pastiche (or to mere 'factuality' again) in an effort to celebrate the postmodern as the best of all possible worlds. Opposition to restructuring is made to appear as extremism, the very hope of resistance becomes tinged with the absurd. Marxism is equated only with totalitarianism; radical feminism becomes the destruction of the family; the anti-nuclear movement and radical environmentalism become Luddite foolsplay smashing the job-machines of benevolent high technology; socialist programmes become anachronistic visions of unobtainable utopias stupidly out-of-synch with an infinitely malleable capitalism. The end of modernism is joyfully proclaimed as if the creation of a radical and resistant postmodern political culture were impossible, as if the problems addressed by the various modern movements had disappeared, melted entirely into air.

The development of a radical political culture of postmodernism will accordingly require moving beyond rigorous empirical descriptions which imply scientific understanding but too often hide political meaning; beyond a simplistic anti-Marxism which rejects all the insights of historical materialism in the wake of an exposure of its contemporary weaknesses and gaps; beyond the disciplinary chauvinisms of an outdated academic division of labour desperately clinging to its old priorities; beyond a Marxist geography that assumes that a historical geographical materialism has already been created by merely inserting a second adjective. A new 'cognitive mapping' must be developed, a new way of seeing through the gratuitous veils of both reactionary postmodernism and late modern historicism to encourage the creation of a politicised spatial consciousness and a radical spatial praxis. The most important postmodern geographies are thus still to be produced.

NOTES

1. The most widely used term to describe this recent reconfiguration of capitalism has been 'post-industrial'. The term has its appeal, but misdirects our attention away from the continuing

centrality of industrial production and the labour process in the contemporary restructuring of capitalist societies. It is as absurd in its way as describing what has been happening as 'post-capitalism' or 'the end of ideology'.

2. In 1984, Jameson, Lefebvre, and I took a spiralling tour around the centre of Los Angeles, starting at the Bonaventure Hotel.

3. Despite a very sympathetic treatment of Foucault's spatialisations, Rabinow continues to describe Foucault's work, misleadingly I would argue, as 'a form of critical historicism'.

4. The spatial analytics of Foucault are being recaptured with particular *élan* by Derek Gregory and his students at the University of Cambridge. See Gregory (1994).

5. Massey's work has inspired a new obsession with 'localities' in British geographical research, a privileging of the particularities of place that has yet to prove particularly fruitful. The emphasis on localities has in turn engendered a growing debate on the theoretical implications of what is described as radical geography's 'empirical turn'. See the many recent articles on this debate in *Antipode* (Cooke, 1987; Smith, 1987; Cochrane, 1987; Gregson, 1987).

6. See especially the molehill of embittered commentaries instigated by Saunders and Williams (1986), a crude radical-baiting attack on the alleged Marxist-realist orthodoxy that the authors claim has captured British urban and regional studies. David Harvey's personal response (to what was indeed a personal attack), along with a series of largely self-serving reactions to the bubbling confusion of misrepresentations and shadow-boxing feints and left-crosses, has recently been published in *Society and Space* (Harvey et al., 1987) under the presumptuous title: 'Reconsidering Social Theory: a Debate'.

7. I use the term 'Late Modern' to refer to a continued defence of the modern intellectual division of labour – including Western Marxism and Modern Geography – but with a few contemporary and adaptive twists, such as recognising the impact of postfordist and postmodern restructuring processes. A brilliant example of this flexible halfway house of Late Modern Marxist geography is Harvey's paper, 'Flexible Accumulation Through Urbanization: Reflections on "Post-Modernism" in the American City' (1987).

BIBLIOGRAPHY

Bhaskar, R. (1979) *The Possibility of Naturalism*, Brighton: Harvester Press.

Bhaskar, R. (1975) *A Realist Theory of Science*, Leeds: Alma.

Castells, M. (1985) 'High Technology, Economic Restructuring, and the Urban-regional Process in the United States', in Castells (ed.) *High Technology, Space, and Society*, Beverly Hills: Sage, 11–40.

Castells, M. (1983) *The City and the Grass Roots*, Berkeley and Los Angeles: University of California Press.

Castells, M., and Godard, F. (1974) *Monopolville: l'entreprise, l'état, l'urbain*, Paris: Mouton.

Cochrane, A. (1987) 'What a Difference the Place Makes: the New Structuralism of Locality', *Antipode* 19, 354–63.

Cooke, P. (1987) 'Clinical Inference and Geographic Theory', *Antipode* 19, 69–78.

Eagleton, T. (1986) *Against the Grain: Essays 1975–1985*, London: Verso.

Gregory, D. (1994) *Geographical Imaginations*, Oxford: Blackwell.

Gregory, D., and Urry, J. (eds) (1985) *Social Relations and Spatial Structures*, London: Macmillan; and New York: St Martin's.

Gregson, N. (1987) 'The CURS Initiative: Some Further Comments', *Antipode* 19, 364–70.

Harre, R. (1970) *The Principles of Scientific Thinking*, London: Macmillan.

Harre, R., and Madden, E. (1975) *Causal Powers*, Oxford: Basil Blackwell.

Harvey, D. (1987) 'Flexible Accumulation Through Urbanisation: Reflections on "Post-modernism", in the American city', *Antipode* 19, 260–86.

Harvey, D. (1985b) *Consciousness and the Urban Experience*, Baltimore: Johns Hopkins University Press; and Oxford: Basil Blackwell.

Harvey, D. (1985c) 'The Geopolitics of Capitalism', in Gregory and Urry (eds) *Social Relations and Spatial Structures*, 126–63.

Harvey, D. (1982) *The Limits to Capital*, Oxford: Basil Blackwell; and Chicago: University of Chicago Press.

Harvey, D. et al. (1987) 'Reconsidering Social Theory: a Debate', *Environment and Planning D: Society and Space* 5, 367–434.

Jameson, F. (1984) 'Postmodernism', or the Cultural Logic of Late Capitalism', *New Left Review* 146, 53–92.

Keat, R. and Urry, J. (1982) *Social Theory as Science*, London: Routledge and Kegan Paul.

Lynch, K. (1960) *The Image of the City*, Cambridge, MA; and London, MIT Press.

Mandel, E. (1975) *Late Capitalism*, London: Verso.

Massey, D. (1984) *Spatial Divisions of Labour: Social Structures and the Geography of Production*, London and Basingstoke; Macmillan.

Rabinow, P. (ed.) (1984) *The Foucault Reader*, New York: Pantheon Books.

Saunders, P., and Williams, P. (1986) 'The New Conservatism: Some Thoughts on Recent and Future Development in Urban Studies', *Environment and Planning D: Society and Space* 4, 393–99.

Saunders, P. (1981; second ed. 1986) *Social Theory and the Urban Question*, London: Hutchinson.

Sayer, A. (1985) 'The Difference that Space Makes', in Gregory and Urry (eds), 49–66.

Sayer, A. (1984) *Method in Social Science: A Realist Approach*, London: Hutchinson.

Sayer, A. (1982) 'Explanation in Economic Geography: Abstraction versus Generalization', *Progress in Human Geography* 6, 68–88.

Scott, A., and Storper, M. (eds) (1986) *Production, Work, Territory: The Geographical Anatomy of Industrial Capitalism*, Boston: Allen and Unwin.

Smith, N. (1987) 'Dangers of the Empirical Turn: Some Comments on the CURS Initiative', *Antipode* 19, 59–68.

Smith, N. (1984) *Uneven Development*, Oxford: Basil Blackwell.

13

INTERNATIONAL RELATIONS
AS POLITICAL THEORY†

R. B. J. Walker

International Relations (IR) is an area in which Marxism has played a critical role, and the development of post-Marxism has considerable implications for the field. IR has been largely structured on a debate between two opposing factions: the Realists and the Idealists. Realists adopt a fairly empirical approach to issues of global power politics, whereas Idealists are operating within some form or other of universal theory (or 'grand narrative', in Lyotard's formulation). In the latter camp we find Marxists and neo-Marxists (the latter emphasising the conflicts between transnational capital and the nation State). The credibility of the Idealist paradigm has come under attack in recent years, given the collapse of the Soviet Empire and the general decline of Marxism as a global political force. Coupled with this shift in political paradigms has been a shift in theoretical paradigms, which also has posed problems for disciplines such as IR. Given the critique of the notion of identity and the championship of difference in postmodernism and poststructuralism, for example, it becomes increasingly difficult to defend the traditional conception of political sovereignty, where states are assumed to have clearly-definable national identities. One would have to say that the field of IR is, at the very least, receptive *to post-Marxist theorising. Rob Walker's work makes gestures in a post-Marxist direction from a broadly postmodernist perspective. In the extract from* Inside/Outside: International Relations as Political Theory *(1993) below, Walker insists that it is now necessary, post-Cold War, to rethink the nature, methodology, and assumptions of IR as a discipline. Walker's anti-universalist stance recalls that advanced in Laclau and Mouffe's model of post-Marxism.*

HISTORICAL MOMENTS

Attempts to come to terms with the complexities, contradictions and opportunities of contemporary political life participate in a widespread sense of accelerations, disjunctions and uncertainties. The swift succession of events is already enough to induce vertigo, even among journalists, policy-advisors and other mediators of the moment.

† From R. B. J. Walker, *Inside/Outside: International Relations as Political Theory*, Cambridge: Cambridge University Press, 1993 (pp. 1–11, 13–14).

Moreover, passing events draw much of their significance from broader readings of the twentieth century – and of modernity more generally – as an age of unprecedented innovations and transformations. 'All that is solid melts into air,' observed Marx in his paradigmatic account of the increasing dynamism of the modern world.[1] Paradoxically, perhaps, this remark has become more prescient than ever, despite, or perhaps even in part because of evaporating hopes for an alternative to the capitalism that has so completely transformed human life over the past half-millennium.

The most trenchant reminder that ours is an age of speed and temporal accelerations has been the simultaneous dissolution of Cold War geopolitics and rapid entrenchment of a globally organised capitalism across the territorial divisions of Europe. The year 1989 is now firmly enshrined as a symbol of historical ruptures that have been felt everywhere. Structural rigidities and ideological certainties have given way to social revolutions and territorial fluidities. Ritualised attitudes and postures have atrophied, scholarly literatures have been declared redundant and policy-making elites have been forced to regroup. Even the most up-to-date cartographies have acquired the antique aura of mid-century maps of a world carved into formal colonies and empires.

No doubt there are still suspicions that beneath the surprises and contingencies lies a fundamental continuity of human behaviour, some hidden hand of utilitarian efficiency or tragic necessity that must soon reappear. The eternal return of power politics or the decisive confirmation of established teleologies: these, it might be argued, offer a more appropriate interpretation of contemporary trajectories than wild claims about innovation and transformation. The latest news of geopolitical aggression or the arrogance of great powers readily inspires old memories. Claims about the vindication of favoured philosophies of history – about the slightly delayed end-of-ideology and the final supremacy of capitalism and/or modernity and/or liberalism – have become a central motif of contemporary political debate. Established orthodoxies still retain the courage – and self-righteousness – of their convictions.

Focusing upon dramatic events, it is undoubtedly tempting to exaggerate the novelty of novelty. Dissolutions of Cold War and the re-writing of Europe seem misleadingly momentous when interpreted only in relation to the entrenched expectations of a world carved up at Yalta and Bretton Woods. An old order may be giving way to the new but, it might be said, we are likely to see the emergence of a new order that looks suspiciously like the old. The players or the polarities may change but the rules of the game are likely to stay more or less the same. This, after all, is the lesson that continues to be taught in so many appeals to a canonical tradition of political realism and to be reenforced through claims about the core principles of an international balance of power.

Even so, neither the drama of apparently familiar geopolitical conflict nor the celebration of ideological victories have been able to erase a pervasive sense that the search for a lasting and stable order – for a resilient architecture that might withstand the assaults and erosions of temporal change, unexpected dangers and volatile fortunes – is increasingly tenuous. The demolition of the Berlin Wall may have signalled an opening across territorial space, but it equally signalled an awareness of temporal velocities and incongruities. Ancient memories and burnished resentments have meshed simultaneously with expanded credit and a sharp eye for the main chance. Nineteenth-century nationalisms thaw while geopolitical inertia gives way to an all-consuming global economy. Yalta may have established a settled order at the architectonic centre of world politics for almost half a century, but the speed of dissolution is more in keeping with the accelerative tendencies that have been charted by almost every account of modern economies, technologies and cultures as the most distinctive characteristic of the century itself. Dissolutions in Europe may have been followed by the concerted reassertion of great power dominance in the Persian Gulf, but even the imposition of a global military order by the greatest of great powers has seemed unlikely to restrain the unpredictable volatilities of regional antagonisms or the aspirations of oppressed peoples.

As a grand cliché about modernity, the claim that we live in an era of rapid transformations has even become a form of continuity among diverse currents of contemporary social and political thought. Ever since the possibility of a progressive history was elaborated during the European Enlightenment, modern thinkers have struggled to grasp the succession of events as an unfolding of a more or less reasonable, even rational process.

For early-modern writers like Hobbes, reason and order – both cosmological and socio-political – could be envisaged in relation to the discovery of permanent principles, the secular guarantees of a geometry that seemed to offer at least as good a bet as the increasingly dubious guarantees of Heaven. From the late eighteenth century, the guarantees of Reason were converted into the promises of History. For some, like Rousseau, these promises were distinctly ambiguous. For others, like Hegel, they were magnificent. Whether as Comtean positivism, Benthamite utilitarianism, Marxian revolution or Weberian disenchantment, subsequent social and political thought and practice has been articulated around powerful claims about change, novelty and transformation that have been common intellectual currency for at least two hundred years. Contemporary sociological research, for example, remains deeply indebted to the concern – shared by all the classical sociologists like Durkheim, and echoing Hobbes in a more historically minded age – with how a stable modern society can exist at all given the transformative quality of modern life.

In this context, contemporary vertigo has already acquired its own trusted antidote. The sense of acceleration that impressed so many thinkers in the late nineteenth and early twentieth centuries is easily turned from a problematic into a celebration. History, it can be said, is simply working out as it should. Development is evolutionary and progressive. The end of ideology is undeniably at hand. Modernity shall indeed be our salvation. If full-blooded Hegelianism or a crude theory of Progress seem to have too many side-effects, too much of the chauvinistic arrogance of nineteenth-century empires, a more benign treatment of rational choice theory, utilitarian ethics and the freedom of the market will suffice. And for those not wanting to seem too naive or trusting, the antidote may be swallowed with an appropriate coating of Rousseauean or Weberian scepticism. Modernity brings both emancipation and loss: not heaven on earth but the struggles of Sisyphus, the boring of hard boards, the demands of responsibility and community in a world in which secular principles have lost their heavenly glow.

Claims to novelty, in short, already have an appropriate location within the established conventions of contemporary intellectual life. Even the startling dissolutions and reconstitutions of 1989 can seem like business as usual once one is sedated by contemporary philosophies of history, by scholarly procedures that, no less than established political interests, are ready and willing to put novelties and uncertainties in their proper place.

Nevertheless, philosophies of history that depend on an affirmation – even a highly qualified affirmation – of the European Enlightenment or nineteenth-century theories of progress have themselves come to appear as artifacts of a world that has transformed beyond the imagination of eighteenth- and nineteenth-century prophets. Those philosophies of history are still captivated by a pervasive sense of space and territoriality. They promise to take us from here to there, from tradition to modernity, from modernity to postmodernity, from primitive to developed, from darkness into light. In this sense, they reproduce the fixing of temporality within spatial categories that has been so crucial in the construction of the most influential traditions of Western philosophy and socio-political thought. Whether moving from the dangers of sophistry to the eternal forms, from the sins of earth to the redemptions of eternity or from the vagaries of individual subjectivity to the objective certainties of nature, modern accounts of history and temporality have been guided by attempts to capture the passing moment within a spatial order: within, say, the invariant laws of Euclid, the segmented precision of the clock or the sovereign claims of territorial states.[2]

Interpretations of momentous events have again begun to sediment into manageable routines. Speculations about grand civilisational transformations have become more familiar as the blinkers of Cold War fade and a new millennium beckons. But the experience of temporality, of speed, velocity and acceleration, is more and more bewildering.

Despite the bewilderment, this experience is now richly inscribed in the contemporary imagination.[3] Discourses of military strategy express worries about contracting response times and instantaneous decisions rather than about the logistics of extended territorial spaces. Discourses of political economy speak about the enhanced mobility of capital compared with territorial constraints experienced by governments and labour. The language of probabilities and accelerations now familiar from astrophysics contrasts sharply with the restrained dynamics expressed in the great Newtonian synthesis of cosmic order. A popular culture of freeze-frames, instant replays and video simulations is widely interpreted as an expression of a rapidly changing world of speed and contingency that increasingly eludes the comprehension even of all those theories, those one dimensional echoes of Durkheim, Weber and Marx, that once captured the unprecedented dynamics of modernity with such conviction.

Whether in the context of traumatic events, of accounts of modernity as variations on the themes of spatial extension and historical progress, or of more recent readings of what has been characterised variously as a posthistorical or postmodern condition, contemporary claims about novelty pose a range of fundamental problems for contemporary political thought and practice. I am concerned to explore some of these problems by examining how they have come to be expressed by contemporary theories of international relations.[4]

Theories of international relations, I will argue, are interesting less for the substantive explanations they offer about political conditions in the modern world than as expressions of the limits of the contemporary political imagination when confronted with persistent claims about and evidence of fundamental historical and structural transformation. They can be read, as I will read them here, as expressions of a historically specific understanding of the character and location of political life in general. They can also be read, as I will also read them here, as a crucial site in which attempts to think otherwise about political possibilities are constrained by categories and assumptions that contemporary political analysis is encouraged to take for granted.

Theories of international relations are more interesting as aspects of contemporary world politics that need to be explained than as explanations of contemporary world politics. As such, they may be read as a characteristic discourse of the modern state and as a constitutive practice whose effects can be traced in the remotest interstices of everyday life. To ask how theories of international relations demarcate and discipline the horizons beyond which it is dangerous to pursue any political action that aspires to the rational, the realistic, the sensible, the responsible or even the emancipatory, is to become acutely aware of the discursive framing of spatiotemporal options that has left its mark in the quiet schism between theories of political possibility within and theories of mere relations beyond the secure confines of the modern territorial state. To ask how theories of international relations manage to constrain all intimations of a chronopolitics within the ontological determinations of a geopolitics, within the bounded geometric spaces of here and there, is to become increasingly clear about the rules under which it has been deemed possible to speak about politics at all. As discourses about limits and dangers, about the presumed boundaries of political possibility in the space and time of the modern state, theories of international relations express and affirm the necessary horizons of the modern political imagination. Fortunately, the necessary horizons of the modern political imagination are both spatially and temporally contingent.

HISTORICITY AND SPATIALITY

The problematic character of modern theories of international relations has been widely discussed, especially in relation to the presumed bankruptcy of established intellectual traditions, the untidy proliferation of research strategies, an unseemly dependence on the interests of specific states and cultures, and the hubris of empirical social science. In the readings to be developed here, however, I want to show how this general sense of dissatisfaction must become especially acute when the historically specific understandings of space and time that inform the primary categories and traditions of international relations theory are challenged by speculations about the accelerative tendencies of contemporary political life.

The most important expression of these understandings, indeed the crucial modern political articulation of all spatiotemporal relations, is the principle of state sovereignty. They are also apparent in persistent debates about the validity of claims about political realism in relation to equally persistent claims about historical and structural transformation. Consequently, much of my analysis is explicitly concerned with the specific spatiotemporal valorisations that may be traced in claims about state sovereignty and political realism. I will argue that, as they have been articulated as theories of international relations, claims about political realism are a historically specific consequence of contradictory ontological possibilities expressed by the principle of state sovereignty, and not, as is so often asserted, an expression of ahistorical essences and structural necessities.

At the very least, I am concerned to show that much more is going on in the construction of claims about state sovereignty and political realism than is usually apparent from even the most theoretically and methodologically sophisticated literature in the field. If it is true, as so many have concluded on the basis of diverse research strategies, that claims about state sovereignty and political realism simply fail to grasp the dynamics of contemporary world politics, then it is necessary to be clear about the conditions under which it has been assumed to be possible to engage with contemporary rearticulations of spatiotemporal relations. Familiar controversies about whether states are obstinate or obsolete, or whether so-called non-state actors play a significant role in contemporary world politics, or even whether states are becoming caught within networks of interdependence or functional regimes, do not take us very far in this respect. On the contrary, a large proportion of research in the field of international relations remains content to draw attention to contemporary innovations while simply taking a modernist framing of all spatiotemporal options as an unquestionable given. While it is not surprising that a discipline largely constituted through categories of spatial extension should experience difficulties coming to terms with problems of historical transformation and temporal acceleration, the implications of these difficulties have remained rather elusive.

Part of my aim in reading persistent claims about state sovereignty and political realism as attempts to resolve, or more usually to forget about, the spatiotemporal conditions of contemporary political practice, is to explore some of the implications of recent attempts to canvass the possibility of an explicitly critical attitude within the theory of international relations. Few would argue that such an attitude is now flourishing. Many even seem to feel that such an attitude would be undesirable. Certainly, the absence of a moment of critique in this context has provided one of the conventional measures by which to distinguish international relations theory from most other areas of contemporary social and political analysis. In fact, I will argue, the absence of a critical edge to most theories of international relations is a rather special case. The distinction between theories of international relations and other forms of social and political analysis is itself an expression of the limits of a political practice that seeks to be other than what it has already become within the spatial horizons of the territorial state.

While my analysis draws upon ideas and strategies of investigation that have become familiar from broad and still controversial literatures about postmodernity and poststructuralism, I am primarily concerned to show how moments of critique that are already present in modern theories of international relations have been lost or forgotten through textual strategies that conflate, polarise and reify specifically modern accounts of spatiotemporal relations. In this context, for example, I am interested not only in the pervasive discourses in which political realists constantly confront idealists and utopians, but also the manner in which the possibility of a critical theory of international relations has been erased by a privileging of epistemological and methodological prescriptions that simply take historically specific-modern-ontological options as a given. The spatial framing of the relation between an autonomous subject set apart from the objective world is especially crucial, for it resonates with the same modernist dichotomies that have been reified so smoothly within claims about state sovereignty and political realism. Epistemologies that simply affirm these dichotomies are not obviously the most appropriate place from which to investigate a world in which boundaries are so evidently shifting and uncertain.

As a theory, or complex of theories, constituted through claims about sovereign identity in space and time, international relations simply takes for granted that which seems to me to have become most problematic. I prefer to assume that any analysis of contemporary world politics that takes the principle of sovereign identity in space and time as an unquestioned assumption about the way the world is – as opposed to an often very tenuous claim made as part of the practices of modern subjects, including the legitimation practices of modern states – can only play with analogies and metaphors taken from discourses in which this assumption is also taken for granted: hence much of the contemporary appeal of utilitarian micro-economic theory as a way of explaining patterns of conflict and cooperation between states. For all that they have been advanced under the banner of an epistemologically rigorous social science, utilitarian stories about rational action remain explicitly literary devices and carry enormous ontological and ideological baggage. Shifting allusions from that which is assumed to be known – the rational action of sovereign individuals in a market – to that which has to be explained – the rational/irrational action of sovereign states in an anarchical system/society – they especially have encouraged the uncritical affirmation of claims to sovereign identity in space and time that might be better placed under rather more critical suspicion.

While my explicit focus is on modern Anglo-American theories of international relations, and on attempts to develop a critical posture towards them, I am also concerned with broader theoretical analyses of the rearticulation of spatiotemporal relations in late or postmodernity, and with what the specific experiences of international relations theory might tell us about the limits of our ability to comprehend and respond to contemporary spatiotemporal transformations more generally. Reading theories of international relations as a constitutive horizon of modern politics in the territorial state, I want to clarify some of the difficulties besetting attempts to envisage any other kind of politics, whether designated as a world politics encompassing the planet, as a local politics arising from particular places, or as somehow both at once

– the possibility that seems to me to be both the most interesting but also the one that is explicitly denied by modernist assumptions about sovereign identity in space and time.

In this broader context, especially, it is difficult to avoid two sources of controversy that have become apparent in the contrasting meanings now assigned to modernity and to the designation of the present as either post or late. Both the character and contemporary fate of modernity are difficult to pin down in this respect. On the one hand, modernity has been characterised as either a privileging of space over time or as a culture of historical and temporal self-consciousness. On the other, contemporary accelerations have been understood as a reassertion of either temporality or spatiality.

As they have descended from claims about the ancients and the moderns, claims about modernity usually refer to a form of life associated with the emergence of those autonomous subjectivities and unbridgeable chasms charted by Descartes, Galileo and Hobbes, celebrated by Kant, and reified in popular characterisations of Enlightentment reason. As they have descended from various cultural movements over the past century or so, they refer more to a sensitivity to the fragility of those autonomous subjectivities and the impossibility of those chasms between subject and object, language and world or knower and known. The theme of modernity as an era not only of rapid socio-political, economic and technological transformations but also of a new consciousness of temporality and the contingency of specifically modern experiences, has been especially familiar since the late nineteenth century. In fact, much of the recent literatures on the dynamics of late or postmodernity, as on late capitalism, may be read as a recovery and extension of ideas once associated with, say, Baudelaire, Bergson and Nietzsche as well as Marx.[5] Many of these ideas have long been explored in relation to literature and aesthetics under the rubric of modernism, although they have been largely erased from the dominant currents of social and political thought in favour of the progressivist teleologies of modernisation theory. Where many of the characteristic themes of postmodern and poststructuralist thought seem strange and even dangerous in the context of ideologies of modernisation, they are more likely to seem quite familiar to those who understand modern cultural forms precisely as responses to the renewed appreciation of temporality and contingency that was so characteristic of late nineteenth- and early twentieth-century intellectual life in Europe.

While much of the contemporary concern with speed and acceleration may be found in intellectual currents that are modern in this latter sense, as well as in currents that are more convinced that modernity is an evaporating condition, theories of international relations remain deeply informed by the ontological horizons of early modernity, although many elements of the late-nineteenth-century crisis of historicism are readily visible in some versions of the claim to political realism. In fact, I will argue, reiterated appeals to political realism simply obscure contradictions that have long been troublesome to theorists of modernity. This is especially the case with recently influential attempts to articulate a so-called structural or neorealist theory of international relations, attempts which I read as yet another attempt to avoid serious ontological difficulties through a gratuitous appeal to epistemological necessities.

The double diagnosis of modernity as a field of spatial separations or of historical consciousness encourages a double diagnosis of contemporary trajectories. Some writers identify modernity in relation to characteristic claims about evolutionary teleology and progressive history. Impressed by the speed and accelerations of the contemporary era, they speak of a new spatial awareness, characterising postmodernity as a transition from time to space, from temporal continuities to spatial dislocations. Others, focusing more on the constitutive moments of early-modern thought, analyse modernity primarily in spatial terms, notably in relation to the spatial separation of the self-conscious ego from the objective world of nature, the aesthetics of three dimensional perspective, and the demarcations of the territorial state. Contemporary conditions are then understood as a revalorisation of temporality.

The historical and theoretical problems posed by these contrasting conceptions of the spatio-temporal character of modernity are obviously very complex, and pose serious difficulties for the analysis of contemporary political life. They are implicated, for example, in an important tension within the literature on modern political economy. Much of this literature has inherited Marx's insight that the dynamic character of capitalism implied the inevitable destruction of space by time: all that is solid melts into air. Analyses of the capitalist state, however, have had to explain the ability of political structures to preserve a sense of spatial integrity, whether in the name of territoriality or national identity. This tension is felt in the continuing rift between international relations and international political economy as forms of enquiry, a rift that is often, and not very helpfully, characterised as one between base and superstructure or between high and low politics.[6] They are also implicated in analytical procedures and disciplinary boundaries that simply reproduce obsolete distinctions between space and time in a world that seems more appropriately characterised by patterns of intricate connections. Nevertheless, especially because my explicit focus is on a discipline that has been constituted as an analysis of relations between states conceived primarily as spatial entities, I treat the primacy of space in the cultural and intellectual experience of the early modern era as crucial, as setting the conditions under which later accounts of temporality – including those given by Marx – could be articulated as a linear and thus measurable progression. [. . .]

To pursue speculations about the transformative quality of contemporary trajectories with any theoretical rigour, I will argue, is necessarily to put in doubt the spatial resolution of all philosophical options that is expressed by the principle of state sovereignty – a resolution which is in any case always in doubt and subject to constant deferral, as well as subject to constant attempts to affirm its natural necessity. To put the point as succinctly as possible: if it is true that contemporary political life is increasingly characterised by processes of temporal acceleration, then we should expect to experience increasingly disconcerting incongruities between new articulations of power and accounts of political life predicated on the early-modern fiction that temporality can be fixed and tamed within the spatial coordinates of territorial jurisdictions. [. . .]

Furthermore, to the extent that contemporary accounts of temporal accelerations evade the familiar clichés of modern philosophies of history, they also put in doubt the manner in which challenges to the principle of state sovereignty are conventionally advanced; that is, on the ground of universalising claims about peace, justice, reason and humanity in general. This ground is precisely the condition under which claims about state sovereignty were advanced in the first place. It cannot offer the possibility of effective critique.

This is one of the key insights that have been sustained by at least some contributors to the postmodern turn in twentieth-century social and political theory.[7] It is an insight that I want to pursue here in a series of meditations on the discursive rituals through which modern theories of international relations have been constructed as a clearly defined but only intermittently problematised horizon of modern political thought and practice. Approaching questions about political identity and historical change by reflecting on the implications of the postmodern turn for theories of international relations, I want to explore how we are now able, or unable, to conceive of other possibilities, other forms of political identity and community, other histories, other futures.

NOTES

1. Karl Marx, *The Communist Manifesto*, 1848.
2. The relevant literature here is enormous, encompassing, say, the link between geometry and Platonist accounts of truth, beauty and goodness, the categorical schemes of Kantian philosophy, and the spatiotemporal modalities of capitalist economies. My own reading of this theme is especially influenced by the literature on the relationship between spatial extension and the articulation of autonomous subjectivities in late-medieval theology and early-modern science and philosophy. In this context, see especially such classic texts as Ernst Cassirer, *Individual and Cosmos in Renaissance Philosophy* (1927) trans. M. Domandi (New York: Harper and Row, 1963); Pierre Duhem, *Medieval Cosmology: Theories of Infinity, Place, Time, Void, and the Plurality of Worlds* (abridged edition of *Le Système du monde*, 10 vols, 1913–1959), trans. and ed. Roger Ariew (Chicago: University of Chicago Press, 1985); Edmund Husserl, *The Crisis of European Sciences and Transcendental Phenomenology: An Introduction to Phenomenological Philosophy* (1954) trans. David Carr (Evanston: Northwestern University Press, 1970); and Michel Foucault, *The Order of Things* (London: Tavistock, 1970).
3. The most sustained exploration of this theme in the context of contemporary world politics is the work of James Der Derian; see his 'The (S)pace of International Relations: Simulation, Surveillance and Speed', *International Studies Quarterly*, 34: 3, September 1990, 295–310; and *Anti-Diplomacy: Speed, Spies and Terror in International Relations* (Oxford: Basil Blackwell, 1992). It has become especially apparent in some of the most thoughtful interpretations of the Gulf War and its aftermath; see especially Stephen Gill, 'Reflections on Global Order and Sociohistorical Time', *Alternatives*, 16:3, Summer 1991, 275–314; and Timothy W. Luke, 'The Discipline of Security Studies and the Codes of Containment; Learning from Kuwait', *Alternatives*, 16:3, Summer 1991, 315–44. Among the many recent general texts that affirm both the significance of and the difficulty of responding to this theme in the specific context of international relations theory, see especially James N. Rosenau, *Turbulence in World Politics: A Theory of Change and Continuity* (Princeton: Princeton University Press, 1990); and Ernst-Otto Czempiel and J. N. Rosenau, eds, *Global Change and Theoretical Challenges* (Lexington: Lexington Books, 1989).

   As I suggest later in this chapter, much of the pertinent general literature expresses an ambivalence as to whether modernity and its contemporary expressions are best characterised as a privileging of space or of time, an ambivalence that I interpret as a crucial effect of the modern resolution of all philosophical options through a claim to an autonomous subject capable of preserving its self-identity in time and space (see note 2 above). For especially provocative discussions, see Paul Virilio, *Speed and Politics* (New York: Semiotext(e), 1987);

Virilio, *War and Cinema: The Logistics of Perception* (New York: Verso, 1989); and Gilles Deleuze, *Bergsonism*, trans. Hugh Tomlinson and Barbara Habberjam (New York: Zone Books, 1988). See also Donald M. Lowe, *History of Bourgeois Perception* (Chicago: University of Chicago Press, 1982); Timothy W. Luke, *Screens of Power: Ideology, Domination and Resistance in Informational Society* (Urbana and Chicago: University of Illinois Press, 1989); Harold A. Innis, *The Bias of Communication* (Toronto: University of Toronto Press, 1951); Marshall McLuhan, *The Gutenberg Galaxy* (Toronto: University of Toronto Press, 1962); Steven Connor, *Postmodernist Culture: An Introduction to Theories of the Contemporary* (Oxford: Basil Blackwell, 1989); Fredric Jameson, *Postmodernism, or The Cultural Logic of Late Capitalism* (Durham, NC: Duke University Press, 1991); Douglas Kellner, ed., *Postmodernism/Jameson/Critique* (Washington, DC: Maisonneuve Press, 1989); David Harvey, *The Condition of Postmodernity* (Oxford: Basil Blackwell, 1989); Edward Soja, *Postmodern Geographies: The Reassertion of Space in Critical Social Theory* (London: Verso, 1989); and Anthony Giddens, *The Consequences of Modernity* (Cambridge: Polity Press, 1990).

The problem of temporality, of course, has long been treated as a key theme of Western political thought. For my present purposes, it is especially important to remember the degree to which early-modern political thought involved a struggle to take the temporal realm seriously in relation to the claims of Heaven. In the shadow of Augustine's grand schism, of the devaluation of a life on earth in relation to the transcendental guarantees of eternity, a Machiavelli or a Hobbes can be read – as I tend to read them in this book – as moments in a broader attempt to constitute a positive vision of human existence in time. On this general theme, see, for example, John Gunnell, *Political Philosophy and Time*, 2nd edn, (Chicago: Chicago University Press, 1987); and Sheldon Wolin, *Politics and Vision* (Boston: Little Brown, 1960). See also John Bender and David E. Wellberg, eds, *Chronotypes: The Construction of Time* (Stanford: Stanford University Press, 1991).

4. I refer to international relations as a specific Anglo-American academic discipline that developed as a semi-autonomous enterprise from the 1920s onwards, and especially since 1945; to theories of international relations as an analytical and prescriptive literature produced by that discipline; to relations between states or the states system as the primary substantive concern of those theories; and to world politics as a broader array of processes – also often the focus of those theories – that extend beyond the territoriality and competence of particular states.

All these terms are highly problematic. Loose usages of the term international relations, for example, tend to reify a specific convergence between state and nation; references to the states system encourage a conflation of accounts of the state as territorial space and as governmental apparatus; ambivalent references to international relations and international politics signify some uncertainty about exactly what it is that goes on between states; most significantly, world politics appears both as a synonym for relations between states and as a way of referring to processes that largely escape prevailing analytical categories. The significance of the manner in which such terms slip from being innocuous synonyms to indicators of profound theoretical controversy should become clearer as the analysis proceeds.

The development of international relations as a discipline is explored in Kenneth W. Thompson, 'The Study of International Relations: Trends and Developments', *Review of Politics*, XIV, October 1952, 433–67; Hedley Bull, 'The Theory of International Politics, 1919–1969', in Brian Porter, ed., *International Politics 1919–1969: The Aberystwyth Papers* (Oxford: Oxford University Press, 1972), 30–55; Stanley Hoffman, 'An American Social Science: International Relations', *Daedalus*, 106, Summer 1977, 41–59; and William Olson and Nicholas Onuf, 'The Growth of a Discipline: Reviewed' in Steve Smith, ed., *International Relations: British and American Perspectives* (Oxford: Basil Blackwell, 1985), 1–28.

Recent attempts to assess the general achievements and present status of the discipline include Smith, ed., *International Relations*; K. J. Holsti, *The Dividing Discipline: Hegemony and Diversity in International Theory* (Boston: Allen and Unwin, 1985); Hayward R. Alker Jr, and Thomas J. Biersteker, 'The Dialectics of World Order: Notes for a Future Archeologist of International Savoir faire', *International Studies Quarterly*, 28: 2, June 1984, 121–42; Yale Ferguson and Richard W. Mansbach, *The Elusive Quest: Theory and International Politics* (Columbia: University of South Carolina Press, 1988); Richard Higgott, ed., *New Directions in International Relations? Australian Perspectives*, Canberra Studies in World Affairs, No. 23, (Canberra: Australian National University Department of International Relations, 1988); Richard Higgott and J. L.

Richardson, eds, *International Relations: Global and Australian Perspectives on an Evolving Discipline* (Canberra: Department of International Relations, Australian National University, 1991); and Hugh Dyer and Leon Mangasarian, eds, *The Study of International Relations: The State of the Art* (London: Macmillan, 1989).

For more focused controversies about the significance of converging claims about empirical social science, rational choice theory and 'neo-realism', on the one hand, and about emerging forms of 'critical theory', on the other, see especially Robert O. Keohane, ed. *Neorealism and Its Critics* (New York: Columbia University Press, 1986); Hayward Alker and Richard K. Ashley, eds, *After Neo-Realism: The Institutions of Anarchy in World Politics* (in preparation); and Richard K. Ashley and R. B. J. Walker, eds, 'Speaking the Language of Exile: Dissidence in International Studies', special issue of *International Studies Quarterly*, 34: 3, September 1990. These controversies provide the most immediate context in which the present analysis has been framed.

5. For helpful introductions to this theme see, for example, Marshall Berman, *All That is Solid Melts into Air: The Experience of Modernity* (New York: Simon and Schuster, 1982); David Frisby, *Fragments of Modernity: Theories of Modernity in the Work of Simmel, Kracauer and Benjamin* (Cambridge, MA: The MIT Press, 1986); and Stephen Kern, *The Culture of Time and Space, 1880–1918* (Cambridge, MA: Harvard University Press, 1983).

6. Because I am primarily concerned with the analysis of controversies that have developed within the theory of international relations, I pay relatively little attention to important literatures that have challenged the manner in which theories of international relations have been developed on the basis of a systematic amnesia about the international and global organisation of economic life. And because I am concerned to problematise the principle of state sovereignty, I also largely ignore literatures that challenge the absence of much analysis of the state as a complex historical phenomenon, an absence that has permitted so much empty speculation about the behaviour of black boxes, national interests, rational actors and the like. I share much of the critique that emerges from such literatures while remaining concerned about the extent to which it often remains caught within modernist assumptions about the character and location of political practice or informed by reductionist assumptions about the relative autonomies of economy, polity, society and culture. Many of the most helpful commentaries on literatures which I marginalise here have been informed by the counter-reductionist account of hegemony associated with Antonio Gramsci. See especially Robert W. Cox, *Production, Power, and World Order: Social Forces in the Making of History* (New York: Columbia University Press, 1987); Stephen Gill and David Law, *The Global Political Economy* (Baltimore: Johns Hopkins University Press, 1988); Gill, *American Hegemony and the Trilateral Commission* (Cambridge: Cambridge University Press, 1990); Craig Murphy and Roger Tooze, eds, *The New International Political Economy* (Boulder: Lynne Rienner, 1991); and Enrico Augelli and Craig Murphy, *America's Quest for Supremacy and the Third World: A Gramscian Analysis* (London: Francis Pinter, 1988).

The key connection between this literature and the present analysis is a shared concern with practices of reification, although I focus more explicitly on some aspects of the discursive economy of the modern state. Consequently, I also adopt a broader interpretation of the meaning of economy than is usual among economists, though it is one that has become increasingly familiar in the analysis of political discourse. See, for example Jean-Joseph Gouz, *Symbolic Economies: After Marx and Freud*, trans. Jennifer Curtis Gage (Ithaca, NY: Cornell University Press, 1990); Friedrich A. Kittler, *Discourse Networks, 1800/1900*, trans. Michael Metteer (Stanford: Stanford University Press, 1990); Michael Shapiro, 'Sovereignty and Exchange in the Orders of Modernity', *Alternatives*, 16:4, Fall 1991, 447–77; and Shapiro, *Reading the Postmodern Polity: Political Theory as Textual Practice* (Minneapolis: University of Minnesota Press, 1992).

7. It is, moreover, an insight that has been developed in quite diverse directions by Michel Foucault, Jacques Derrida, and the now extensive litany of names associated with postmodernist critique. This litany ought to be enough to forestall any expectations of a single poststructuralist approach to international relations/world politics. As with the more general literature, the differences among poststructuralist approaches in this context are often more striking than the convergences. Compare, for example, Richard K. Ashley, *Statecraft as Mancraft* (in preparation); William Connolly, *Identity/Difference: Democratic Negotiation of Political Paradox* (Ithaca: Cornell

University Press, 1991); Michael Shapiro, *The Politics of Representation* (Madison: University of Wisconsin Press, 1988); and David Campbell, *Writing Security: United States Foreign Policy and the Politics of Identity* (Manchester: Manchester University Press, 1992). On the heterogeneity of sources at work in such literature, see Jim George and David Campbell, 'Patterns of Dissent and the Celebration of Difference: Critical Social Theory and International Relations', in Ashley and Walker, eds, *Speaking the Language of Exile*, 269–93.

Attempts to depict some central insight of postmodern and poststructural thought are notoriously fraught with contradictions, as with Lyotard's well-known sweeping narrative about the end of 'master narratives'; see Jean-François Lyotard, *The Postmodern Condition: A Report on Knowledge*, trans. Geoff Bennington and Brian Massumi (Minneapolis: University of Minnesota Press, 1984). In a related manner, Jameson argues that it is 'safest to grasp the concept of the postmodern as an attempt to think the present historically in an age that has forgotten how to think historically in the first place'; Jameson, *Postmodernism*, ix. In each case, totalising claims pose severe difficulties, although I take it that the contradictory character of such diagnoses expresses a serious philosophical, cultural and political problematic rather than a simple minded failure of logic. In the case of Lyotard, it is a problematic that can be linked to the dissolution of modern conceptions of the transparency of language, while in the case of Jameson it can be linked to the difficulty of analysing late capitalism. Though both avenues of inquiry are undoubtedly crucial for analyses of contemporary world politics, they are beyond the scope of the present inquiry.

Contrary to such totalising strategies, I prefer to treat the postmodern turn and the literature of poststructuralism as opening up a range of critical possibilities, many of them at odds with each other, rather than as names for yet another grand solution to all philosophical and political puzzles. For helpful discussions of the difficulties of precise navigation in these waters, see Spivak, *The Post-Colonial Critic* (London: Routledge, 1990); William Connolly, *Politics and Ambiguity* (Madison: University of Wisconsin Press, 1987); and Zygmunt Bauman, *Modernity and Ambivalence* (Cambridge: Polity Press, 1991).

14

IN THE NAME OF THE REVOLUTION†

Jacques Derrida

Derrida had often hinted at correspondences between his philosophy of deconstruction and Marxism, without ever engaging very directly with the Marxist canon. Spectres of Marx *(1994) changed all that, although not perhaps in the way that his detractors on the left would have preferred. Whereas most of the latter were looking for an endorsement by Derrida, such that deconstruction could be enlisted in the service of a radical left-wing politics with specific cultural objectives, what they are offered here is something altogether less precise. This is not the Marx of classical Marxism, but Marx as plural, the generator of many different, sometimes conflicting, cultural traditions, whose work cannot be reduced to any single meaning. It is typically iconoclastic of Derrida to turn to Marx at a time when the latter's reputation and influence is on the wane, but he wants to insist that Marx is central to our intellectual inheritance, a spectral presence behind almost all our cultural debates in the West — and one that cannot simply be exorcised from our memory once and for all. Given the persistence of that spectre it makes no sense to Derrida, as he insists in the extract below, to talk of the 'end of history', and he opposes himself to all Fukuyama-style proclamations to this effect. Such is the strength of Marx's cultural legacy, particularly to someone of Derrida's generation, that it is not possible simply to cut oneself free from it (as, say, Lyotard had claimed to do) by some grand gesture. Convoluted though Derrida's argument can be on occasion, and singularly lacking in comfort for old-style Marxists, it represents nevertheless a plea for a retention of the spirit of Marxism, as well as an acknowledgement of the power of Marx's thought. Uncongenial though the current cultural circumstances may appear to be, that body of thought remains, for Derrida, of continuing relevance. In his own eccentric way, therefore, Derrida can be considered an exponent of post-Marxism.*

It will always be a fault not to read and reread and discuss Marx – which is to say also a few others – and to go beyond scholarly 'reading' or 'discussion'. It will be more and more a fault, a failing of theoretical, philosophical, political responsibility. When the dogma machine and the 'Marxist' ideological apparatuses (States, parties, cells, unions,

† From J. Derrida, *Spectres of Marx: The State of the Debt, the Work of Mourning, and the New International*, trans. Peggy Kamuf, New York: Routledge, 1994 (pp. 13–15, 37–48).

and other places of doctrinal production) are in the process of disappearing, we no longer have any excuse, only alibis, for turning away from this responsibility. There will be no future without this. Not without Marx, no future without Marx, without the memory and the inheritance of Marx: in any case of a certain Marx, of his genius, of at least one of his spirits. For this will be our hypothesis or rather our bias: *there is more than one of them, there must be more than one of them.*

Nevertheless, among all the temptations I will have to resist today, there would be the temptation of memory: to recount what was for me, and for those of my *generation* who shared it during a whole lifetime, the experience of Marxism, the quasi-paternal figure of Marx, the way it fought in us with other filiations, the reading of texts and the interpretation of a world in which the Marxist inheritance was – and still remains, and so it will remain – absolutely and thoroughly determinate. One need not be a Marxist or a communist in order to accept this obvious fact. We all live in a world, some would say a culture, that still bears, at an incalculable depth, the mark of this inheritance, whether in a directly visible fashion or not.

Among the traits that characterise a certain experience that belongs to my generation, that is, an experience that will have lasted at least forty years, and which is not over, I will isolate first of all a troubling paradox. I am speaking of a troubling effect of 'déjà vu', and even of a certain 'toujours déjà vu'. I recall this malaise of perception, hallucination, and time because of the theme that brings us together this evening: 'whither Marxism?' For many of us the question has the same age as we do. In particular for those who, and this was also my case, opposed, to be sure, *de facto* 'Marxism' or 'communism' (the Soviet Union, the International of Communist Parties, and everything that resulted from them, which is to say so very many things . . .), but intended at least never to do so out of conservative or reactionary motivations or even moderate right-wing or republican positions. For many of us, a certain (and I emphasise *certain*) end of communist Marxism did not await the recent collapse of the USSR and everything that depends on it throughout the world. All that started – all that was even *déjà vu*, indubitably – at the beginning of the 1950s. Therefore, the question that brings us together this evening – 'whither Marxism?' – resonates like an old repetition. It was already, but in an altogether different way, the question that imposed itself on the many young people who we were at the time. The same question had already *sounded*. The same, to be sure, but in an altogether different way. And the difference in the sound, that is what is echoing this evening. It is still evening, it is always nightfall along the 'ramparts', on the battlements of an old Europe at war. With the other and with itself.

Why? It was the same question, already, as final question. Many young people today (of the type 'readers-consumers of Fukuyama' or of the type 'Fukuyama' himself) probably no longer sufficiently realise it: the eschatological themes of the 'end of history', of the 'end of Marxism', of the 'end of philosophy', of the 'ends of man', of the 'last man' and so forth were, in the 1950s, that is, forty years ago, our daily bread. We had this bread of apocalypse in our mouths naturally, already, just as naturally as that which I nicknamed after the fact, in 1980, the 'apocalyptic tone in philosophy'.

What was its consistency? What did it taste like? It was, *on the one hand*, the reading or analysis of those whom we could nickname the *classics of the end*. They formed the canon of the modern apocalypse (end of History, end of Man, end of Philosophy, Hegel, Marx, Nietzsche, Heidegger, with their Kojevian codicil and the codicils of Kojève himself). It was, *on the other hand and indissociably*, what we had known or what some of us for quite some time no longer hid from concerning totalitarian terror in all the Eastern countries, all the socio-economic disasters of Soviet bureaucracy, the Stalinism of the past and the neo-Stalinism in process (roughly speaking, from the Moscow trials to the repression in Hungary, to take only these minimal indices). Such was no doubt the element in which what is called deconstruction developed – and one can understand nothing of this period of deconstruction, notably in France, unless one takes this historical entanglement into account. Thus, for those with whom I shared this singular period, this double and unique experience (both philosophical and political), for us, I venture to say, the media parade of current discourse on the end of history and the last man looks most often like a tiresome anachronism. At least up to a certain point that will have to be specified later on. Something of this tiresomeness, moreover, comes across in the body of today's most *phenomenal culture*: what one hears, reads, and sees, what is most *mediatised* in Western capitals. As for those who abandon themselves to that discourse with the jubilation of youthful enthusiasm, they look like latecomers, a little as if it were possible to take still the last train after the last train – and yet be late to an end of history.

How can one be late to the end of history? A question for today. It is serious because it obliges one to reflect again, as we have been doing since Hegel, on what happens and deserves the name of *event*, after history; it obliges one to wonder if the end of history is but the end of a *certain* concept of history. Here is perhaps one of the questions that should be asked of those who are not content just to arrive late to the apocalypse and to the last train of the end, if I can put it like that, without being out of breath, but who find the means to puff out their chests with the good conscience of capitalism, liberalism, and the virtues of parliamentary democracy – a term with which we designate not parliamentarism and political representation *in general*, but the *present*, which is to say in fact, *past* forms of the electoral and parliamentary apparatus. [. . .]

In proposing this title, *Spectres of Marx*, I was initially thinking of all the forms of a certain haunting obsession that seems to me to organize the *dominant* influence on discourse today. At a time when a new world disorder is attempting to install its neo-capitalism and neo-liberalism, no disavowal has managed to rid itself of all of Marx's ghosts. Hegemony still organises the repression and thus the confirmation of a haunt-ing. Haunting belongs to the structure of every hegemony.[1] But I did not have in mind first of all the exordium of the *Manifesto*. In an apparently different sense, Marx–Engels spoke there already, in 1847–48, of a spectre and more precisely of the 'spectre of communism' (*das Gespenst des Kommunismus*). A terrifying spectre for all the powers of old Europe (*alle Mächte des alten Europa*), but spectre of a communism then *to come*. Of a communism, to be sure, already namable (and well before the League of the Just or the Communist League), but still to come beyond its name. Already promised but only promised. A spectre all the more terrifying, some will say. Yes, on the condition that one can never distinguish between the future-to-come and the coming-back of a spectre. Let us not forget that, around 1848, the First International had to remain quasi-secret. The spectre was there (but what is the *being-there* of a spectre? what is the mode of presence of a spectre? that is the only question we would like to pose here). But that of which it was the spectre, communism (*das Gespenst des Kommunismus*), was itself not there, by definition. It was dreaded as communism to come. It had already been announced, with this name, some time ago, but it was not yet *there*. It is only a spectre, seemed to say these allies of old Europe so as to reassure themselves; let's hope that in the future it does not become an actual, effectively present, manifest, non-secret reality. The question old Europe was asking itself was already the question of the future, the question 'whither?': 'whither communism?' if not 'whither Marxism?' Whether one takes it as asking about the future of communism or about communism in the future, this anguished question did not just seek to know how, in the future, communism would affect European history, but also, in a more muffled way, already whether there would still be any future and any history at all for Europe. In 1848, the Hegelian discourse on the end of history in absolute knowledge had already resounded throughout Europe and had rung a consonant note with many other knells (*glas*). And communism was essentially distinguished from other labour movements by its *international* character. No organised political movement in the history of humanity had ever yet presented itself as *geo-political*, thereby inaugurating the space that is now ours and that today is reaching its limits, the limits of the earth and the limits of the political.

The representatives of these forces or all these powers (*alle Mächte*), namely the States, wanted to *reassure* themselves. They wanted to be sure. So they were sure, for there is no difference between 'being sure' and 'wanting to be sure'. They were sure and certain that between a spectre and an actually present reality, between a spirit and a *Wirklichkeit*, the dividing line was assured. It *had* to be safely drawn. It *ought* to be assured. No, it *ought to have been* assured. The sureness of this certainty is something they shared, moreover, with *Marx himself*. (This is the whole story, and we are coming to it: Marx thought, to be sure, on his side, from the other side, that the dividing line between the ghost and actuality ought to be crossed, like utopia itself, by a realisation, that is, by a revolution; but *he too* will have continued to believe, to try to believe in the existence of this dividing line as real limit and conceptual distinction. He too? No, someone in him. Who? The 'Marxist' who will engender what for a long time is going to prevail under the name of 'Marxism'. And which was also haunted by what it attempted to foreclose.)

Today, almost a century and a half later, there are many who, throughout the world, seem just as worried by the spectre of communism, just as convinced that what one is dealing with there is only a spectre without body, without present reality, without actuality or effectivity, but this time it is supposed to be a past spectre. It was only a spectre, an illusion, a phantasm, or a ghost: that is what one hears everywhere today ('Horatio saies, 'tis but our Fantasie,/ And will not let beleefe take hold of him'). A still worried sigh of relief: let us make sure that in the future it does not come back! At bottom, the spectre is the future, it is always to come, it presents itself only as that which could come or come back; in the future, said the powers of old Europe in the last century, it must not incarnate itself, either publicly or in secret. In the future, we hear everywhere today, it must not re-incarnate itself; it must not be allowed to come back since it is past.

What exactly is the difference from one century to the next? Is it the difference between a past world – for which the spectre represented a coming threat – and a present world, today, where the spectre would represent a threat that some would like to believe is past and whose return it would be necessary again, once again in the future, to conjure away?

Why in both cases is the spectre felt to be a threat? What is the time and what is the history of a spectre? Is there a present of the spectre? Are its comings and goings ordered according to the linear succession of a before and an after, between a present-past, a present-present, and a present-future, between a 'real time' and a 'deferred time'?

If there is something like spectrality, there are reasons to doubt this reassuring order of presents and, especially, the border between the present, the actual or present reality of the present, and everything that can be opposed to it: absence, non-presence, non-effectivity, inactuality, virtuality, or even the simulacrum in general, and so forth. There is first of all the doubtful contemporaneity of the present to itself. Before knowing whether one can differentiate between the spectre of the past and the spectre of the future, of the past present and the future present, one must perhaps ask oneself whether the *spectrality effect* does not consist in undoing this opposition, or even this dialectic, between actual, effective presence and its other. One must perhaps ask oneself whether this opposition, be it a dialectical opposition, has not always been a closed field and a common axiomatic for the antagonism between Marxism and the cohort or the alliance of its adversaries.

Pardon me for beginning with such an abstract formulation.

In the middle of the last century, an alliance was constituted against this spectre, to drive off the evil. Marx did not call this coalition a Holy Alliance, an expression he plays with elsewhere. In the *Manifesto*, the alliance of the worried conspirators assembles, more or less secretly, a nobility and a clergy – in the old castle of Europe, for an unbelievable expedition against what will have been haunting the night of these masters. At twilight, before or after a night of bad dreams, at the presumed end of history, it is a 'holy hunt against this spectre': 'All the powers of old Europe have joined [*verbündet*] into a holy hunt against this spectre [*zu einer heiligen Hetzjagd gegen dies Gespenst*].'

It would thus be possible to form a secret alliance against the spectre. If Marx had written his *Manifesto* in my language, and if he had had some help with it, as a Frenchman can always dream of doing, I am sure he would have played on the word *conjuration*. Then he would have diagnosed today the same *conjuration*, this time not only in old Europe but in the new Europe, the New World, which already interested him very much a century and a half ago, and throughout the world, in the new world order where the hegemony of this new world, I mean the United States, would still exercise a more or less critical hegemony, more and less assured than ever.

The word *conjuration* has the good fortune to put to work and to produce, without any possible reappropriation, a forever errant surplus value. It capitalises first of all two orders of semantic value. What is a 'conjuration'?

The French noun *conjuration* gathers up and articulates the meanings of two English words – and also two German words.

1.   *Conjuration* signifies, *on the one hand*, 'conjuration' (its English homonym) which itself designates two things at once:

a.   *On the one hand*, the conspiracy (*Verschwörung* in German) of those who promise solemnly, sometimes secretly, by swearing together an oath (*Schwur*) to struggle against a superior power. It is to this conspiracy that Hamlet appeals, evoking the 'Vision' they have just seen and the 'honest ghost', when he asks Horatio and Marcellus to swear ('swear't', 'Consent to swear'). To swear upon his sword, but to swear or to swear together *on the subject of the spectral apparition itself*, and to promise secrecy on the subject of the apparition of an honest ghost that, from beneath the stage, conspires with Hamlet to ask the same thing from the sworn: ('*The Ghost cries from under the stage:* Sweare'). It is the apparition that enjoins them to conspire to *silence the apparition*, and to promise secrecy on the subject of the one who demands such an oath from them: one must not know whence comes the injunction, the conspiracy, the promised secret. A son and the 'honest ghost' of the father, the supposedly honest ghost, the spirit of the father, conspire together to bring about such an event.

b.   'Conjuration' signifies, *on the other hand*, the magical incantation destined to *evoke*, to bring forth with the voice, to *convoke* a charm or a spirit. Conjuration says in sum the appeal that causes to come forth *with the voice* and thus it makes come, by definition, what *is not there* at the present moment of the appeal. This voice does not describe, what it says certifies nothing; its words cause something to happen. This is the usage encountered again in the words of the Poet at the opening of *Timon of Athens*. After having asked 'How goes the world?' and after the Painter has told him 'It wears, sir, as it grows,' the Poet exclaims:

> Ay, that's well known;
> But what particular rarity, what strange,
> Which manifold record not matches? – See,
> Magic of bounty, all these spirits thy power
> Hath *conjur'd* to attend. I know the merchant. (I, i)

Marx evokes more than once *Timon of Athens*, as well as *The Merchant of Venice*, in particular in *The German Ideology*. The chapter on 'The Leipzig Council – Saint Max', also supplies, and we will say more about this later, a short treatise on the spirit or an interminable theatricalisation of ghosts. A certain 'Communist Conclusion' appeals to *Timon of Athens*.[2] The same quotation will reappear in the first version of *A Contribution to the Critique of Political Economy*. In question is a spectralising disincarnation. Apparition of the bodiless body of money: not the lifeless body or the cadaver, but a life without personal life or individual property. Not without identity (the ghost is a 'who', it is not of the simulacrum in general, it has a kind of body, but without property, without 'real' or 'personal' right of property). One must analyse the proper of property and how the general property (*Eigentum*) of money neutralises, disincarnates, deprives of its difference all personal property (*Eigentümlichkeit*). The genius of Shakespeare will have understood this phantomalisation of property centuries ago and said it better than anyone. The *ingenium* of his paternal geniality serves as reference, guarantee, or confirmation in the polemic, that is, in the ongoing war – on the subject, precisely, of the monetary spectre, value, money or its fiduciary sign, gold: 'It was known to Shakespeare better than to our theorizing petty bourgeois [*unser theoretisierender Kleinbürger*] ... [h]ow little connection there is between money, the most general form of property [*die allgemeinste Form des Eigentums*], and personal peculiarity [*mit der persönlichen Eigentümlichkeit*].'[3]

The quotation will also make apparent (as a supplementary benefit but in fact it is altogether necessary) a theologising fetishisation, the one that always links ideology irreducibly to religion (to the idol or the fetish) as its principal figure, a species of 'invisible god' to which adoration, prayer, and invocation are addressed ('Thou visible god'). Religion, and we will come back to this, was never one ideology among others for Marx. What, Marx seems to say, the genius of a great poet – and the spirit of a great father – will have uttered in a poetic flash, with one blow going faster and farther than our little bourgeois colleagues in economic theory, is the becoming-god of gold, which is at once ghost and idol, a god apprehended by the senses. After having marked the heterogeneity between the property of money and personal property (there is 'little connection' between them), Marx adds, and it is not a negligible clarification it seems to me, that in truth they are not only different but opposed (*entgegensetzt*). And it is then that, cutting into the body of the text and making choices that should be analysed closely, he wrests a long passage from that prodigious scene in *Timon of Athens* (IV, iii). Marx loves the words of this imprecation. One must never keep silent about the imprecation of the just. One must never silence it in the most analytic text of Marx. An imprecation does not theorise, it is not content to say how things are, it cries out the truth, it promises, it provokes. As its name indicates, it is nothing other than a prayer. Marx appropriates the words of this imprecation with a kind of delight whose signs are unmistakable. Declaring his hatred of the human race ('I am Misanthropos and hate mankind'), with the anger of a Jewish prophet and sometimes the very words of Ezechiel, Timon curses corruption, he casts down anathema, he swears against prostitution – prostitution in the face of gold and the prostitution of gold itself. But he takes the time to analyse, nevertheless, the transfiguring alchemy, he denounces the reversal of values, the falsification and especially the prejury of which it is the law. One imagines the impatient patience of Marx (rather than Engels) as he transcribes in his own hand, at length, in German, the rage of a prophetic imprecation:

> ... Thus much of this will make
> Black white, foul fair, wrong right,
> Base noble, old young, coward valiant.
>
> This yellow slave
> Will ...
> Make the hoar leprosy adored ...

> This is it
> That makes the wappered widow wed again.
> She whom the spittle house and ulcerous sores
> Would cast the gorge at, this embalms and spices
> To th' April day again . . .
>
> Thou visible god,
> That sold'rest closest impossibilities
> And mak'st them kiss . . .
>
> *sichtbare Gottheit,*
> *Die du Unmöglichkeiten eng verbrüderst*
> *Zum Kusz sie zwingst!*

Among all the traits of this immense malediction of malediction, Marx will have had to efface, in the economy of a long citation, those that are most important for us here, for example the aporias and the double bind that carry the act of swearing and conjuring off into the history of venality itself. At the moment he goes to bury the gold, a shovel in his hand, the prophet-gravedigger, anything but a humanist, is not content to evoke the breaking of vows, the birth and death of religions ('This yellow slave/ Will knit and break religions; bless the accurs'd'); Timon also begs [*conjure*] the other, he pleads with him to promise, but he conjures thus by perjuring and by confessing his perjury in a same and single bifid gesture. In truth, he conjures *by feigning the truth*, by feigning at least to make the other promise. But if he feigns to make the other promise, it is in truth to make the other promise not to keep his promise, that is, not to promise, even as he pretends to promise: to perjure or to abjure in the very moment of the oath; then following from this same logic, he begs him to spare all oaths. As if he were saying in effect: I beg you (*je vous en conjure*), do not swear, abjure your right to swear, renounce your capacity to swear, moreover no one is asking you to swear, you are asked to be the non-oathables that you are ('you are not oathable'), you, the whores, you who are prostitution itself, you who give yourselves to gold, you who give yourselves for gold, you who are destined to general indifference, you who confuse in equivalency the proper and the improper, credit and discredit, faith and lie, the 'true and the false', oath, perjury, and abjuration, and so forth. You the whores of money, you would go so far as to abjure ('forswear') your trade or your vocation (of perjured whore) for money. Like a madam who would give up even her whores for money.

The very essence of humanity is at stake. Absolute double bind on the subject of the *bind* or the *bond* themselves. Infinite misfortune and incalculable chance of the performative – here named literally ('perform', 'perform none' are Timon's words when he asks (*conjure*) the other *to promise not to keep a promise*, calling therefore for perjury or abjuration). Force, as weakness, of an ahuman discourse on man. Timon to Alcibiades: 'Promise me friendship, but perform none. If thou wilt promise, the gods plague thee, for thou art a man. If thou dost not perform, confound thee, for thou art a man' (IV, iii). Then to Phyrnia and Timandra who ask for gold – and whether Timon has any more:

> Enough to make a whore forswear her trade,
> And to make wholesomeness a bawd. Hold up, you sluts,
> Your aprons mountant. You are not oathable,
> Although I know you'll swear, terribly swear,
> Into strong shudders and to heavenly agues
> Th'immortal gods that hear you. Spare your oaths;
> I'll trust to your conditions. Be whores still . . .

Addressing himself to prostitution or to the cult of money, to fetishism or to idolatry itself, Timon trusts. He gives faith, he believes, he indeed wants to *credit* ('I'll trust') but only in the imprecation of a paradoxical hyperbole: he himself pretends to trust in that which, from the depths of abjuration, from the depths of that which is not even capable or worthy of an oath ('you are not oathable'), remains nevertheless faithful to a natural instinct, as if there were a pledge of instinct, a fidelity to itself of instinctual nature, an oath of living nature before the oath of convention, society, or law. And it is the fidelity to infidelity, the constancy in perjury. This life enslaves itself regularly, one can trust it to do so, it never fails to kneel to indifferent power, to that power of mortal indifference that is money. Diabolical, radically bad in that way, nature is prostitution, it enslaves itself faithfully, one can have confidence here in it, it enslaves itself to what is betrayal itself, perjury, abjuration, lie, and simulacrum.

Which are never very far from the spectre. As is well known, Marx always described money, and more precisely the monetary sign, in the figure of appearance or simulacrum, more exactly of the ghost. He not only described them, he also defined them, but the figural presentation of the concept seemed to describe some spectral 'thing', which is to say, 'someone'. What is the necessity of this figural presentation? What is its relation to the concept? Is it contingent? That is the classic form of our question. As we do not believe in any contingency here, we will even begin to worry about the classical (basically Kantian) form of this question which seems to marginalise or keep at a distance the figural schema even as it takes it seriously. *The Critique of Political Economy* explains to us how the existence (*Dasein*) of money, metallic *Dasein*, gold or silver, produces a *remainder*.[4] This remainder is – it remains, precisely – but the shadow of a great name: '*Was übrigbleibt ist* magni nominis umbra.' 'The body of money is but a shadow [*nur noch ein Schatten*].'[5] The whole movement of idealisation (*Idealisierung*) that Marx then describes, whether it is a question of money or of ideologems, is a production of ghosts, illusions, simulacra, appearances, or apparitions (*Scheindasein* of the *Schein-Sovereign* and of the *Schein-gold*). Later he will compare this spectral virtue of money with that which, in the desire to hoard, speculates on the use of money *after death*, in the other world (*nach dem Tode in der andern Welt*).[6] *Geld, Geist, Geiz*: as if money (*Geld*) were the origin both of spirit (*Geist*) and of avarice (*Geiz*). 'Im Geld liegt der Ursprung des Geizes,' says Pliny as quoted by Marx right after this. Elsewhere, the equation between *Gaz* and *Geist* will be joined to the chain.[7] The metamorphosis of commodities (*die Metamorphose der Waren*) was already a process of transfiguring idealisation that one may legitimately call spectropoetic. When the State emits paper money at a fixed rate, its intervention is compared to 'magic' (*Magie*) that transmutes paper into gold. The State appears then, for it is an appearance, indeed an apparition; it 'seems now to transform paper into gold by the magic of its imprint [*scheint jetzt durch die Magie seines Stempels Papier in Gold zu verwandeln*; Marx is referring to the imprint that stamps gold and prints paper money].'[8] This magic always busies itself with ghosts, it does business with them, it manipulates or busies *itself*, it becomes a business, the business it does in the very element of haunting. And this business attracts the undertakers, those who deal with cadavers but so as to steal them, to make the departed disappear, which remains the condition of their 'apparition'. Commerce and theatre of gravediggers. In periods of social crisis, when the social 'nervus rerum' is, says Marx, 'buried [*bestattet*] alongside the body whose sinew it is' (131), the speculative burying of the treasure inters only a useless metal, deprived of its monetary soul (*Geldseele*). This burial scene recalls not only the great scene of the cemetery and gravediggers in *Hamlet*, when one of them suggests that the work of the 'grave-maker' lasts longer than any other: until Judgement Day. This scene of burying gold also evokes more than once, and still more exactly, *Timon of Athens*. In Marx's funerary rhetoric, the 'useless metal' of the treasure once buried becomes like the burnt-out ashes (*ausgebrannte Asche*) of circulation, like its *caput mortuum*, its chemical residue. In his wild imaginings, in his nocturnal delirium (*Hirngespinst*), the miser, the hoarder, the speculator becomes a martyr to exchange-value. He now refrains from exchange because he dreams of a pure exchange. (And we will see later how the apparition of exchange-value, in *Capital*, is precisely an apparition, one might say a vision, a hallucination, a *properly* spectral apparition if this figure did not prevent us from speaking here properly of the proper.) The hoarder behaves then like an alchemist (*alchimistich*), speculating on ghosts, the 'elixir of life', the 'philosophers' stone'. Speculation is always fascinated, bewitched by the spectre. That this alchemy remains devoted to the apparition of the spectre, to the haunting or the return of *revenants* is brought out in the literality of a text that translations sometimes overlook. When, in this same passage, Marx describes the transmutation, there is haunting at stake. What operates in an alchemical fashion are the exchanges and mixtures of *revenants*, the *madly spectral* compositions or conversions. The lexicon of haunting and ghosts (*Spuk, spuken*) takes centre stage. Whereas the English translation speaks of the 'alchemist's apparitions' ('The liquid form of wealth and its petrification, the elixir of life and the philosophers' stone are wildly mixed together like an alchemist's apparitions'), the French translation drops the reference to ghosts (*spuken alchimistisch toll durcheinander*) with the phrase 'fantasmagorie d'une folle achimie'.[9]

In short, and we will return to this repeatedly, Marx does not like ghosts any more than his adversaries do. He does not want to believe in them. But he thinks of nothing else. He believes rather in what is supposed to distinguish them from actual reality, living effectivity. He believes he can oppose them, like life to death, like vain appearances of the simulacrum to real presence. He believes enough in the dividing line of this opposition to want to denounce, chase away, or exorcise the spectres but by means of critical analysis and not by some counter-magic. But how to distinguish between the analysis that denounces magic and the counter-magic that it still risks being? We will ask ourselves this question again, for example, as regards *The German Ideology*. 'The Leipzig Council – Saint Max' (Stirner) also organises, let us recall once more before coming back to it later, an *irresistible* but *interminable* hunt for ghosts (*Gespenst*) and for *revenants* or spooks (*Spuk*). *Irresistible* like an effective critique, but also like a compulsion; *interminable* as one says of an analysis, and the comparison would not be at all fortuitous.

This hostility towards ghosts, a terrified hostility that sometimes fends off terror with a burst of laughter, is perhaps what Marx will always have had in common with his adversaries. He too will have tried to *conjure* (away) the ghosts, and everything that was neither life nor death, namely, the re-apparition of an apparition that will never be either the appearing or the disappeared, the phenomenon or its contrary. He will have tried to conjure (away) the ghosts *like* the conspirators [*conjurés*] of old Europe on whom the *Manifesto* declares war. However inexpiable this war remains, and however necessary this revolution, it conspires [*conjure*] *with them* in order to *exorc-analyse* the spectrality of the spectre. And this is today, as perhaps it will be tomorrow, our problem.

2.   For 'conjuration' means, on the other hand, 'conjurement' (*Beschwörung*), namely, the magical exorcism that, on the contrary, tends to expulse the evil spirit which would have been called up or convoked (*OED*: 'the exorcising of spirits by invocation', 'the exercise of magical or occult influence').

A conjuration, then, is first of all an alliance, to be sure, sometimes a political alliance, more or less secret, if not tacit, a plot or a conspiracy. It is a matter of neutralising a hegemony or overturning some power. (During the Middle Ages, *conjuratio* also designated the sworn faith by means of which the bourgeois joined together, sometimes against a prince, in order to establish free towns.) In the occult society of those who have sworn together (*des conjurés*), certain subjects, either individual or collective, represent forces and ally themselves together in the name of common interests to combat a dreaded political adversary, that is, also, to conjure it away. For to conjure means *also* to exorcise: to attempt both to destroy and to disavow a malignant, demonised, diabolised force, most often an evil-doing spirit, a spectre, a kind of ghost who comes back or who still risks coming back *post mortem*. Exorcism conjures away the evil in ways that are also irrational, using magical, mysterious, even mystifying practices. Without excluding, quite to the contrary, analytic procedure and argumentative ratiocination, exorcism consists in repeating in the mode of an incantation that the dead man is really dead. It proceeds by *formulae*, and sometimes theoretical formulae play this role with an efficacity that is all the greater because they mislead as to their magical nature, their authoritarian dogmatism, the occult power they share with what they claim to combat.

But effective exorcism pretends to declare the death only in order to put to death. As a coroner might do, it certifies the death but here it is in order to inflict it. This is a familiar tactic. The constative form tends to reassure. The certification is effective. It wants to be and it must be *in effect*. It is *effectively* a performative. But here effectivity phantomalizes itself. It is in fact *en effet* a matter of a performative that seeks to reassure but first of all to reassure itself by assuring itself, for nothing is less sure, that what one would like to see dead is indeed dead. It speaks in the name of life, it claims to know what that is. Who knows better than someone who is alive? it seems to say with a straight face. It seeks to convince (itself) there where it makes (itself) afraid: now, it says (to itself), what used to be living is no longer alive, it does not remain effective in death itself, don't worry. (What is going on here is a way of not wanting to know what everyone alive knows without learning and without knowing, namely, that the dead can often be more powerful than the living; and that is why to interpret a philosophy as philosophy or ontology of life is never a simple matter, which means that it is always too simple, incontestable, like what goes without saying, but finally so unconvincing, as unconvincing as a tautology, a rather heterological tauto-ontology, that of Marx or whomever, which relates everything back to life only on the condition of including there death and the alterity of its other without which it would not be what it is.) In short, it is often a matter of pretending to certify death there where the death certificate is still the performative of an act of war or the impotent gesticulation, the restless dream, of an execution.

NOTES

1. For a novel elaboration, in a 'deconstructive' style, of the concept of *begemony*, I refer to Ernesto Laclau and Chantal Mouffe, *Hegemony and Socialist Strategy: Towards a Radical Democratic Politics* (London: Verso, 1985).
2. Karl Marx and Frederick Engels, *The German Ideology*, in *Collected Works*. (New York: International Publishers, 1976), pp. 230–1).
3. *The German Ideology*, p. 230.
4. *A Contribution to the Critique of Political Economy*, chapter 2, part 2 b ('The Circulation of Money') (New York: International Publishers, 1970).
5. *Critique*, p. 109.
6. *Critique*, p. 132.
7. *Critique*, p. 142. This is a semantic chain that we have examined in *Glas* (in Hegel) and in *Of Spirit: Heidegger and the Question*.
8. *Critique*, pp. 119, 140.
9. *Critique*, p. 134.

III

POST-MARXISM/POST-*MARXISM*: FEMINIST INTERVENTIONS

15

THE UNHAPPY MARRIAGE OF MARXISM AND FEMINISM: TOWARDS A MORE PROGRESSIVE UNION†

Heidi Hartmann

The accommodation between Marxism and feminism has been at best an uneasy one, and serious divisions between the relevant parties began to reveal themselves with increasing frequency from the 1960s onwards. Heidi Hartmann's essay 'The Unhappy Marriage of Marxism and Feminism' (1981) represents one of the most influential, as well as most trenchant, interventions in the debate between Marxists and feminists (not to mention laying claim to being one of the most memorable titles). What the author seeks is a 'more progressive union' that corrects the current imbalance of power, where feminism is simply subsumed under Marxism as a secondary struggle only, of less importance than, for example, issues of class. In Hartmann's reading, however, feminism and Marxism need each other and should be considered more in the nature of equal partners; only then will the powerful alliance that has grown up between patriarchy and capitalism be meaningfully challenged – to the ultimate benefit of the socialist cause as a whole. Marxism cannot go on in its traditional, sex-blind fashion, but will have to change; otherwise, as Hartmann warns in her no-nonsense way, the only sensible alternative from a feminist perspective is 'divorce'.

The 'marriage' of marxism and feminism has been like the marriage of husband and wife depicted in English common law: marxism and feminism are one, and that one is marxism.[1] Recent attempts to integrate marxism and feminism are unsatisfactory to us as feminists because they subsume the feminist struggle into the 'larger' struggle against capital. To continue our simile further, either we need a healthier marriage or we need a divorce.

The inequalities in this marriage, like most social phenomena, are no accident. Many marxists typically argue that feminism is at best less important than class conflict and at worse divisive of the working class. This political stance produces an analysis that

† From H. Hartmann, 'The Unhappy Marriage of Marxism and Feminism: Towards a More Progressive Union', in L. Sargent, ed., *The Unhappy Marriage of Marxism and Feminism: A Debate on Class and Patriarchy*, London: Pluto Press, 1981, pp. 1–41 (pp. 2–11, 30–3). [Published in America as *Women and Revolution: A Discussion of the Unhappy Marriage between Marxism and Feminism*, Boston, MA: South End Press, 1981.]

absorbs feminism into the class struggle. Moreover, the analytic power of marxism with respect to capital has obscured its limitations with respect to sexism. We will argue here that while marxist analysis provides essential insight into the laws of historical development, and those of capital in particular, the categories of marxism are sex-blind. Only a specifically feminist analysis reveals the systemic character of relations between men and women. Yet feminist analysis by itself is inadequate because it has been blind to history and insufficiently materialist. Both marxist analysis, particularly its historical and materialist method, and feminist analysis, especially the identification of patriarchy as a social and historical structure, must be drawn upon if we are to understand the development of western capitalist societies and the predicament of women within them. In this essay we suggest a new direction for marxist feminist analysis.

Part I of our discussion examines several marxist approaches to the 'woman question'. We then turn, in Part II, to the work of radical feminists. After noting the limitations of radical feminist definitions of patriarchy, we offer our own. In Part III we try to use the strengths of both marxism and feminism to make suggestions both about the development of capitalist societies and about the present situation of women. We attempt to use marxist methodology to analyse feminist objectives, correcting the imbalance in recent socialist feminist work, and suggesting a more complete analysis of our present socioeconomic formation. We argue that a materialist analysis demonstrates that patriarchy is not simply a psychic, but also a social and economic structure. We suggest that our society can best be understood once it is recognised that it is organised both in capitalistic and in patriarchal ways. While pointing out tensions between patriarchal and capitalist interests, we argue that the accumulation of capital both accommodates itself to patriarchal social structure and helps to perpetuate it. We suggest in this context that sexist ideology has assumed a peculiarly capitalist form in the present, illustrating one way that patriarchal relations tend to bolster capitalism. We argue, in short, that a partnership of patriarchy and capitalism has evolved.

In the concluding section, Part IV, we argue that the *political* relations of marxism and feminism account for the dominance of marxism over feminism in the left's understanding of the woman question. A more progressive union of marxism and feminism, then, requires not only improved intellectual understanding of relations of class and sex, but also that alliance replace dominance and subordination in left politics.

MARXISM AND THE WOMAN QUESTION

The woman question has never been the 'feminist question'. The feminist question is directed at the causes of sexual inequality between women and men, of male dominance over women. Most marxist analyses of women's position take as their question the relationship of women to the economic system, rather than that of women to men, apparently assuming the latter will be explained in their discussion of the former. Marxist analysis of the woman question has taken three main forms. All see women's oppression in our connection (or lack of it) to production. Defining women as part of the working class, these analyses consistently subsume women's relation to men under workers' relation to capital. First, early marxists, including Marx, Engels, Kautsky, and

Lenin, saw capitalism drawing all women into the wage labour force, and saw this process destroying the sexual division of labour. Second, contemporary marxists have incorporated women into an analysis of everyday life in capitalism. In this view, all aspects of our lives are seen to reproduce the capitalist system and we are all workers in the system. And third, marxist feminists have focused on housework and its relation to capital, some arguing that housework produces surplus value and that houseworkers work directly for capitalists. These three approaches are examined in turn.

Engels, in *Origins of the Family, Private Property and the State*, recognised the inferior position of women and attributed it to the institution of private property.[2] In bourgeois families, Engels argued, women had to serve their masters, be monogamous, and produce heirs who would inherit the family's property and continue to increase it. Among proletarians, Engels argued, women were not oppressed, because there was no private property to be passed on. Engels argued further that as the extension of wage labour destroyed the small-holding peasantry, and women and children were incorporated into the wage labour force along with men, the authority of the male head of household was undermined, and patriarchal relations were destroyed.[3]

For Engels, then, women's participation in the labour force was the key to their emancipation. *Capitalism* would abolish sex differences and treat all workers equally. Women would become economically independent of men and would participate on an equal footing with men in bringing about the proletarian revolution. After the revolution, when all people would be workers and private property abolished, women would be emancipated from capital as well as from men. Marxists were aware of the hardships women's labour force participation meant for women and families, which resulted in women having two jobs, housework and wage work. Nevertheless, their emphasis was less on the continued subordination of women in the home than on the progressive character of capitalism's 'erosion' of patriarchal relations. Under socialism housework too would be collectivised and women relieved of their double burden.

The political implications of this first marxist approach are clear. Women's liberation requires first, that women become wage workers like men, and second, that they join with men in the revolutionary struggle against capitalism. Capital and private property, the early marxists argued, are the cause of women's particular oppression just as capital is the cause of the exploitation of workers in general.

Though aware of the deplorable situation of women in their time the early marxists failed to focus on the *differences* between men's and women's experiences under capitalism. They did not focus on the feminist questions – how and why women are oppressed as women. They did not, therefore, recognise the vested interest men had in women's continued subordination. [. . .] [M]en benefited from not having to do housework, from having their wives and daughters serve them, and from having the better places in the labour market. Patriarchal relations, far from being atavistic leftovers, being rapidly outmoded by capitalism, as the early marxists suggested, have survived and thrived alongside it. And since capital and private property do not cause the oppression of women as *women*, their end alone will not result in the end of women's oppression.

Perhaps the most popular of the recent articles exemplifying the second marxist approach, the everyday life school, is the series by Eli Zaretsky in *Socialist Revolution*.[4] Although Zaretsky, in agreement with feminist analysis, argues that sexism is not a new phenomenon produced by capitalism, he stresses that the particular form sexism takes now has been shaped by capital. He focuses on the differential experiences of men and women under capitalism. Writing a century after Engels, once capitalism had matured, Zaretsky points out that capitalism has not incorporated all women into the labour force on equal terms with men. Rather capital has created a separation between the home, family, and personal life on the one hand and the workplace on the other.[5]

Sexism has become more virulent under capitalism, according to Zaretsky, because of this separation between wage work and home work. Women's increased oppression is caused by their exclusion from wage work. Zaretsky argues that while men are oppressed by having to do wage work, women are oppressed by not being allowed to do wage work. Women's exclusion from the wage labour force has been caused primarily by capitalism, because capitalism both creates wage work outside the home and requires women to work in the home in order to reproduce wage workers for the capitalist system. Women reproduce the labour force, provide psychological nurturance for workers, and provide an island of intimacy in a sea of alienation. In Zaretsky's view women are labouring for capital and not for men; it is only the separation of home from work place, and the privatisation of housework brought about by capitalism, that creates the *appearance* that women are working for men privately in the home. The difference between the *appearance*, that women work for men, and the *reality*, that women work for capital, has caused a misdirection of the energies of the women's movement. Women should recognise that they, too, are part of the working class, even though they work at home.

In Zaretsky's view, 'the housewife emerged, alongside the proletarian [as] the two characteristic laborers of developed capitalist society',[6] and the segmentation of their lives oppresses both the husband-proletarian and the wife-housekeeper. Only a reconceptualisation of 'production' which includes women's work in the home and all other socially necessary activities will allow socialists to struggle to establish a society in which this destructive separation is overcome. According to Zaretsky, men and women together (or separately) should fight to reunite the divided spheres of their lives, to create a humane socialism that meets all our private as well as public needs. Recognising capitalism as the root of their problem, men and women will fight capital and not each other. Since capitalism causes the separation of our private and public lives, the end of capitalism will end that separation, reunite our lives, and end the oppression of both men and women.

Zaretsky's analysis owes much to the feminist movement, but he ultimately argues for a redirection of that movement. Zaretsky has accepted the feminist argument that sexism predates capitalism; he has accepted much of the marxist feminist argument that housework is crucial to the reproduction of capital; he recognises that housework is hard work and does not belittle it; and he uses the concepts of male supremacy and sexism. But his analysis ultimately rests on the notion of separation, on the concept of *division*, as the crux of the problem, a division attributable to capitalism. Like the 'complementary spheres' argument of the early twentieth century, which held that women's and men's spheres were complementary, separate but equally important, Zaretsky largely denies the existence and importance of *inequality* between men and women. His focus is on the relationship of women, the family, and the private sphere to capitalism. Moreover, even if capitalism created the private sphere, as Zaretsky argues, why did it happen that *women* work there, and *men* in the labour force? Surely this cannot be explained without reference to patriarchy, the systemic dominance of men over women. From our point of view, the problem in the family, the labour market, economy, and society is not simply a division of labour between men and women, but a division that places men in a superior, and women in a subordinate, position.

Just as Engels sees private property as the capitalist contribution to women's oppression, so Zaretsky sees privacy. Because women are labouring privately at home they are oppressed. Zaretsky and Engels romanticise the preindustrial family and community – where men, women, adults, children worked together in family centred enterprise and all participated in community life. Zaretsky's humane socialism will reunite the family and re-create that 'happy workshop'.

While we argue that socialism *is* in the interest of both men and women, it is not at all clear that we are all fighting for the same kind of 'humane socialism', or that we have the same conception of the struggle required to get there, much less that capital alone is responsible for our current oppression. While Zaretsky thinks women's work *appears* to be for men but in reality is for capital, we think women's work in the family *really is* for men – though it clearly reproduces capitalism as well. Reconceptualising production may help us think about the kind of society we want to create, but between now and its creation, the struggle between men and women will have to continue along with the struggle against capital.

Marxist feminists who have looked at housework have also subsumed the feminist struggle into the struggle against capital. Mariarosa Dalla Costa's theoretical analysis of housework is essentially an argument about the relation of housework to capital and the place of housework in capitalist society and not about the relations of men and women as exemplified in housework.[7] Nevertheless, Dalla Costa's political position, that women should demand wages for housework, has vastly increased consciousness of the importance of housework among women in the women's movement. The demand was and still is debated in women's groups all over the United States.[8] By making the claim that women at home not only provide essential services for capital by reproducing the labour force, but also create surplus value through that work,[9] Dalla Costa also vastly increased the left's consciousness of the importance of housework, and provoked a long debate on the relation of housework to capital.[10]

Dalla Costa uses the feminist understanding of housework as real work to claim legitimacy for it under capitalism by arguing that it should be waged work. Women should demand wages for housework rather than allow themselves to be forced into the traditional labour force, where, doing a 'double day', women would still provide housework services to capital for free as well as wage labour. Dalla Costa suggests that women who receive wages for housework would be able to organise their housework collectively, providing community child care, meal preparation, and the like. Demanding wages and having wages would raise their consciousness of the importance of their work; they would see its *social* significance, as well as its private necessity, a necessary first step toward more comprehensive social change.

Dalla Costa argues that what is socially important about housework is its necessity to capital. In this lies the strategic importance of women. By demanding wages for housework and by refusing to participate in the labour market women can lead the struggle against capital. Women's community organisations can be subversive to capital and lay the basis not only for resistance to the encroachment of capital but also for the formation of a new society.

Dalla Costa recognises that men will resist the liberation of women (that will occur as women organise in their communities) and that women will have to struggle against them, but this struggle is an auxiliary one that must be waged to bring about the ultimate goal of socialism. For Dalla Costa, women's struggles are revolutionary not because they are feminist, but because they are anti-capitalist. Dalla Costa finds a place in the revolution for women's struggle by making women producers of surplus value, and as a consequence part of the working class. This legitimates women's political activity.[11]

The women's movement has never doubted the importance of women's struggle because for feminists the *object* is the liberation of women, which can only be brought about by women's struggles. Dalla Costa's contribution to increasing our understanding of the social nature of housework has been an incalculable advance. But like the other marxist approaches reviewed here her approach focuses on capital – not on relations between men and women. The fact that men and women have differences of interest, goals, and strategies is obscured by her analysis of how the capitalist system keeps us all down, and the important and perhaps strategic role of women's work in this system. The rhetoric of feminism is present in Dalla Costa's writing (the oppression of women, struggle with men) but the focus of feminism is not. If it were, Dalla Costa might argue for example, that the importance of housework as a social relation lies in its crucial role in perpetuating male supremacy. That women do housework, performing labour for men, is crucial to the maintenance of patriarchy.

Engels, Zaretsky, and Dalla Costa all fail to analyse the labour process within the family sufficiently. Who benefits from women's labour? Surely capitalists, but also surely men, who as husbands and fathers receive personalised services at home. The content and extent of the sevices may vary by class or ethnic or racial group, but the fact of their receipt does not. Men have a higher standard of living than women in terms of luxury consumption, leisure time, and personalised services.[12] A materialist approach ought not ignore this crucial point.[13] It follows that men have a material interest in women's continued oppression. In the long run this may be 'false consciousness', since the majority of men could benefit from the abolition of hierarchy within the patriarchy. But in the short run this amounts to control over other people's labour, control which men are unwilling to relinquish voluntarily.

While the approach of the early marxists ignored housework and stressed women's labour force participation, the two more recent approaches emphasise housework to such an extent they ignore women's current role in the labour market. Nevertheless, all three attempt to include women in the category working class and to understand women's oppression as another aspect of class oppression. In doing so all give short shrift to the object of feminist analysis, the relations between women and men. While our 'problems' have been elegantly analysed, they have been misunderstood. The focus of marxist analysis has been class relations; the object of marxist analysis has been understanding the laws of motion of capitalist society. While we believe marxist methodology *can* be used to formulate feminist strategy, these marxist feminist approaches discussed above clearly do not do so; their marxism clearly dominates their feminism.

As we have already suggested, this is due in part to the analytical power of marxism itself. Marxism is a theory of the development of class society, of the accumulation process in capitalist societies, of the reproduction of class dominance, and of the development of contradictions and class struggle. Capitalist societies are driven by the demands of the accumulation process, most succinctly summarised by the fact that production is oriented to exchange, not use. In a capitalist system production is important only insofar as it contributes to the making of profits, and the use value of products is only an incidental consideration. Profits derive from the capitalists' ability to exploit labour power, to pay labourers less than the value of what they produce. The accumulation of profits systematically transforms social structure as it transforms the relations of production. The reserve army of labour, the poverty of great numbers of people and the near-poverty of still more, these human reproaches to capital are by-products of the accumulation process itself. From the capitalist's point of view, the reproduction of the working class may 'safely be left to itself'.[14] At the same time, capital creates an ideology, which grows up along side it, of individualism, competitiveness, domination, and in our time, consumption of a particular kind. Whatever one's theory of the genesis of ideology one must recognise these as the dominant values of capitalist societies.

Marxism enables us to understand many aspects of capitalist societies: the structure of production, the generation of a particular occupational structure, and the nature of the dominant ideology. Marx's theory of the development of capitalism is a theory of the development of 'empty places'. Marx predicted, for example, the growth of the proletariat and the demise of the petit bourgeoisie. More precisely and in more detail, Braverman among others has explained the creation of the 'places' clerical worker and service worker in advanced capitalist societies.[15] Just as capital creates these places indifferent to the individuals who fill them, the categories of marxist analysis, class, reserve army of labour, wage-labourer, do not explain why particular people fill particular places. They give no clues about why *women* are subordinate to *men* inside and outside the family and why it is not the other way around. *Marxist categories, like capital itself, are sex-blind.* The categories of marxism cannot tell us who will fill the empty places. Marxist analysis of the woman question has suffered from this basic problem. [. . .]

FEMINISM AND THE CLASS STRUGGLE

Historically and in the present, the relation of feminism and class struggle has been either that of fully separate paths ('bourgeois' feminism on one hand, class struggle on the other), or, within the left, the dominance of feminism by marxism. With respect to the latter, this has been a consequence both of the analytic power of marxism, and of the power of men within the left. These have produced both open struggles on the left, and a contradictory position for marxist feminists.

Most feminists who also see themselves as radicals (antisystem, anti-capitalist, anti-imperialist, socialist, communist, marxist, whatever) agree that the radical wing of the women's movement has lost momentum while the liberal sector seems to have seized the time and forged ahead. Our movement is no longer in that exciting, energetic period when no matter what we did, it worked – to raise consciousness, to bring more women (more even than could be easily incorporated) into the movement, to increase the visibility of women's issues in the society, often in ways fundamentally challenging to both the capitalist and patriarchal relations in society. Now we sense parts of the movement are being coopted and 'feminism' is being used against women – for example, in court cases when judges argue that women coming out of long-term marriages in which they were housewives don't need alimony because we all know women are liberated now. The failure to date to secure the passage of the Equal Rights Amendment in the United States indicates the presence of legitimate fears among many women that feminism will continue to be used against women, and it indicates a real need for us to reassess our movement, to analyse why it has been coopted in this way. It is logical for us to turn to marxism for help in that reassessment because it is a developed theory of social change. Marxist theory is well developed compared to feminist theory, and in our attempt to use it, we have sometimes been sidetracked from feminist objectives.

The left has always been ambivalent about the women's movement, often viewing it as dangerous to the cause of socialist revolution. When left women espouse feminism, it may be personally threatening to left men. And of course many left organisations benefit from the labour of women. Therefore, many left analyses (both in progressive and traditional forms) are self-serving, both theoretically and politically. They seek to influence women to abandon attempts to develop an independent understanding of women's situation and to adopt the 'left's' analyses of the situation. As for our response to this pressure, it is natural that, as we ourselves have turned to marxist analysis, we would try to join the 'fraternity' using this paradigm, and we may end up trying to justify our struggle to the fraternity rather than trying to analyse the situation of women to improve our political practice. Finally, many marxists are satisfied with the traditional marxist analysis of the women question. They see class as the correct framework with which to understand women's position. Women should be understood as part of the working class; the working class's struggle against capitalism should take precedence over any conflict between men and women. Sex conflict must not be allowed to interfere with class solidarity.

As the economic situation in the United States has worsened in the last few years, traditional marxist analysis has reasserted itself. In the 1960s the civil rights movement, the student free speech movement, the antiwar movement, the women's movement, the environmental movement, and the increased militancy of professional and white collar groups all raised new questions for marxists. But now the return of obvious economic problems such as inflation and unemployment had eclipsed the importance of these demands and the left has returned to the 'fundamentals' – working-class (narrowly defined) politics. The growing 'marxist-leninist preparty' sects are committed antifeminists, in both doctrine and practice. And there are signs that the presence of feminist issues in the academic left is declining as well. Day care is disappearing from left conferences. As marxism or political economy become intellectually acceptable, the 'old boys'' network of liberal academia is replicated in a sidekick 'young boys'' network of marxists and radicals, nonetheless male in membership and outlook despite its youth and radicalism.

The pressures on radical women to abandon this silly stuff and become 'serious' revolutionaries have increased. Our work seems a waste of time compared to inflation and unemployment. It is symptomatic of male dominance that *our* unemployment was never considered in a crisis. In the last major economic crisis, the 1930s, the vast unemployment was partially dealt with by excluding women from many kinds of jobs – one wage job per family, and that job was the man's. Capitalism and patriarchy recovered – strengthened from the crisis. Just as economic crises serve a restorative function for capitalism by correcting imbalances, so they might serve patriarchy. The 1930s put women back in their place.

The struggle against capital and patriarchy cannot be successful if the study and practice of the issues of feminism is abandoned. A struggle aimed only at capitalist relations of oppression will fail, since their underlying supports in patriarchal relations of oppression will be overlooked. And the analysis of patriarchy is essential to a definition of the kind of socialism useful to women. While men and women share a need to overthrow capitalism they retain interests particular to their gender group. It is not clear – from our sketch, from history, or from male socialists – that the socialism being struggled for is the same for both men and women. For a humane socialism would require not only consensus on what the new society should look like and what a healthy person should look like, but more concretely, it would require that men relinquish their privilege.

As women we must not allow ourselves to be talked out of the urgency and importance of our tasks, as we have so many times in the past. We must fight the attempted coercion, both subtle and not so subtle, to abandon feminist objectives.

This suggests two strategic considerations. First, a struggle to establish socialism must be a struggle in which groups with different interests form an alliance. Women should not trust men to liberate them after the revolution, in part, because there is no reason to think they would know how; in part, because there is no necessity for them to do so. In fact their immediate self-interest lies in our continued oppression. Instead we must have our own organisations and our own power base. Second, we think the sexual division of labour within capitalism has given women a practice in which we have learned to understand what human interdependence and needs are. While men have long struggled *against* capital, women know what to struggle *for*.[16] As a general rule, men's position in patriarchy and capitalism prevents them from recognising both human needs for nurturance, sharing, and growth, and the potential for meeting those needs in a nonhierarchical, nonpatriarchal society. But even if we raise their consciousness, men might assess the potential gains against the potential losses and choose the status quo. Men have more to lose than their chains.

As feminist socialists, we must organise a practice which addresses both the struggle against patriarchy and the struggle against capitalism. We must insist that the society we want to create is a society in which recognition of interdependence is liberation rather than shame, nurturance is a universal, not an oppressive practice, and in which women do not continue to support the false as well as the concrete freedoms of men.

NOTES

1. Often paraphrased as 'the husband and wife are one and that one is the husband', English law held the 'by marriage, the husband and wife are one person in law: that is, the very being or legal existence of the woman is suspended during the marriage, or at least is incorporated and consolidated into that of the Husband', I. Blackstone, *Commentaries*, 1965, pp. 442–5, cited in Kenneth M. Davidson, Ruth B. Ginsburg, and Herma H. Kay, *Sex Based Discrimination* (St Paul, Minn.: West Publishing Co., 1974), p. 117.
2. Frederick Engels, *The Origin of the Family, Private Property and the State*, edited, with an introduction by Eleanor Burke Leacock (New York: International Publishers, 1972).
3. Frederick Engels, *The Condition of the Working Class in England* (Stanford, Calif.: Stanford University Press, 1958). See esp. pp. 162–6 and p. 296.
4. Eli Zaretsky, 'Capitalism, the Family, and Personal Life', *Socialist Revolution*, Part I in No. 13–14 (January–April 1973), pp. 66–125, and Part II in No. 15 (May–June 1973), pp. 19–70. Also Zaretsky, 'Socialist Politics and the Family', *Socialist Revolution* (now *Socialist Review*). No. 19 (January–March 1974), pp. 83–98, and *Capitalism, the Family and Personal Life* (New York: Harper & Row, 1976). Insofar as they claim their analyses are relevant to women, Bruce Brown's *Marx, Freud, and the Critique of Everyday Life* (New York: Monthly Review Press, 1973) and Henri Lefebvre's *Everyday Life in the Modern World* (New York: Harper & Row, 1971) may be grouped with Zaretsky.
5. In this Zaretsky is following Margaret Benston ('The Political Economy of Women's Liberation', *Monthly Review*, Vol. 21, No. 4 [September 1961], pp. 13–27), who made the cornerstone of her analysis that women have a different relation to capitalism than men. She argued that women at home produce use values, and that men in the labour market produce exchange values. She labelled women's work precapitalist (and found in women's common work the basis for their political unity). Zaretsky builds on this essential difference in men's and women's work, but labels them both capitalist.
6. Zaretsky, 'Personal Life', Part I, p. 114.
7. Mariarosa Dalla Costa, 'Women and the Subversion of the Community', in *The Power of Women and the Subversion of the Community* by Mariarosa Dalla Costa and Selma James (Bristol, England: Falling Wall Press, 1973; second edition) pamphlet, 78 pps.
8. It is interesting to note that in the original article (cited in n. 7 above) Dalla Costa suggests that wages for housework would only further institutionalise woman's housewife role (pp. 32, 34) but in a note (n. 16, pp. 52) she explains the demand's popularity and its use as a consciousness-raising tool. Since then she has actively supported the demand. See Dalla Costa, 'A General Strike', in *All Work and No Pay: Women, Housework, and the Wages Due*, ed. Wendy Edmond and Suzie Fleming (Bristol, England: Falling Wall Press, 1975).
9. The text of the article reads: 'We have to make clear that, within the wage, domestic work produces not merely use values, but is essential to the production of surplus value' (p. 31). Note 12 reads: 'What we mean precisely is that housework as work is *productive* in the Marxian sense, that is, producing surplus value' (p. 52, original emphasis). To our knowledge this claim has never been made more rigorously by the wages for housework group. Nevertheless marxists have responded to the claim copiously.
10. The literature of the debate includes Lise Vogel, 'The Earthly Family', *Radical America*, Vol. 7, no. 4–5 (July–October 1973), pp. 9–50; Ira Gerstein, 'Domestic Work and Capitalism', *Radical America*, Vol. 7, no. 4–5 (July–October 1973), pp. 101–28; John Harrison, 'Political Economy of Housework', *Bulletin of the Conference of Socialist Economists*, Vol. 3, no. 1 (1973); Wally Seccombe, 'The Housewife and her Labour under Capitalism', *New Left Review*, no. 83 (January–February 1974), pp. 3–24; Margaret Coulson, Branka Magas, and Hilary

Wainwright, '"The Housewife and her Labour under Capitalism," A Critique,' *New Left Review*, no. 89 (January–February 1975), pp. 59–71; Jean Gardiner, 'Women's Domestic Labour', *New Left Review*, no. 89 (January–February 1975), pp. 47–58; Ian Gough and John Harrison, 'Unproductive Labour and Housework Again', *Bulletin of the Conference of Socialist Economists*, Vol. 4, no. 1 (1975); Jean Gardiner, Susan Himmelweit and Maureen Mackintosh, 'Women's Domestic Labour', *Bulletin of the Conference of Socialist Economists*, Vol. 4, no. 2 (1975); Wally Seccombe, 'Domestic Labour: Reply to Critics', *New Left Review*, no. 94 (November–December 1975), pp. 85–96; Terry Fee, 'Domestic Labor: An Analysis of Housework and its Relation to the Production Process', *Review of Radical Political Economics*, Vol. 8, no. 1 (Spring 1976), pp. 1–8; Susan Himmelweit and Simon Mohun, 'Domestic Labour and Capital', *Cambridge Journal of Economics*, Vol. 1, no. 1 (March 1977), pp. 15–31.

11. In the US, the most often heard political criticism of the wages for housework group has been its opportunism.

12. Laura Oren documents this for the working class in 'Welfare of Women in Laboring Families: England, 1860–1950', *Feminist Studies*, Vol. 1, no. 3–4 (Winter–Spring 1973), pp. 107–25.

13. The late Stephen Hymer pointed out to us a basic weakness in Engels' analysis in *Origins*, a weakness that occurs because Engels fails to analyse the labour process within the family. Engels argues that men enforced monogamy because they wanted to leave their property to their own children. Hymer argued that far from being a 'gift', among the petit bourgeoisie, possible inheritance is used as a club to get children to work for their fathers. One must look at the labour process and who benefits from the labour of which others.

14. This is a paraphrase. Karl Marx wrote: 'The maintenance and reproduction of the working class is, and must ever be, a necessary condition to the reproduction of capital. But the capitalist may safely leave its fulfillment to the labourer's instincts of self-preservation and propagation.' [*Capital* (New York: International Publishers, 1967), Vol. 1, p. 572.]

15. Harry Braverman, *Labor and Monopoly Capital* (New York: Monthly Review Press, 1975).

16. Lise Vogel, 'The Earthly Family' (see n. 10).

THE WOMAN QUESTION AND THE EARLY MARXIST LEFT†

Rosalind Coward

Rosalind Coward has been another persistent voice calling for a re-examination of the relationship between Marxism and feminism, or as one of her early essays put it, the necessity of 'Rethinking Marxism' to take account of a new cultural climate informed by the researches of feminism. In the following extract, taken from her book Patriarchal Precedents *(1983), Coward goes right back to the origins of classical Marxism (Engels for example), in order to trace why so little progress has been made on the position of women, and the more general issue of sexual relations, despite Marxism's liberationist pretensions. She regards Marxism as feminism's 'natural ally', but it is an alliance that has generally been an unequal one, as witness the conspicuously poor record of Marxist-socialist countries when it comes to women's liberation. What lies behind this poor record, Coward argues, is the tendency of early Marxist theorists to prioritise issues of economic relations over those of sexual relations. Thus it could be assumed by male theorists that once the economic function of marriage and family life had been destroyed, sexual emancipation would follow. As Coward points out, the issue of sexual relations was never really addressed in any detail, and has remained significantly undertheorised in Marxism right up to the present day.*

There appears to be a central paradox confronting any consideration of marxism's adequacy to deal with the position of women in society; why, given the theoretical importance of these concerns, were they rarely brought to the forefront in social and political programmes? Was 'the woman question' central only in so far as the history of the family and the theoretical consideration of the status of women were the bearers of all other considerations on social relations? Or, was it the priority given to the idea of the working-class party and economic class antagonisms which meant that 'the woman question' rarely became more than a theoretical debate? On the answers to these questions hangs the issue of whether marxism can ever be useful for understanding sexual division in society.

† From R. Coward, *Patriarchal Precedents: Sexuality and Social Relations*, London: Routledge and Kegan Paul, 1983 (pp. 163–9, 186–7).

Some might say that marxism naturally neglects women's politics because marxists are mainly men and that men as an interest group would not seek to further women's interests. This is an argument which ignores the evidence. It would be difficult to ignore the commitment which socialism above any other political philosophy has shown to challenging the subordinate position of women in society. Rather than consider the family sacrosanct, marxism insisted on the variability of familial forms. And such has been marxism's concern with the position of women in society that those societies in whose development marxist theory has been crucial often afford women's *formal* equality a significant place in their constitutions.[1] Who can doubt that marxism, with such commitments, would in its history have been both a natural ally for feminism and, indeed, in some cases, the point of origin for some forms of feminism? Both in the centrality which it gave to the concept of the family and in its offer of understanding forms of subordination in society in a 'materialist' fashion, the question of the subordinate position of women in society has rarely been totally absent from marxism's concerns.

Marx, Engels, Lenin and Stalin all at some point considered the 'woman question'. Lafargue, the head of the French Communist Party, wrote a book considering the history of women's position in society.[2] August Bebel, leader of the German Social Democratic Party, wrote *Woman under Socialism*, a book which was to have enormous influence in social democratic politics. All believed that equality between the sexes was integrally linked with a wholesale transformation of society into an egalitarian, that is, socialist, society. Nor did this mean that the specific struggle for equality between the sexes was neglected. Marx and Engels, for example, were responsible for such actions as an amendment to the minimum programme of the French Workers' Party of 1880 where a legal measure was added there to the economic and political demands for women's emancipation; 'The abolition of all paragraphs of law which . . . put women in a subordinate position to men.'[3]

Lenin initiated changes in marriage, divorce and abortion laws and frequently stressed the role of socialism in the 'emancipation' of women. In 1921, he celebrated International Women's Day with an article in *Pravda* insisting on the need for the struggle against women's oppression to be joined to the cause of socialist construction:[4]

> The main and fundamental thing in Bolshevism and in the Russian October Revolution is the drawing into politics of precisely those who were most oppressed under capitalism . . . And it is impossible to draw the masses into politics without also drawing in the women; for under capitalism, the female half of the human race suffers under a double yoke. The working woman and the peasant woman are oppressed by capital but in addition to that, even in the most democratic of bourgeois republics, they are, firstly, in an inferior position because the law denies them equality with men, and secondly . . . they are 'in domestic slavery', they are 'domestic slaves' crushed by the most petty, most menial, most arduous, and most stultifying work of the kitchen and by isolated domestic, family economy in general.

A few years later, even Stalin is no less effusive in his insistence on the crucial role women have to play in advancing socialism.[5]

> The fate of the proletarian movement, the victory or defeat of proletarian power depends on whether or not the reserve of women will be for or against the working class. That is why the first task of the proletariat and its advance detachment, the Communist Party, is to engage in decisive struggle for the freeing of women workers and peasants from the influence of the bourgeoisie, for political education and organisation of women workers and peasants beneath the banner of the proletariat.

Why is it, then, with all this apparent concern for women's position in society, that the relationship between feminism and socialism has been at best stormy, and the record of socialist countries in achieving equality between the sexes and the liberation of women ranges between somewhat limited to absolutely dire? [I]t will be argued that socialist politics concerning the position of women were always limited by their political and theoretical priorities. Women were simultaneously viewed as a 'natural' group and at the same time submerged in the concept of the family and the political priorities dictated by the integration of this concept with those of the state and classes.[6]

THE FAMILY, THE LABOUR MARKET AND 'TRUE SEX LOVE'

The politics advanced towards the family in *The Origins* are characteristic of much subsequent marxist writing on the subject. The disintegration of the family is seen as a sign of the hypocrisy of the bourgeoisie, who champion the family but who use women as a source of cheap labour. Nevertheless, women's increased role in production is welcomed by marxists because it simultaneously offers women freedom from economic dependence (and therefore slavery) and consequently destroys the economic basis for marriage, hence undermining a cornerstone of bourgeois society. It is only through the destruction of the economic basis of marriage that free and equal sexual relations will be achieved. For although the proletariat have no economic motive for marriage, their marriages have nevertheless been influenced by the patriarchal ideology of bourgeois society, installing the father as absolute authority with the wife as little better than the chief servant. Once economic dependency has ceased to distort relations, all humans will be able to choose their mates in the same way as the proletariat, that is, uninfluenced by economic considerations and expressing 'true sex love' which, for Engels, is monogamous, heterosexual and permanent.

There are two elements in the political goals expressed here – two elements whose lack of necessary integration explain much of marxism's difficult relation with feminism. On the one hand, there is the concern with increasing women's involvement in production and the destruction of the *economic function* of marriage. On the other hand, there is a concern that the quality of the relations between the sexes should be transformed, in other words, a transformation of moral and sexual relations.

The insistence on the need for women to become involved in production is characteristic of much marxist writing on the family. This is because it is assumed that the family has an economic function which must be destroyed. Marx, for example, assumes a degree of inevitability for women's increased role in production. Women will necessarily be drawn into production, and therefore waged labour, in the logic of technical development. Although the capitalist ceases to have to pay a family wage, there are more workers available from whom surplus value can be extracted.

We saw earlier how Marx insisted that surplus value is extracted from 'undifferentiated' agents and how the wage is supposed to represent only the value of labour power and the creation of surplus, being indifferent to social categories of value. At other times, however,[7] Marx starts out with an original 'family' wage, adequate not just for the reproduction of the labourer but for the reproduction of wife and children as well. Thus destruction of the family unit will be a source of increased levels of exploitation; the capitalist may initially have to pay more, but increased productivity will lead to higher profits. Increased exploitation will lead to increasing social contradictions and hence the eventual overthrow of capitalist social relations.

This position insists that marriage has an economic function belonging to a particular mode of production which must be overthrown. It led to the kind of politics advanced by Engels in the second half of his formulation, his moral politics. For Engels, as for many subsequent marxists, it is the economic element which is the source of oppression within marriage. Once this element has been removed, sexual morality will pursue its 'true' course, that of heterosexual, monogamous love.

RELATIONS OF PRODUCTION, SEXUAL RELATIONS AND FEMINISM

The fact that marxists were prepared to consider sexual relations as likely to change and to speculate on the possibilities under socialism meant that marxism was open to the emergent discourses around sexual relations. These discourses were also profoundly structured by the debates about the family and sexuality which were traced earlier. Many socialists considered these questions to be central. There were also many sexologists who were socialists. Some socialist programmes even adopted quite radical perspectives on sexual relations.

But when this question was raised with any systematicity, as with Stella Browne in England, or Kollontai in Russia, marxism was distinctly unsympathetic to any specific intervention within sexuality. The explanation for this seems to be that the two aspects of marxist politics towards sexual relations – the destruction of the economic function of the family and the transformation of the relations between the sexes – were hegemonised by the first element. All aspects of the relations between men and women were deemed to be dependent on the economic function of marriage.

The reason for this hegemony was because marxism insisted at the level of theoretical and political necessity that the struggle for women's emancipation should be integrated to the struggle for socialism. In the previous chapter we saw how the marxist political priority was to transform economic antagonism and that the social division between the sexes was excluded from consideration. What is more, the insistence on the necessity for the transformation in the relations of production was translated into a political assessment of which forces will effect this transformation; that is, forces around the relations of production. In this assessment, the possibility of seeing a specific dynamic in the relations between the sexes disappears. The marxist conceptualisation of the family insists on a necessary relation between the relations of production and the oppressed condition of women, a relation mediated by the economic function of the family. In this tradition of marxism, there is an insistence that socialism must achieve the emancipation of women and that any true emancipation of women must entail socialism. The insistence on the theoretical integration of the two elements through the economic function of the family means that the differential effects of social relations on the sexes were suppressed.

This suppression of the possibility that the forms taken by sexual relations might entail different relations of power characterised much writing on the woman question by the early marxist left. There was an intense hostility to what was branded 'bour-geois' feminism, or to whatever attempted to examine sexual relations apart from the economic relations of production. The feminist movement, or, more correctly, movements, emerged in the second half of the nineteenth century. They aimed at transforming sexual relations regardless of economic relations. Some involved extremely radical criticisms of traditional morality and existing social relations. Others were confined to campaigns against legal and political discrimination. Feminism, then, as now, was by no means a homogeneous political movement with a clear set of aims and objectives. It encompassed a multitude of tendencies; movements for legal and political reform, gradually crystallising around the suffrage movement; agitation for sexual and moral reform; advocacy of and opposition to birth control; sometimes agitation for the elevation of motherhood. Quite often, feminism was no more than a relatively spontaneous organisation around disparate women's issues, for example the campaign which surrounded the Contagious Diseases Act.[8] The effects of such campaigns, however, was sometimes to produce far-ranging critiques of existing social relations.

A minimalist definition of the feminism encountered by the early marxist left was that it was concerned with the position of women in society. Elements within it were, however, completely beyond the theoretical scope of marxism. Questions of sexual behaviour, masculine behaviour, questions of control and expression of sexuality, questions of female autonomy were all in contradiction with marxism's hierarchy of analytic and political priorities given in the deterministic of account of sexual and familial relations. [. . .]

The integration of the family with theorisation of class and political represen-tation, meant that the issue of women's subordination found an all too easy place in marxist schemes. We have seen in the previous chapter that the concept of 'family' in fact belonged to a tradition of speculation on general social relations. Through a certain sleight of hand, Engels made the position of women synonymous with the family. It was this which gave the woman question such a ready place within marxism but which blocked any real theorisation of women or any real acceptance of the centrality of transforming sexual relations. Because of the particular function which the family fulfilled in Engels's work – as the place of individual interest, the family also was easily submerged by socialism to some notion of individualism. It became the realm of freedom to which the state addressed its activities. (It is interesting to reflect that there is a high coincidence between statist notions of socialism and their adherence to traditional forms of the family – as if the family were sufficient expression of individual freedom.)

The bourgeois feminist approach of that period correctly specified on the one hand the non-reducibility of movements to transform the relations between the sexes to an economic (orthodox marxist) notion of socialism. On the other hand, elements of bourgeois feminism were able to stress the radical implications of birth control for women in a way that marxism was unable or unwilling to do, hamstrung by the lack of space possible for the theorisation of the relations between the sexes. In this way a more radical challenge was launched on the family from outside rather than inside marxism. At the same time, however, this feminism which, in the past, took a relatively technicist view of equality rather than striking at more fundamental inequalities, failed to see that the cause of all women cannot be bettered without a fundamental restructuring of social relations, including the ways in which the means of production are controlled.

We can conclude, then, that a certain tradition emerged within marxism, where the family was, paradoxically, both to the forefront of political and theoretical concerns, and, simultaneously, inadequately theorised. In so far as Engels's account of the family insisted on the analytic and political priority of the relations of production, the specific dynamic of relations between the sexes could not be adequately treated. For example, the insistence on the family as economic unit made it impossible to consider the differential effects of family relations on the sexes. Far from marriage binding the sexes together as an economic unit, marriage and the ideologies of sexual division have put the sexes in radically different positions. Men and women have different relations to the labour market, to child-bearing and child-care, and to the state. This tradition of marxism might argue that the state represents the interests of the bourgeoisie; it might equally well be argued that the state differently affects men and women, women constructed in a relationship of dependency on men.

NOTES

1. See M. Molyneaux, 'Socialist Societies Old and New', *Feminist Review*, no. 8, 1981.
2. P. Lafargue, *La Question de la Femme*, Paris, Editions de L'Oeuvre Nouvelle.
3. Quoted in W. Thönnessen, *The Emancipation of Women*, London, Pluto Press, 1973, p. 35.
4. V. I. Lenin, quoted in *The Woman Question: Selected writings of Marx, Engels, Lenin and Stalin*, International Publishers Co., 1951, p. 47.
5. J. V. Stalin, 'International Women's Day 1925', quoted in *The Woman Question*, p. 44.
6. The re-evaluation of the place of feminism within socialism and the relationship between the two is now under investigation.
   Barbara Taylor's 'The Feminist Theory and Practice of the Socialist Movement in Britain 1820–45', PhD, University of Sussex, is an important exploration of the relationship between feminism and socialism in pre-marxist socialism. Other studies can be found in: S. Rowbotham, and J. Weeks, *Socialism and the New Life*, London, Pluto Press, 1977; S. Rowbotham, *Stella Brown, Socialist and Feminist*, London, Pluto Press, 1978; J. Weeks, *Sex, Politics and Society*, London, Longman, 1981.
7. K. Marx, *Das Kapital*, London, Lawrence & Wishart, 1974, vol. 1, p. 391.
8. For a full account of the context and politics surrounding this see J. Walkewitz, *Prostitution in Victorian England*, Cambridge, Cambridge University Press, 1980.

17

FEMINISM AND THE
PROBLEM OF PATRIARCHY†

Caroline Ramazanoglu

For Caroline Ramazanoglu, Marxist feminism is an inherently problematical position that inevitably involves feminists in a series of contradictions. Identifying herself nevertheless as a Marxist feminist, Ramazanoglu proceeds to address these contradictions in Feminism and the Contradictions of Oppression *(1989), arguing that once we understand what causes them we shall be able to set about improving the effectiveness of feminism's political strategies. In this particular extract, the concept of patriarchy is taken as an example of how these contradictions can manifest themselves. The very concept itself has helped to crystallise second-wave feminism, where patriarchy equals women's common enemy; but patriarchy means different things to a radical feminist and a Marxist feminist. To the former it carries connotations of biological determinism (men can't change), while to the latter it is a historically constructed phenomenon (men can change). The concept therefore forces Marxist feminists to rethink their Marxism (where the concept does not really exist), while contesting its precise meaning and field of application. Once again it is a case of there needing to be dialogue between Marxism and feminism as equal partners, and of Marxism being asked to address its sex-blindness.*

MARXIST FEMINISM

Marxist feminism is in a way more inherently contradictory than radical feminism. Socialism is a struggle for the interests of a particular class at a particular historical stage of human development. Marxist feminists are, therefore, in the contradictory situation of having a commitment to struggle for the interests of women as women, regardless of our class, power or economic interests, while at the same time having a commitment to struggle for the interests of the exploited working class, which entails struggling with some men and against some women. New-wave marxist feminism grew out of reactions to marxism, inspired by radical feminism. Radical feminist assertions of

† From C. Ramazanoglu, *Feminism and the Contradictions of Oppression*, London: Routledge, 1989 (pp. 13–14, 15–16, 33–42).

women's common oppression were incompatible with classical marxist analysis. The new radical feminist insights which exposed women's common oppression as women, and celebrated sisterhood in oppression, had a powerful influence on marxist women's thinking. The rise of radical feminism, for example, raised women's consciousness of the subordinate roles they were expected to play in left-wing political organisations and protest movements. Reactions to the sexism of left-wing and black men brought awareness of conflicts of interest between women and men, and of class and racial divisions in capitalist societies. While marxist analysis could not explain women's oppression by men, radical feminist analyses did not address the problems of divisions between women.

Previously, socialist women had taken up the cause of oppressed working-class women, but had seen the struggle for women's issues as subordinate to the more general class struggle within capitalism. Feminism was dismissed as a bourgeois expression of women's interests, which did not act in the real interests of working-class women. The explosion of radical feminism allowed socialist women to become feminists in pursuit of women's goals, which, to some extent at least, transcended class. This made marxist feminism inherently problematic from its inception. [. . .]

Marxist feminists questioned the adequacy of marxist theory and politics, since socialism, although it could produce improved material conditions for women, clearly did not produce women's liberation from men. But at the same time, they also reacted against what they saw as the unjustified universality of radical feminist analysis. Because they were very conscious of the class divisions between women, and of the legacy of colonialism and imperialism, the assumption of one form of oppression affecting all women equally was treated as problematic. Marxism and feminism have not been integrated (Rowbotham *et al.* 1979; Sargent 1981), but radical feminism's influence on marxism led marxists to ask new questions. Marxist feminism came into conflict with radical feminism, particularly in Britain, and has remained in a state of some tension ever since.

Like radical and unlike liberal feminism, marxist feminism focused on power differences between women and men. Marxist scholarship offers little analysis here, so marxist feminists drew on radical feminist notions of patriarchy (the generalised power of men over women) and on the notion of sexual politics (the general struggle of women against men's power over them). Both radical and marxist feminists drew on Engels's essay on the family although not uncritically.[1] The concept of patriarchy then became one of the most central, but also one of the most confused terms in feminist use.

My own inclination favours marxist feminism. My bias in this direction has come largely from working in South Wales, Uganda and Turkey, where I experienced both the limits of other social theories in explaining labour migration and, at a personal level, the enormous differences of interest between women. But this is a statement of my bias, rather than an assertion that marxist feminism provides everything we need to know in order to change society. There is, however, no way of being all things to all women within feminism, and if my biases had been more towards radical feminism, the balance of this book would, no doubt, have been different.

I prefer the term marxist feminism to the politically more ambivalent socialist feminism, because it was Marx's method of social analysis that enabled feminists to produce knowledge of the wider context of women's varying oppression through history. I do not think that a commitment to marxist feminism need entail commitment to a masculine vision of socialism, nor approval of the quality of women's lives in male-dominated, totalitarian states. Nor does it mean that marxist feminism is independent of radical feminism. All versions of feminism have strengths and weaknesses, and marxist feminism could not exist in the forms that it does now if there had been no liberal or radical feminism. Radical feminism was in part a reaction against marxist explanation. But radical feminist ideas have also been taken into marxist feminism, creating new contradictions, but also positive and creative understandings of society. It is through debates between schools that we have to find effective political strategies for feminism. [. . .]

THE PROBLEM OF PATRIARCHY

Patriarchy is a key concept used by feminists in recent years. It encapsulates the mechanisms, ideology and social structures which have enabled men throughout much of human history to gain and to maintain their domination over women, Any term with such a wide-ranging task is likely to present problems. Patriarchy is not only a central concept in feminist thought, it is also the term most disputed between feminists, and it is used by different feminists in very different ways. Different versions of the concept of patriarchy are used to present different accounts of the nature and causes of men's domination of women.

Patriarchy, in the sense of the power of the father over his kinship group, had been developed in social theory prior to feminists' use of the term and had been used by anthropologists. But in the early 1970s the use of the term was transformed as it took on political significance in new-wave feminist discourse. Since the concept of patriarchy was developed as a means of both identifying and challenging men's power over women, theories of patriarchy are, implicitly or explicitly, theories which explain the creation and maintenance of men's social, ideological, sexual, political, and economic dominance.

The term patriarchy was taken up by radical feminists because existing social theories had no general concepts to account for men's domination. Social theories which had developed in the west from views elaborated in the eighteenth and nineteenth centuries took men's superiority for granted. The absence of concepts for understanding male domination followed from the lack of questioning of male dominance. Men's dominant position in society was publicly taken for granted as the normal and desirable state of affairs. The unequal relations between men and women were not seen as needing explanation. (Though it should not be forgotten that throughout this period such complacency was repeatedly challenged by women at all levels of society, albeit with varying results.) Once feminists asked questions about why the relations between men and women were as they were, and how they could be changed, they had to create new concepts for answering their questions.

However patriarchy is defined, it is a concept used to attempt to grasp the mechanisms by which men in general manage to dominate women in general. It refers to ideas and practices ranging from the most intimate of sexual encounters to the most general economic and ideological factors. It came to mean not only the power of men in general over women in general, but also the hierarchical character of male power, and the ideological legitimation of this power as natural, normal, right, and just. It enabled feminists to 'see' the common oppression of all women in relation to all men. Radical feminists initially treated patriarchy as a universal characteristic of human society. Marxist feminists tried to take account of both mode of production and patriarchy in their understanding of men's dominance. This gave them the problem of approaching the universal concept of patriarchy historically.

Patriarchy as Universal

The assumption that male dominance could be explained in general terms initially led feminists to search for a single overriding source of male power over women (e.g. Millett 1977; Daly 1978). This ahistorical view of patriarchy is most characteristic of 1970s American radical feminism, but has variants and qualified versions in America and elsewhere. It is this view of patriarchy which has probably attracted the most criticism, because it raises very directly issues of biological reductionism and conceptions of the innate essences of being male and being female. Because this approach is particularly vulnerable to criticism, attacks on this version of patriarchy have often been seen as disposing of the power of radical feminist argument in general. The overgeneral use of patriarchy, however, was politically very effective in drawing women's attention to the extent of male dominance. It drew attention to the existence of power relations between men and women, not only in the public but also in the private domain of family, household, and sexual relations. The idea of patriarchy enabled women to see their personal experiences as part of a general sexual politics in which they shared interests with other women. It made the subordination and oppression of women by men visible and illegitimate, and stimulated political action.

The problem of treating patriarchy as socially constructed but still as universal is that it is difficult to avoid falling into the trap of biological determinism. If, for example, feminists are dealing with immediate practical issues, such as that of male violence towards women, they may assert that patriarchy is a cause but without being able to explain variation in male violence. Patriarchy does not just label men's power over women, it also creates a need for explanations of why men have this power and of how they maintain it. Where patriarchy is taken to be a universal characteristic of the relations between men and women, then, since all that women have in common is their biological sex, it is hard to avoid the assumption that patriarchy must be rooted in an essential masculine nature.

The conception of patriarchy as universal is logically based on the conception of woman as a universal category. Whether or not women are explicitly conceived of as a class whose interests are opposed to those of men as a class (a position taken, for example, by Firestone (1979) and Millett (1977)), men are seen as having and defending power over women. Criticism of biological determinism has been countered to some extent by those who have defined patriarchy as the institutionalisation of male power, rather than as an innate property of being male (e.g. Spender 1985: 36). Spender argues that all men derive benefit from patriarchy so that all men are politically in opposition to women, but she qualifies this universalising position by claiming that politics is only one dimension of existence so that individual men need not be treated as personal enemies (Spender 1985 and Spender 1986: 217).

Delphy (1984: 17–18) also modifies the initial radical feminist position. She rejects the universal notion of patriarchy in favour of patriarchy defined as the system of subordination of women by men in contemporary industrial society. This system has an economic base rooted in what Delphy terms the domestic mode of production. Where women have been subordinated elsewhere, or in the past, separate explanations are needed. Although Delphy's conception of the domestic mode of production has attracted criticism (e.g. Barrett and McIntosh 1979) Delphy maintains (1984: 22), against the radical feminist position, that it is useless to seek a single cause of women's oppression. But she also argues (180), against marxist feminists, that women do constitute a class with interests antagonistic to those of men.

Radical feminists also successfully used the conception of patriarchy to challenge conventional knowledge of society as patriarchal, that is, as constructed by men in men's interests. This conception of patriarchal ideology as a characteristic of western thought, however, has been more enduring than initial attempts to use an abstract concept of patriarchy to explain the whole history of relationships between women and men.

Patriarchy slipped into feminist discourse as a loose general category of explanation, particularly as 'patriarchal society'. Radical feminist approaches to patriarchy as an explanation of male dominance were mainly countered by feminists who drew more directly on marxist thinking. The influence of Marx's analysis of human history led marxist feminists to see patriarchy as a historical product, created by people in the course of their daily lives. This approach meant that patriarchy could not be taken for granted as a characteristic of the relations between men and women, but needed to be identified and explained in a variety of different historical situations.

Patriarchy as Historical

In the 1970s, there were varied feminist attempts to treat both patriarchy and capitalism as generalised abstractions with the consequent problem of having to explain in very general terms the relationships between them. This was done either by locating patriarchy as an intervening variable between the mode of production and the oppression of women or by conflating patriarchy and capitalism into a system of capitalist patriarchy, or patriarchal capitalism (Patriarchy Conference 1978; Kuhn and Wolpe 1978; Eisenstein 1979; Sargent 1981). The way in which this was done varied between different authors, but is always problematic (Brittan and Maynard 1984: 58–9). All these attempts faced common problems of specifying the relations between capitalism and patriarchy *in general*. In these approaches, capitalism is seen as historically intertwined with patriarchy in characteristic ways, giving rise to a patriarchal family/household system, a patriarchal state, the domination of education by patriarchal ideology, and so on.

Hartmann (1981: 18–19) argued that capitalism and patriarchy were two different forms of oppression each with its own material base: 'the material base of patriarchy is men's control over women's labour power'. The way in which men gained and exercised this control through marriage, childcare, domestic labour, economic dependence on men, and social institutions constituted capitalism as patriarchal capitalism. McDonough and Harrison (1978: 11) took a somewhat different view, arguing that patriarchy should be seen as a historical concept, but that in general, 'patriarchal relations take their form from the dominant mode of production'. The problem with this view is that there is no clear way in which we can know how, or even whether, these variables are interconnected. How can we determine whether patriarchy is independent of capitalism, or any other mode of production? Is patriarchy produced by capitalism, and feudalism, but not by every mode of production? Or, is patriarchy semi-autonomous, that is, partially dependent on the way production is organised? How can such questions be answered in general? There is no reason to assume that such connections must take the same form in different situations.

These views attracted criticism within feminism. Criticisms focused on the very generalised conceptions of both capitalism and patriarchy, which resulted in the assertion of very general relations between them. Walby (1983) picked on a crucial weakness of this marxist feminist approach when she pointed out (102) that these analyses lacked any notion of contradiction: 'many existing analyses of the relation between patriarchy and capitalism, or between gender inequality and capitalism, assume that there is a harmonious articulation between the two'.

Adlam (1979) argues that conflating capitalism and patriarchy renders any explanation of male dominance insoluble. It reduces explanation to generalised abstractions, and ignores the specificity of sexual divisions which do not need to be reduced to other factors such as class, biology, or property. Adlam sees no need to treat women as a unitary category with the same essential interests (1979: 101). Rowbotham (1981: 365) goes further in rejecting the concept of patriarchy on the ground that it cannot escape being an ahistorical term. She argues that it is a word that fails to convey movement, the complexities of the relations between men and women, or the extent of women's resistance to and transformation of male power. Dorothy Smith (1983: 99) comments that any generalised conception of patriarchy, or assertion of a generalised relationship between patriarchy and mode of production, works against our ability to explain history. No matter how similar they may appear, household relationships and the articulation of households with the rest of society have changed through time. Smith goes on to claim (101) that the near universality of patriarchy has simply been produced by feminists' conceptions of social hierarchies, and by disregarding the variability of history.

Cockburn (1983) suggested replacing the ahistorical notion of patriarchy indicating generalised male supremacy with a conception of sex/gender system. A sex/gender system could produce patriarchal ideology but would require further explanation of how this ideology was produced and maintained through its historical development. Any such explanation would entail some knowledge of the organisation of production. Cockburn's study of the male dominance of the British craft printing industry indicates the complexity of the historical relations between class, gender, and technological change in the struggle to establish male supremacy in printing. The situation in other industries and in other countries led to rather different struggles with different outcomes.

Other marxist feminists have been more cautious in rejecting the concept of patriarchy completely. There is always the danger of throwing the baby out with the bath water. It was the crude universality of the radical feminist conception of patriarchy which forced marxist feminists to rethink their marxism. If the relations between sexuality, production and ideology are historically variable, it is probable that the extent to which women share common interests across class lines is variable. But we still need some general concept of patriarchy to enable us to see the extent to which women are oppressed as women, although the male domination of women has to be identified and explained in each situation in which it is found.

Considerable problems remain of explaining exactly how men gain power in different situations, and in different modes of production, and whether such power has any basis in biological difference. Sylvia Walby (1986: 50) argues that the complexity of social existence is such that too many factors need to be explained in an unstructured way. This criticism, however, would be equally applicable to the whole of social theory. It can be countered by the argument that the relevant factors for explanation are identified through theoretical analysis and women's critical consciousness of their experiences.

Walby (1986: 69) conceives of patriarchy as a mode of production comprising domestic work, paid work, the state, male violence, and sexuality. Gender inequality then has to be explained through the intersection of patriarchy, capitalism and racist structures, in specific areas such as in the use of women's labour. This is useful in focusing problems of explanation on the historical connections between areas of women's lives normally seen as separate, but it is not clear how conceiving patriarchy as a mode of production successfully bridges historical and general explanation.

Radical and marxist feminist attempts to specify general connections between patriarchy and capitalism have been unsuccessful because they cannot take adequate account of history or struggle. It cannot be assumed that patriarchy routinely benefits capitalism, and Walby argues that in practice it does not, for example, where men can prevent women from undercutting their labour. Neither can it be assumed that capitalism always serves the needs of dominant men. Cockburn (1983) argues that men are robbed of warmth, creativity, full sexuality, and caring, and that they encounter tensions in their domestic lives.

Feminism at present has no agreement on a possible resolution of the problem of patriarchy. Universal theories of the general male dominance of women founder on the rocks of biological reductionism and historical variability. Abstracted marxist feminist explanations of capitalist patriarchy or patriarchal capitalism do not solve the problem of dealing with the contradictions of historical developments rather than with abstracted generalities. They do not explain why or how men have managed to oppress women in so many different situations. But if we abandon patriarchy altogether and adopt 'an historical approach to sex-gender relations' (Rowbotham 1981: 368), we are left with no general understanding of why variable historical struggles between men and women have so many similar outcomes. As Kuhn and Wolpe (1978: 9) pointed out, 'a materialist approach to the question of women's situation constantly comes up against the problem of the transhistorical character of women's oppression, which immediately problematises the relationship between such oppression and the mode of production.' Treating patriarchy historically does not resolve the problem of how biology can be taken into account in understanding men's dominance over women. The term patriarchy then leaves open historical questions of how it is that men generally dominate women, rather than female dominance or some balance of power.

Rather than patriarchy constituting a general explanation of the relations between men and women, these relations remain a problem to be explained. Patriarchy has enabled feminists to see mechanisms in sexual relations, work, and public and private life through which men dominate women, but problems of explanation remain. It is not at all clear that if it was men who bore and suckled babies they would be able to maintain their extensive dominance over women. We do not need to reduce patriarchy to biology, but equally, we do not need to ignore biology without good reasons. Yet if we abandon patriarchy we are in danger of losing our political conception of what needs to be changed. The problem of using a single term with disputed meanings to cover the enormous complexity of the relations between men and women, between sex and gender and between gender relations and mode of production, throughout history, is still with us.

THE PROBLEM OF UNIVERSALITY

A general problem with feminism is the tendency towards universal generalisation, which has characterised not only radical feminism but also, in somewhat different ways, marxist feminism. The use of universal generalisations derived from theory and divorced from experience are characteristic of much western social theory. I have criticised elsewhere (Ramazanoglu 1985) the ways in which universal generalisations can make women's experience invisible. The adequacy of feminist argument, however, has been weakened by the uncritical application of feminist generalisations to situations which are insufficiently known or understood.

Universal generalisations about male domination prevent us from seeing the contradictions in women's lives. The concept of contradiction is one that feminists have taken from marxism. The power of Marx lies not so much in the conclusions he drew in the 1860s or 1870s, but in the questions which his approach to human history enable us to ask today. The relevant marxist question for feminists, then, is not 'are women oppressed?' but 'what are the sources of the contradictions which determine and limit the opportunities for women (or workers or ethnic minorities) to live as whole, free, human beings in control of their own lives?' If the question is put in this way, then quite clearly there cannot be one standard answer that will apply to all women or in all circumstances.

Marxist feminism has frequently been treated as about capitalist societies, and capitalism is taken to be an abstraction which takes the same form in different places and times.[2] Marx's own sense of historical variability, his outrage at the appalling conditions in which nineteenth-century workers lived and died, and his ability to weave their individual experiences into his general analysis of the capitalist mode of production, had no place in the generalities of 1970s marxist feminism. Marx was quite clear that while the abstract concept of capitalism was a general tool for identifying the character of capitalist societies, each historical capitalist society was unique (Marx 1976: 876). More recently, Heyzer (1986) has pointed out that while women in South-East Asia are oppressed as women, the form that their oppression takes depends on the extent and manner of the integration of local production and kinship systems into the capitalist mode of production, and also on the presence or absence of grass-roots resistance by women.

Having said this, it does not follow that unique situations have nothing in common with each other. While each situation needs its own investigation and explanation, the very general occurrence of the oppression of women by men indicates that there will be shared circumstances even over time and across cultures, economies and classes. We need a general feminist theory in order to look for combinations of underlying determinants which over and over again create and re-create the circumstances of oppression. But we also need a theory which can take account of the differences and divisions that develop between women. Male domination is contradictory for women, in that patriarchal societies allow some women power over others.

The value of marxist analysis for feminism, therefore, is to end the search for a single cause of women's oppression or for a generalised relationship between patriarchy and capitalism. Rather the lessons of marxism should alert feminists to the incredibly complex and variable situations in which women come to be oppressed. Rather than taking the prevalence of oppression for granted, we should see every instance of oppression as a problem in which combinations of shared and unique factors need to be identified and explained.

We still need to establish much more clearly how women have come to be in the social situations that they are in; how the balance of power between men and women is maintained, and what forms resistance has taken and might take in future. These investigations must be clearly located in feminist theory which can take account of history and of contradiction. Historical research has already shown significant variation in women's experiences during industrialisation and the variety of working experience even among working-class women (Lewenhak 1980; Sarsby 1985). What is wrong with much of feminist theory is the tendency towards abstract generalisation, even though this is often grounded in personal experience and so does not necessarily seem abstract. If abstract generalisations are imposed in a variety of unresearched and unexamined situations, the understanding of why some women are more oppressed than others is actively discouraged.

NOTES

1. Engels (1970). There have been a number of critical appraisals of Engels's work (Sacks 1975; Sayers *et al.* 1987).
2. Capitalism is widely discussed in feminist work, but is rarely defined. In using the term I have in mind the following definition. All societies which are recognised as capitalist must have these characteristics:
   1. private ownership of productive forces based on exploitation;
   2. general production of commodities for a market (things to be bought and sold);
   3. separation of people who produce things from the things that they produce, and from the means of producing them (in contrast to peasants with their own land, or craft workers);
   4. labour power as a commodity (that aspect of people's labour which is bought and sold for wages, as opposed to labour on things which people produce and control themselves);
   5. creation of surplus value. Surplus value is created when workers produce more value than they consume as wages, and this surplus is appropriated by a class of capitalists, as the basis of the accumulation of capital;
   6. the expanded reproduction of capital. The continuation of the capitalist mode of production in any society depends on the continuous expansion of the processes of production and accumulation;
   7. the operation of the economy and the political control of the economy are *apparently*, but not essentially, separated.

Any society which is dominated by the characteristics listed above will be a capitalist society. But each historical society will be a unique configuration of economic, political, and social factors. No two capitalist societies can, therefore, be exactly the same, and every capitalist society is in a process of change. The capitalist mode of production is an abstract notion and cannot be observed as such.

BIBLIOGRAPHY

Adlam, D. (1979), 'The case against capitalist patriarchy', *M/F*, 3: 83–102.

Barrett, M. and McIntosh, M. (1979), 'Christine Delphy: towards a materialist feminism?', *Feminist Review*, 1: 95–106.

Brittan, A. and Maynard, M. (1984), *Sexism, Racism and Oppression*, Oxford, Blackwell.

Cockburn, C. (1983), *Brothers: Male Dominance and Technological Change*, London, Pluto.

Daly, M. (1978), *Gyn/Ecology: The Metaethics of Radical Feminism*, Boston, Beacon Press.

Delphy, C. (1984), *Close To Home: A Materialist Analysis of Women's Oppression*, London, Hutchinson.

Eisenstein, Z. (1979), *Capitalist Patriarchy and the Case for Socialist Feminism*, New York, Monthly Review Press.

Engels, F. (1970), 'The origin of the family, private property and the state', in K. Marx and F. Engels, *Selected Works*, vol. 3, Moscow, Progress Publishers.

Firestone, S. (1979), *The Dialectic of Sex*, London, Women's Press.

Hartmann, H. (1981). 'The unhappy marriage of Marxism and feminism: towards a more progressive union', in Sargent (1981).

Heyzer, N. (1986), *Working Women in South-East Asia: Development, Subordination and Emancipation*, Milton Keynes, Open University Press.

Kuhn, A. and Wolpe, A.-M. (1978), *Feminism and Materialism*, London, Routledge & Kegan Paul.

Lewenhak, S. (1980), *Women and Work*, London, Fontana.

McDonough, R. and Harrison, R. (1978), 'Patriarchy and relations of production', in Kuhn and Wolpe (1978).

Marx, K. (1976), *Capital*, vol. I, Harmondsworth, Penguin.

Millett, K. (1977), *Sexual Politics*, London, Virago.

Patriarchy Conference (1978), *Papers on Patriarchy*, Brighton, PDC and Women's Publishing Collective.

Ramazanoglu, C. (1985), 'Labour migration in the development of Turkish capitalism', in H. Ramazanoglu (ed.), *Turkey in the World Capitalist System*, Aldershot, Gower.

Rowbotham, S. (1981), 'The trouble with "patriarchy"', in R. Samuel (ed.), *People's History and Socialist Theory*, London, Routledge & Kegan Paul.

Rowbotham, S., Segal, L., and Wainwright, H. (1979), *Beyond the Fragments: Feminism and the Making of Socialism*, London, Merlin.

Sacks, K. (1975), 'Engels revisited: women, the organisation of production, and private property', in R. R. Reiter (ed.), *Toward an Anthropology of Women*, New York, Monthly Review Press.

Sargent, L. (ed.) (1981), *Women and Revolution: A Discussion of the Unhappy Marriage of Marxism and Feminism*, London, Pluto Press.

Sarsby, J. (1985), 'Sexual segregation in the pottery industry', *Feminist Review*, 21: 67–93.

Sayers, J., Evans, M., and Redclift, N. (1987), *Engels Revisited: New Feminist Essays*, London, Tavistock.

Smith, D. (1983), 'Women, class and family', in R. Miliband and J. Savile (eds), *Socialist Register 1983*, London, Merlin Press.

Spender, D. (1985), *For the Record*, London, Women's Press.

Spender, D. (1986), 'What is feminism? A personal answer', in J. Mitchell and A. Oakley (eds), *What is feminism?* Oxford, Blackwell.

Walby, S. (1983), 'Women's unemployment, patriarchy and capitalism', *Socialist Economic Review 1983*, London, Merlin Press.

Walby, S. (1986), *Patriarchy at Work*, Cambridge, Polity Press.

18

PAID EMPLOYMENT AND HOUSEHOLD PRODUCTION†

Sylvia Walby

The place of women's labour, both paid and unpaid, within the capitalist mode of production, has been a contentious issue in both Marxist and feminist circles. In the following extract from Theorizing Patriarchy *(1990), Sylvia Walby examines several different Marxist accounts of women's employment under capitalism, only to find wanting their various explanations for women's lower participation rate in paid employment, as well as lower wage levels overall. Yet again it is a case of sex-blindness, with, in this instance, capital–labour relations being prioritised over gender relations. Like Coward, Walby also looks at classical Marxist conceptions of the family, although she is significantly kinder to Engels than Coward proves to be. For Walby, Engels's identification of the importance of economic considerations in marriage, flawed though it is in many respects, provides the basis for an understanding of women's subordination by the type of labour (domestic) they normally perform in familial situations. An appreciation of the role of unpaid domestic labour, or 'household production', within capitalist production in general is therefore extremely useful to feminists, even if this does not entirely explain the existence of gender inequality in our society.*

MARXIST AND MARXIST FEMINIST ANALYSIS

Marxist and Marxist feminist writers explain the pattern of women's employment as determined by capitalist relations. Women's lower pay and lesser labour force participation are critically shaped by the capital-labour relation. Women are seen as a subordinate and marginal category of worker whose greater exploitation benefits employers, although a sub-group of this school sees women's position in the household, rather than paid labour, as an achievement rather than failure of the working class. There is great variation within class analysis as to the explanation of gender relations in paid employment and the significance of this for class relations. I shall identify four variants: first, that initiated by Braverman; second, the cyclical reserve army theory; third, the family wage debate; fourth, Marxist segmentation theory.

† From S. Walby, *Theorizing Patriarchy*, Oxford: Blackwell, 1990 (pp. 33–8, 70–3).

Braverman

Braverman (1974) has a general thesis on the development of capitalism into which he integrates an analysis of gender relations. There are two main parts to his argument: first, that there is a progressive deskilling of jobs in contemporary monopoly capitalism, and that women take most of these new less-skilled jobs; second, that household tasks shift to the factory, reducing the amount of labour to be done in the home and releasing women for waged labour.

Braverman has a model of structural conflict between capital and labour whereby deskilling occurs as a result of the attempt by employers to increase their profits at the expense of the workforce. Deskilling is designed to remove control over the labour process from skilled workers to the capitalist by splitting the conception of the task from its execution. It is also designed to reduce costs by decreasing the need for expensive labour and making it possible to employ cheaper labour on simpler tasks. This cheaper labour is female.

The second part of the argument concerns the changing relationship between the household and the market. Braverman argues that the amount of housework has decreased as a result of the household buying from the market goods it would previously have produced itself. Clothing and pre-prepared foods are examples of things which are cheaper to make under capitalist relations and forces of production than domestic ones. This is considered to release women for waged work.

As a consequence of these two parallel processes, women freed from domestic work are available to take up the new deskilled work in offices and factories. Thus their labour force participation rates rise. At the same time the labour force participation rates for men drop as they are expelled from skilled labour and become unemployed or retire early. Braverman forsees a convergence in the proportions of men and women in the paid workforce.

Both sides of Braverman's provocative and powerful argument have problems. Many have pointed out that the form of managerial control towards which Braverman sees all employers moving is in fact merely one among two or more (Elger, 1979; Friedman, 1977; Wood, 1982); thus there is not such an inevitable tendency to deskilling. Braverman's account of the reduction of the amount of time spent by housewives on housework is contradicted by evidence from time budgets taken over a number of years, which do not show such a decline among housewives (Bose, 1979; Cowan, 1983; Vanek, 1980). However, it should be noted that the proportion of women who are full-time housewives is itself declining ... and women who also do paid work spend fewer hours on housework than their full-time counterparts (Pahl, 1984). The empirical questions appear unresolved in the literature and will be further addressed below.

Reserve Army Theory

Braverman has a conception of women as a long-term reserve of labour which is now being brought into employment by the development of capitalism. Other Marxists, while also viewing women as a reserve army of labour, consider this to be as a short-term or cyclical phenomenon. Marx himself did not discuss the employment of women to any significant extent but he did identify different forms of industrial labour reserve, and argued that it was critical to capital accumulation. The function of a reserve, according to Marx, was to prevent workers being able to bargain up their wages and conditions of employment in times of increased demand for labour (Marx, 1954). This reserve could be of different types: floating, latent or stagnant. The floating was composed of people who had been employed in capitalist industry and been made unemployed. The latent comprised people who had not been employed by capitalist industry previously but who were available as a result of changes in that area of the economy, for instance, underemployed agricultural labourers. The stagnant consisted of those whose employment was at a very low level and intermittent. Later Marxists have argued that the notion of a latent reserve may be applied to married women.

Beechey (1977, 1978), in her early work, applies Marx's theory to women, arguing that they constitute a flexible reserve which can be brought into paid work when boom conditions increase the need for labour, and let go to return to the home in times of economic recession. Married women in particular can be used in this way because they have somewhere to go and something to do when employers no longer need their services.

> They provide a flexible working population which can be brought into production and dispensed with as the conditions of production change . . .
> . . . married women have a world of their very own, the family, into which they can disappear when discarded from production. (Beechey, 1977: 57)

(However, more recently Beechey has changed her position on the usefulness of the reserve army concept (Beechey and Perkins, 1987).)

Bruegel (1979) has extended this analysis into a consideration of recent British experience, arguing that part-time workers in particular form a reserve army of labour. She shows how the number of women part-time workers in electrical engineering fluctuates more extensively with the trade cycle than does total employment in this industry.

There is some supporting evidence from the world wars, in which women were recruited to work, especially in the munitions factories, for the duration, and 'let go' at the end (Braybon, 1981). Further, some studies of job loss suggest that practices such as sacking part-timers first (until this was declared illegal discrimination in the late 1970s) and 'last in, first out' might contribute to the more tenuous hold of women on paid employment in times of economic retrenchment (Bruegel, 1979; MacKay et al., 1971).

However, there are some serious theoretical and empirical problems with this theory. First, the theory has some internal contradictions. If capital is considered to be the determinant of the process in which women lose their jobs before men, then capital would be acting against its own interests if it were to let women go before men, since women can be employed at lower wages than men. The theory does not specify a mechanism by which women would be let go before men which is in the interests of the employer directly concerned.

Second, the empirical evidence does not support the theory. Women did not leave paid employment in greater numbers than men in the 1930s depression in the USA (Milkman, 1976) or in the mid-1970s recession across the Western world (OECD, 1976), neither have they in the recent British recession (Walby, 1989). Indeed in Britain in the 1980s the number of women in paid employment increased overall during the decade, despite a slight dip during the deep recession. While men's employment opportunities have wilted since their mid-1960s peak, those for women have continued to increase.

There have been attempts to rescue the theory from these problems. Milkman (1976) argues that the reserve army effect is merely masked by the effects of job segregation by sex. She describes how the sector which was worst hit by job loss in the USA in the 1930s employed predominantly men, while women were to be found in those sectors which were least affected. The segregation of men from women in employment, with men concentrated in manufacturing and women in services, gave women relative protection from loss of employment.

The correlation identified by Milkman is undoubtedly important. However, as a response to the problems of reserve army theory it raises as many questions as it answers. Why are women concentrated in the most buoyant section of the economy? Why are men not substituted for women in the remaining jobs? In short, occupational segregation has become the central feature of the pattern of gender relations in employment and needs explanation. Yet this is not attempted by reserve army theorists. The relative position of women and men remains unexplained.

Family Wage

The first two versions of Marxist theory on gender relations in employment assume that women are a marginal and hence disadvantaged group within the labour market. In the third, a Marxist account of the family wage, Humphries (1977) argues that women's relative absence from the labour market is a result of the successful struggle of the working class for a family wage against the opposition of capital. In common with other Marxist writers on this topic she considers that women's employment is critically structured by the relationship between capital and labour. However, she considers women's place as full-time homemakers, and hence marginal position in paid employment, to be principally a victory for the working class, rather than a disadvantage for women. Humphries argues that the withdrawal of women from the labour market enables the family to raise its standard of living, ensuring the non-alienated care of the young, the sick and the old, to control the supply of labour to the labour market so as to raise the price of those who enter it, and to assist the solidarity of the working class. This situation is a result of a successful struggle by the organised working class for a family wage for men.

Humphries's argument has been criticised by writers such as Barrett and McIntosh (1980) for the lack of consideration it shows to the disadvantages faced by women in a gender-divided working class. Further, these writers show that, apart from in a minority of families, the family wage has never really existed, except as an idea. Many men who receive a so-called family wage do not support a wife or children; many women who do not receive a family wage do support children. The family wage is an ideology justifying higher wages for men, rather than a reality.

Marxist Segmented Labour Market Theory

These three Marxist approaches have been criticised for paying insufficient attention to divisions within the labour market itself. Traditionally Marxist theory has focused on production rather than the market, the latter being associated with Weberian analyses. However, the significance of divisions by ethnicity and gender within the labour market itself have led to attempts at a Marxist theory of a segmented labour market. The various writings of Edwards, Gordon and Reich, collectively and individually, have argued that labour market segmentation can be understood as an outcome of the struggle between capital and labour (Edwards, Gordon and Reich, 1975; Edwards, 1979; Gordon, 1972). Essentially employers are seen to segment the labour market as a part of a divide-and-rule strategy. This prevents the homogenisation of the proletariat and their ability collectively to resist the demands of capital. This segmentation is not an inevitable response of capital, but part of a historical development, in which employers try one strategy after another to control their workforce. Pre-existing divisions based on ethnicity as well as gender are utilised by employers in this segmentation strategy.

The problems with this analysis stem from two main sources: first, the key question of where these ethnic and gender divisions come from is not explained, leaving a large absence in the account; second, the periodisation provided, which suggests that segmentation is specific to capitalism after the 1920s, is wrong, since ethnic and gender segregation existed long before this. Indeed segregation by gender pre-dates capitalism (Hartmann, 1979; Middleton, 1988), so capitalism cannot be considered its cause. So while the account is important in taking occupational segregation seriously in an analysis of social relations in employment, its explanation of why it takes a gendered form is incomplete.

Marxist accounts of gender relations in paid work are important in contextualising these within the relations between capital and labour. However, they all ultimately fail for this same reason – the overconcentration on the capital–labour relation at the expense of a theorisation of gender as an independent source of inequality. [. . .]

MARXISM AND MARXIST FEMINISM

Marxist feminist analyses start from the significance of class relations and the exploitative economic relations between classes for the understanding of gender relations. These are seen to be importantly implicated in the oppression of women, sufficiently so that women's liberation from the family would not be achievable outside a socialist society. There is no one Marxist feminist approach to the household, but many varied ones, and indeed some Marxist writers have said next to nothing about gender and the household. Approaches range from those which see gender and the family determined principally at an ideological level, to those which view it primarily at an economic one; from those which see the family as neutral in the oppression of women which stems from capitalism, to those which view it as the critical site of women's oppression.

Following Marx's almost total neglect of the topic, Engels (1940) produced an early attempt by a Marxist to take feminist issues seriously. He considered that the basis of women's oppression was to be found in the family. He produced an analysis which grounded gender inequality both in a material division of labour between the sexes and in its significance for class relations. Engels argued within a base-superstructure model of society in which the material base determined the political and ideological super-structure. The material base was composed of two parts: production and reproduction. Production was the production of tools, food and other commodities. Reproduction was the reproduction of the species through biological processes of birth and also the rearing of children. The balance of power between the sexes was dependent upon the relative importance of these two spheres for society. In early human history women were in the ascendancy; later this matriarchy was overthrown. This world historic defeat of the female sex was a result of the growth of class society. With developing productivity in the sphere of production larger surpluses were generated, the control over which became the source of division and conflict between the class which controlled them and the class which generated them. The class which controlled the surpluses sought to impose sexual monogamy on their wives in order to ensure that the heirs were their own biological sons. Hence the development of the monogamous family with male control over women was seen by Engels as part of the strategy of the ruling class to maintain control over the economic surpluses.

Engels's account has been subject to much criticism. In his history of the family and its passage from matriarchy to patriarchy, he appears to have confused matrilineal societies, in which descent is traced through women but in which men still have control, with matriarchal societies, in which women have control (Delmar, 1976). Most scholars do not think matriarchal societies have ever existed, although not all would agree (Stone, 1977). Further, Engels's assumption that proletarian families would not involve the subordination of women, since only bourgeois ones had property to pass to heirs, is clearly empirically incorrect. Another problem is his biologism in the account of why men undertook production and women reproduction, a consequence of conflating the social aspects of child care into the biological aspects of pregnancy and birth.

Despite these serious flaws, Engels's account does provide the basis of a materialist account of women's subordination in his recognition of the material nature of the work that women do. This insight was lost to many subsequent generations of Marxist theorists, for instance Althusser, and has only recently been regained.

Althusser (1971) had a theoretical view of the family as an ideological state apparatus whose function was to socialise children for the capitalist system. The parallels of this Marxist functionalism with the Parsonian functionalism are striking, and the same range of criticisms apply.

The 'domestic labour debate' took place in reaction to this tendency to see women's work in the family as an ideological rather than an economic activity and vigorously asserted the material significance of women's domestic labour for capital. In this debate the relationship between housework, or domestic labour, and capital was systematically examined. The central question was just how central or peripheral domestic labour was for capital, and hence for the determination of the structure of society. The more central it was to capital, the more important were women as political actors. The debate was implicitly about the significance of the feminism of the 1970s. The argument proceeded via a series of technical arguments about 'value', the Marxist unit of economic worth. If domestic labour created this directly, then it was more important than if it did not.

James and Dalla Costa (1973) argued that housework created both value and surplus value, that women's work was central to capitalism, and that women were politically central to a socialist movement. They contended that the work that women did in the household was necessary for workers to be able to go and do their jobs in the factories and offices, and so was essential to the workings of the economy. Capitalism could not function without women cooking, cleaning and keeping house. Hence domestic labour must create value, women must be central to capitalism, and feminism must be central to socialist strategy.

Such writings were accused of sloppy use of Marxist concepts by those who had a more traditional interpretation of Marxism. Indeed one of the themes of the debate was the extent to which Marxist concepts could be developed to take account of gender relations, and to what extent they must retain a narrower usage.

Seccombe (1974) argued that domestic labour created value but not surplus value. He agreed that housework was embodied in the husbands who sold their labour to a capitalist, thus transferring value from the housewife to the capitalist via the husband. However, domestic labourers could not be considered to create surplus value, since housewives did not have a direct relationship with the capitalist, which, Seccombe argued, was theoretically necessary for the creation of value. The implication of this was that there was an equal exchange between husband and wife of housework for maintenance (since no surplus was extracted). This notion was criticised by Gardiner (1975), who pointed out the obvious inequality between spouses and the benefit to the husband of the arrangement.

The debate dealt with a very narrow range of issues related to the household, and an even smaller range of those associated with gender inequality. It did not really address the issue of whether you could read off political implications from degree of exploitation (see Coulson, Magas and Wainwright, 1975) or the non-economic issues within the household (see Molyneux, 1979). Nevertheless, its significance was in unequivocally demonstrating that women's domestic labour should be analysed as work within a Marxist perspective.

The criticism of Marxism in general and Marxist analyses of gender in particular as economistic led to the demise of this debate. Later writers such as Barrett (1980) stressed the importance of a non-economistic analysis. Barrett argued for the importance of ideology in the construction of gender. These ideologies were critically generated around the institution of the family: 'it is within the family that masculine and feminine people are constructed and it is through the family that the categories of gender are reproduced' (p. 77). More precisely Barrett argues that gender is socially constructed 'within an ideology of familialism' (p. 206), in order to take account of those who are not reared in conventional families. The significance that Barrett attaches to ideology is not considered to peripheralise the importance of gender. Rather she argues within a post-Althusserian Marxism which gives greater theoretical weight to ideology than do earlier forms of Marxism, although she does not go so far as to describe ideology as material. This ideology is centrally rooted in the family, making the family the central institution for the oppression of women.

In explaining the existence and form of the family Barrett is ambivalent. Women, she declares, do not benefit, while working-class men and the bourgeoisie may. The answer can only be found in a historical as well as theoretical analysis (p. 223). Through a sophisticated and erudite Marxist feminist analysis Barrett effectively argues that there is no logic of capitalism behind the oppression of women, though capitalist developments are implicated. But the cessation of the analysis at a point at which a historical analysis is demanded means that a final resolution of the theoretical dilemmas for Marxist feminism which she has presented is absent.

This shift away from an economic analysis of women's oppression was reflected in a growing interest in psychoanalytic theory. One of the most influential of these was Mitchell (1975), in her attempt to rehabilitate Freud for feminism. Mitchell's willingness to consider causes of women's oppression other than class and capitalism develops her analysis way beyond the limits of conventional Marxist feminism. [. . .]

The strength of Marxist feminist analysis of gender and production in the household is its exploration of the link with capitalism. Its weakness is the overstating of this at the expense of gender inequality itself. Its strengths and weaknesses are thus the mirror image of those of radical feminism.

BIBLIOGRAPHY

Althusser, Louis (1971), *Lenin and Philosophy and Other Essays* (London: New Left Books).

Barrett, Michele (1980), *Women's Oppression Today: problems in Marxist feminist analysis* (London: Verso).

Barrett, Michele and McIntosh, Mary (1980), 'The "Family Wage": some problems for feminists and socialists', *Capital and Class*, 11, summer, pp. 51–72.

Beechey, Veronica (1977), 'Some notes on female wage labour in capitalist-production', *Capital and Class*, 3, autumn, pp. 45–66.

Beechey, Veronica (1978), 'Women and production: a critical analysis of some sociological theories of women's work', in *Feminism and Materialism: women and modes of production*, ed. Annette Kuhn and AnnMarie Wolpe (London: Routledge).

Beechey, Veronica and Perkins, Tessa (1987), *A Matter of Hours: women, part-time work and the labour market* (Cambridge: Polity).

Bose, Catherine (1979), 'Technology and changes in the division of labour in the American home', *Women's Studies International Quarterly*, 2, pp. 295–304.

Braverman, Harry (1974), *Labor and Monopoly Capital: the degradation of work in the twentieth century* (New York: Monthly Review Press).

Braybon, Gail (1981), *Women Workers in the First World War: the British experience* (London: Croom Helm).

Bruegel, Irene (1979), 'Women as a reserve army of labour: a note on recent British experience', *Feminist Review*, 3, pp. 12–23.

Coulson, Margaret, Magas, Branka, and Wainwright, Hilary (1975), '"The housewife and her labour under capitalism" – a critique', *New Left Review*, 89, pp. 59–71.

Cowan, Ruth Schwartz (1983), *More Work for Mother: the ironies of household technology from the open hearth to the microwave* (New York: Basic Books).

Delmar, Rosalind (1976), 'Looking again at Engels' "Origin of the Family, Private Property and the State"', in *The Rights and Wrongs of Women*, ed. Juliet Mitchell and Ann Oakley (Harmondsworth: Penguin).

Edwards, Richard (1979), *Contested Terrain: the transformation of the work-place in the twentieth century* (London: Heinemann).

Edwards, Richard C., Gordon, David M. and Reich, Michael (1975), *Labour Market Segmentation* (Lexington, Mass.: Lexington Books).

Elger, Anthony (1979), 'Valorisation and deskilling – a critique of Braverman', *Capital and Class*, 7, spring, pp. 58–99.

Engels, Frederick (1940), *The Origin of the Family, Private Property and the State* (London: Lawrence and Wishart).

Friedman, Andy (1977), 'Responsible autonomy vesus direct control over the labour process', *Capital and Class*, 1, pp. 43–57.

Gardiner, Jean (1975), 'Women's domestic labour', *New Left Review*, 89, pp. 47–58.

Gordon, David M. (1972), *Theories of Poverty and Underemployment: orthodox, radical and dual labour market perspectives* (Lexington, Mass: Lexington Books).

Hartmann, Heidi I. (1979), 'Capitalism, patriarchy and job segregation by sex', in *Capitalist Patriarchy*, ed. Zillah R. Eisenstein (New York: Monthly Review Press).

Humphries, Jane (1977), 'Class struggle and the persistence of the working class family', *Cambridge Journal of Economics*, September.

James, Selma and Dalla Costa, Maria (1973), *The Power of Women and the Subversion of the Community* (Bristol: Falling Wall Press).

McKay, D. I., Boddy, D., Brack, J., Diack, J. A. and Jones, N. (1971), *Labour Markets under Different Employment Conditions* (London: Allen and Unwin).

Marx, Karl (1954), *Capital*, vol. 1 (London: Lawrence and Wishart).

Middleton, Chris (1988), 'Gender divisions and wage labour in English history', in *Gender Segregation at Work*, ed. Sylvia Walby (Milton Keynes: Open University Press).

Milkman, Ruth (1976), 'Women's work and economic crisis: some lessons of the Great Depression', *Review of Radical Political Economy*, 8, 1, spring.

Mitchell, Juliet (1975), *Psychoanalysis and Feminism* (Harmondsworth: Penguin).

Molyneux, Maxine (1979), 'Beyond the domestic labour debate', *New Left Review*, 116, pp. 3–27.

OECD (1976), *The 1974–5 Recession and the Employment of Women* (Paris: Organisation for Economic Co-operation and Production).

Pahl, Ray E. (1984), *Divisions of Labour* (Oxford: Blackwell).

Seccombe, Wally (1974), 'The housewife and her labour under capitalism', *New Left Review*, 83, pp. 3–24.

Stone, Lawrence (1977), *The Family, Sex and Marriage in England 1500–1800* (London: Weidenfeld).

Vanek, Joann (1980), 'Time spent in housework', in *The Economics of Women and Work*, ed. Alice H. Amsden (Harmondsworth: Penguin).

Walby, Sylvia (1989), 'Flexibility and the sexual division of labour', in *The Transformation of Work?*, ed. Stephen Wood (London: Unwin Hyman).

Wood, Stephen (ed.) (1982), *The Degradation of Work? Skill, deskilling and the labour process* (London: Hutchinson).

INDEX